Y0-CCP-379

CONTAINING CONFLICT
Cases in
Preventive Diplomacy

edited by
Satō Hideo

JCIE

Tokyo · Japan Center for International Exchange · *New York*

The surnames of the authors and other persons mentioned in this book are
positioned according to country practice.

Copyediting by Kim Gould Ashizawa and Pamela J. Noda
Cover and typographic design by Becky Davis, EDS Inc., Editorial & Design
Services. Typesetting and production by EDS Inc.
Cover photograph © 1999 Cartesia Software/PhotoDisc, Inc.

Printed in Japan
ISBN 4-88907-059-1

Distributed outside Japan by Brookings Institution Press (1775 Massachusetts
Avenue, N.W., Washington, D.C. 20036-2188 U.S.A.) and Kinokuniya
Company Ltd. (5-38-1 Sakuragaoka, Setagaya-ku, Tokyo 156-8691 Japan).

Japan Center for International Exchange
9-17 Minami Azabu 4-chome, Minato-ku, Tokyo 106-0047 Japan
URL: http://www.jcie.or.jp

Japan Center for International Exchange, Inc. (JCIE/USA)
1251 Avenue of the Americas, New York, N.Y. 10020 U.S.A
URL: http://www.jcie.org

Contents

Foreword

I N the wake of the cold war, the likelihood of large-scale wars between major powers significantly decreased, but the international community faced a sudden increase in regional conflicts. Smaller-scale regional and ethnic conflicts of the type seen in Somalia, Rwanda, Bosnia, and Kosovo began to proliferate, presenting a new challenge to strategists and policymakers around the world. While international cooperative structures have progressed markedly in the post–cold war period, the need to strengthen peacekeeping mechanisms and to prevent and resolve conflicts remains a major item on the international agenda.

In response, the Japan Center for International Exchange (JCIE) launched a research project on this topic in October 1999, under its Global ThinkNet (GTN) Fellows program. The Global ThinkNet Fellows program was created by JCIE in 1996 to train and develop Japanese scholars and researchers who can participate in international collaborative policy research and dialogue. The goal of this ambitious human resource development effort was to involve 100 future Japanese intellectual leaders in JCIE projects over the course of five years. Each GTN Fellows project is overseen by a leading senior expert in the field, and the Fellows are expected to participate in regular meetings, conduct fieldwork, and produce publishable policy papers in English.

The project that resulted in this book was led by Professor Satō Hideo, former dean of the Graduate School of International Political Economy at the University of Tsukuba and president of the Japan Association for International Relations, who was at that time a senior advisor to the rector of United Nations University (UNU). Professor Satō is widely known for his work in the area of foreign policy, and particularly on U.S.-Japan relations. During his tenure at UNU, he became increasingly interested in the issue of preventive diplomacy, and suggested it as the focus of this JCIE study group. He saw this as an area where academics could provide useful input into the policymaking process. Accordingly, five GTN Fellows were selected to tackle this issue of preventive diplomacy, examining such topics as UN peacekeeping activities; the peacebuilding process in Croatia; the international commitment to solve refugee problems; re-imaging the concept of the state-nation relationship in Asia; and a new approach to the democratization process in Belarus.

The group met on a monthly basis to discuss their papers and exchange views on various topics related to preventive diplomacy, sometimes with the assistance of outside experts. In November 1999, Takemi Keizō, member of the House of Councillors and former vice-minister for foreign affairs, talked with the group about human security issues in Japanese foreign policy, and in December 1999, Gregory Cooney, political counsellor and consul for the Canadian Embassy in Tokyo, discussed his own experience participating in peacekeeping activities in Yugoslavia in the early 1990s. In the spring of 2000, each member conducted field research, traveling to sites appropriate for their respective papers, including New York, Belarus, Moscow, Oxford, Geneva, and Croatia. Following a preparatory two-day retreat in July 2000, the group then headed to the United States in September for a workshop tour. Workshops were held with the University of Maryland's Center for International and Security Studies, the Center for Strategic and International Studies (CSIS), the Brookings Institution, the United Nations Association of the United States (UNA/USA), the Council on Foreign Relations, the United Nations University office of North America, the United Nations, and Columbia University's East Asian Institute. Additional meetings were held with Congressional staff and specialists from the U.S. Department of State. This tour gave the authors a great deal of feedback, which they then incorporated into their revised papers. JCIE is extremely grateful to all those who worked with us in this process for their invaluable time and insight.

Tragically, Professor Satō was unable to oversee the final phases of this project. He passed away on May 1, 2001, following a prolonged illness. It is our sincere hope that this volume will serve as a fitting memorial for a man who was a true internationalist in every sense of the word, who devoted himself to advancing the field of international relations in Japan, who strongly advocated the search for greater policy relevance in the work of international relations experts in academia, and who, above all, was a strong promoter of and mentor for younger scholars.

I would like to express sincere gratitude to the five authors who participated in this project for the time and serious effort they put into their analyses. This project and the resulting volume would not have been possible without the generous financial support of the Nippon Foundation, to which JCIE extends its special thanks. Finally, I would like to thank Wada Shūichi, Pamela J. Noda, Kim Gould Ashizawa, and Kawaguchi Chie for their tireless efforts to ensure that this publication came to fruition.

YAMAMOTO TADASHI
PRESIDENT
JAPAN CENTER FOR INTERNATIONAL EXCHANGE

Introduction

TOWARD the end of the last century, as cold war hostilities faded away, the fundamental paradigm of conflict shifted. The world witnessed a sudden proliferation of violent conflicts that were occurring not between East and West, nor even between nation-states. Actors at the subnational level —often ethnic or religious groups—became the central players in deadly struggles and even in cases of genocide. Secessionist movements appeared at a pace not seen since the post-colonial period. And long-harbored resentments seemed to take on a new life.

The ramifications of these "internal" conflicts for regional and international stability were irrefutable, and the international community quickly recognized the need for new tools and methods to identify and prevent this new threat. In 1992, a communiqué from the first heads-of-state summit of the United Nations (UN) Security Council called for "recommendations on ways of strengthening . . . the capacity of the United Nations for preventive diplomacy, peace-making and peace-keeping." Secretary-General Boutros Boutros-Ghali responded that year with his groundbreaking report, *An Agenda for Peace*. Many nations heeded this call. In 1994, for example, the United States released its *National Security Strategy of Engagement and Enlargement*, which emphasized preventive diplomacy as a way "to help resolve problems, reduce tensions and defuse conflicts before they become crises." A number of major regional multilateral organizations such as the Organization for Security and Co-operation in Europe (OSCE) and the Organization of African Unity (OAU) also embraced the concept of preventive diplomacy as a more effective alternative for dealing with conflicts. As Boutros-Ghali noted in a speech given in Japan, "In matters of peace and security, as in medicine, prevention is self-evidently better than cure. It saves lives and money and it fore-stalls suffering" (2001, 13).

But despite this apparent recognition of preventive diplomacy's value, millions of lives were lost in violent conflicts and millions more were displaced in the decade following the end of the cold war. The international community is still searching for the best means to respond to and prevent such conflicts. This volume represents the work of five Japanese authors to address these questions. They were gathered together under the guidance of one of Japan's leading po-litical scientists, Satō Hideo, to explore the theme of "New Approaches to Preventive Diplomacy." Their chapters examine such themes as UN reform for the enhancement of preventive diplomacy capabili-ties; post-conflict peacebuilding; the principle of self-determination and ethnic conflict; the impact of forced displacement of populations on conflict prevention efforts; reconceptualizing security communi-ties and power-sharing for preventing conflict; and the connection between human rights, democratization, and preventive diplomacy. By analyzing the international community's responses to conflicts in such locations as the African Great Lakes region, the Balkans, Bela-rus, Myanmar, and Cambodia, the authors draw lessons for manag-ing regional conflict through preventive diplomacy.

The first usage of the term "preventive diplomacy" is often attributed to a 1960s report by Dag Hammarskjöld to the United Nations Gen-eral Assembly. He used it in the context of the cold war and the pre-vention of conflicts that might lead to the involvement of the two superpowers. The use of the term in the context of applying diplo-matic efforts to resolve *internal* disputes before they can develop into violent conflicts is apparently a post–cold war phenomenon. How-ever, there is no agreement even among researchers or practitioners of preventive diplomacy on exactly what the term entails. A general definition is given by Michael Lund, who states, "The term 'preven-tive diplomacy' refers to actions or institutions that are used to keep the political disputes that arise between or within nations from es-calating into armed force. These efforts are needed when and where existing international relations or national politics appear unable to manage tensions without violence erupting" (1995). Nonetheless, as will be seen in the chapters that follow, there are many shades of interpretation when it comes to the content and scope of "preventive diplomacy," or to the phases of conflict in which prevention can prove effective.

The first three chapters in this volume, those by Kikkawa Gen, Hoshino Toshiya, and Miyawaki Noboru, share a common thread in that they challenge certain fundamental assumptions that have guided preventive diplomacy efforts over the past decade. These chapters deal with such basic concepts as democracy, human rights, sovereignty, and self-determination, examining how the international community has sought to apply them in various intrastate conflicts and prescribing new approaches to improve the efficacy of conflict prevention efforts. All three authors call into question what Miyawaki views as an increasing linkage in the post–cold war period between preventive diplomacy and the pursuit of such goals as democracy and human rights. While none would deny the importance of those values in the long-term, they question the way in which the international community has sought to impose those values on societies in conflict. As Miyawaki explains, ". . . While there seems to be a general consensus on the desirability of promoting democracy and human rights, the way in which those targets are promoted and standards are set by the international community, and the appropriate response of the international community when a nation fails to meet those standards, are extremely complex issues."

Hoshino points to the ongoing tension between the international community's pursuit of both democratic governance and strategic stability—two goals which often clash. He notes, ". . . The international community, while it recognizes the value of democratic governance, has made compromises to nondemocratic solutions in favor of strategic stability, which in essence undermines the foundation of the widely held theory of democratic peace." Kikkawa further stresses that the democratic impulse has served to promote conflict in a number of instances as referendums in ethnically divided nations have served to trigger secessionist fighting. He states, "The rallying cry of, and international pressure for, democratization has resulted in something other than effective pluralism; the by-products include upsurges in rampant ethnopopulism and the shattering of fragile democratic institutions."

Miyawaki presents the interesting case of Belarus, a nation that was on the path to democracy, but was sidetracked by the rise of an authoritarian leader to power. Despite clear human rights violations and oppression of political freedoms, the country is remarkably stable, and its relative economic and political isolation from all countries other than Russia has left it seemingly impervious to Western pressures to improve its human rights record. In particular, Miyawaki explores the efforts of the OSCE, an organization originally established to monitor human rights, but which has assumed a more active role since 1990 in promoting democracy, and of which Belarus is a member state. He views the OSCE's failure to have any significant impact on Belarus as being symptomatic of an "asymmetrical regime," under which countries such as Belarus "have maintained their authoritarian regimes with 'democratic' trimmings." This gap between the rhetoric and reality of the current human rights regime (what he calls the "Paris regime," established under the Charter of Paris for a New Europe) is undermining the credibility of the OSCE and the international community.

Democratization is of particular concern as it relates to "post-conflict conflict prevention," or how one can prevent further eruptions of violence in societies that have already been torn apart by ethnic or regional conflicts. Kikkawa's chapter, for example, examines the case of the former Republic of Yugoslavia, where he asserts that despite the international community's desire to "recreate and preserve integrated, multiethnic societies" rather than giving in to partitions along ethnic lines, the end result of post-conflict efforts has in fact been a cementing of the ethnic divide in Bosnia and Serbia through the Dayton Peace Accords. He asserts, "In the post-conflict phase, with ethnic divisions being more distinct than ever, the holding of free elections as a step toward democracy and good governance can actually become another tool through which the parties hope to resolve the unfinished business of war."

Hoshino echoes this sentiment in his discussion of solutions to post-conflict tensions. While agreeing that democratic governance should be the long-term objective, he stresses that indigenous initiatives for democratization are extremely unlikely when a society has undergone severe conflicts. He cites the example of Cambodia, where a power-sharing mechanism—as opposed to a strictly democratic system—was created under the Paris Peace Accord. That allowed UN peacekeepers to work with local political leaders "to bridge the transitional period before the Cambodian government was fully organized," and Hoshino notes that a similar mechanism will be needed in Myanmar.

Hoshino also proposes the promotion of security communities among conflicting actors "as a prescriptive policy goal . . . for conflict prevention and transformation." Shōji Mariko's chapter also raises this point indirectly in her discussion of regional organizations as actors in preventive diplomacy. Hoshino, however, places the security community concept in a broader conceptual context, calling for a reconceptualization of the nation-state "as a security community in and of itself, a community composed of all the sub-state groups, rather than conceiving of a security community solely as one composed of sovereign states." Hoshino calls for the encouragement of security community formation at both the interstate and state-based levels that can assist in institutionalizing "toleration mechanisms" as a way of preventing conflict and promoting a long-term and more practical approach to democratization.

Both Kikkawa and Hoshino explore the complex issues surrounding sovereignty, and the shifting concepts of the "nation-state" and "self-determination." These shifts have been widely acknowledged. In a *Foreign Affairs* piece titled "Power Shift," Jessica Mathews (1997) wrote, "The absolutes of the Westphalian system—territorially fixed states where everything of value lies within some state's borders; a single, secular authority governing each territory and representing it outside its borders; and no authority above states—are all dissolving. . . . International standards of conduct are gradually beginning to override claims of national or regional singularity." Similarly, Graham Alison and Owada Hisashi (1999) point out that the very fact that the international community is now asking what can be done about intrastate conflicts represents a significant shift in views of sovereignty over the second half of the 20th century. They also quote Shiridath Ramphal, cochairman of the Commission on Global Governance, who has argued, "Several of the elements of the nation-states system have become less credible, less assertive, less defining, even less hallowed. Sovereignty, self-determination, even non-intervention have had to yield some of their innocence. We still speak of them in the language of orthodoxy, but we know that global realities have curbed their claims, that they no longer reflect universal truths or represent undiluted norms."

Hoshino frames his discussion of this complex issue in terms of the increasing gap between "nation" and "state" and between "state" and "society." He stresses that these structural fissures are the underlying causes of "ethnic" conflicts and that "group identity has been manipulated by political leaders" in response to these fissures. Thus, solutions to conflict must address the root issues rather than just the superficial triggers of violence.

Kikkawa also stresses that the tendency to dismiss conflicts as intractable ethnic disputes ignores the political and strategic factors underlying conflicts. In particular, he notes the change over the postwar period in the relationship between sovereignty and self-determination. In the process of decolonization, self-determination was seen as a right of those who had been subject to colonial rule. The territorial integrity of states, he contends, was held as paramount and he stresses that, prior to the secessionist movements in Yugoslavia, "there was a deliberate move . . . to discredit the idea of self-determination as understood in ethnonational terms." However, in the wake of the cold war, "modern states are being jeopardized by a trend toward subnational and ethnic re-territorialization. This is partly a reflection of the new political trend that has seen democracy and minority rights becoming the *sine qua non* for validating governance." This has made self-determination a "tool to prove democratic entitlement over the territory inhabited by a people who may wish to exercise their right to democratic government within a separate state entity." Kikkawa stresses that the implications of this shift are "staggering."

As raised in Miyawaki's paper as well, Kikkawa views the selective application of norms and standards as perhaps one of the most critical issues in preventive diplomacy. His description of the international community's response to the breakup of Yugoslavia offers a fascinating study of the impact that external actors had in the region. As the conflict between ethnic groups escalated, he explains, many in the international community became convinced that "preventive recognition" of the breakaway ethnic nations was the only means of intervention available. Recognition transformed a domestic conflict into an international conflict, but it also produced "a chain reaction of national minority independence in Bosnia, Macedonia, and Serbia."

This "selective recognition," and the prospect that a referendum on independence could be used as evidence of democratic support for secession in the appeal for international recognition, set a dangerous precedent that the international community must address.

The final two chapters in this volume address issues of a more practical nature. First, Akizuki Hiroko tackles two complex cases of the African Great Lakes region and Kosovo, in which domestic conflicts sparked mass population movements that not only regionalized the conflict but also threatened to—or did—destabilize the nations that received the refugee populations. In the case of the Democratic Republic of the Congo, the mass influx of refugees from neighboring countries (particularly Rwanda) threatened the country's internal security and led to prolonged internal warfare. In Kosovo, by contrast, the potential destabilization of the asylum country, Macedonia, was avoided through the implementation of a transfer program for the refugees which moved a significant portion of them to third countries. Akizuki raises three important issues in her chapter that bear further consideration by the international community. First, she argues that the Kosovo case demonstrates the need to rethink the established principle of unconditional first asylum, suggesting that burden-sharing programs must be implemented to ensure that the asylum country is not destabilized as a result of fulfilling its international obligations. Second, her study details the inherent conflict between the political and humanitarian aspects of the work of the UN High Commissioner for Refugees (UNHCR), and the need to further consider the role of that organ. And finally, Akizuki, like Kikkawa, notes the impact of the inconsistent reactions of the international community to the two conflicts she examines. While the response in Kosovo was rapid and successful, the lack of reaction to the destabilizing influence of the refugees in Congo (many of whom were parties to the violent conflict in Rwanda) led to the spread of violence and loss of life in that region. She calls for a formal framework that includes the Security Council, the UNHCR, and the member-states of the United Nations to "consider refugee problems in view of conflict prevention and to raise the political will of member-states."

Finally, like her colleagues, Shōji examines the proliferation of intrastate conflicts that involve nonstate actors—ethnic, religious, or other communal groups—but focuses her attention on the question of how the United Nations can adjust to this new type of conflict. She notes that the United Nations is faced with a fundamental contradiction, in that it is an organization of member-states and the principle of domestic jurisdiction prevents it from easily intervening in domestic conflicts. Focusing on four areas of preventive diplomacy—early warning, peaceful settlement, confidence-building, and peacebuilding—she examines ways in which the UN system might better involve nonstate actors in its preventive diplomacy efforts. Much of her chapter focuses on the potential for greater cooperation between the United Nations and regional organizations such as the Organization of American States or the OAU as part of a comprehensive approach to conflict prevention. Shōji also calls for the United Nations to play a more substantial role as "the focus of coordination and cooperation" between a broad range of actors in order to prevent conflicts. She stresses that in order for nonstate actors to be able to participate more fully in preventive diplomacy, there needs to be a forum in which they can state their opinions to the United Nations.

Shōji's chapter thus brings us back to Hoshino's emphasis on the role of "security communities" in preventive diplomacy at both the state and sub-state levels. It also echoes calls by all authors for greater cooperation and consistency within the international community to ensure that their actions are effective in preventing conflict and that their inaction does not induce further violence.

BIBLIOGRAPHY

Alison, Graham, and Owada Hisashi. 1999. "The Responsibilities of Democracies in Preventing Deadly Conflict: Reflections and Recommendations." Discussion paper for the Carnegie Commission on Preventing Deadly Conflict. (July).

Boutros-Ghali, Boutros. 1992. *An Agenda for Peace: Preventive Diplomacy, Peacemaking and Peace-Keeping.* New York: United Nations Department of Public Information.

———. 2001. "Peace, Development, and Democratization." In Japan Institute of International Affairs, ed. *In Quest of Human Security: JIIA 40th Anniversary Symposium.* Tokyo: Japan Institute of International Affairs.

Lund, Michael S. 1995. "Underrating Preventive Diplomacy." *Foreign Affairs* 74(4): 160–163.

Mathews, Jessica T. 1997. "Power Shift." *Foreign Affairs* 76(1): 50–66.

Containing Conflict

CHAPTER ONE

Preventing Ethnic Conflicts: A Reconsideration of the Self-Determination Principle

Kikkawa Gen

ONE remarkable feature of the post–cold war era has been the growing consensus in the international community on the importance of preventive diplomacy. This has resulted partly in reaction to the catastrophic ethnic conflicts in Rwanda, the Soviet Union, Yugoslavia, and elsewhere, and partly from a realization that it may be easier and less costly to tackle disputes early, before they reach the point of armed conflict.

Armed conflicts have both general and specific causes. Attempts at conflict prevention must therefore attend to both the generic conditions that make societies prone to armed conflict and the potential catalysts that might imminently translate the propensity for war into armed conflict. In this regard, preventive diplomacy measures by international actors can be divided into two categories: short-term preventive diplomacy (or "light preventive diplomacy") and long-term preventive diplomacy (or "deep preventive diplomacy") (Zaagman 1996, 30; Miall, Ramsbotham, and Woodhouse 1999, 97). Short-term preventive diplomacy aims at preventing or containing a crisis from escalating into an armed conflict. Examples of such action include diplomatic interventions—sending diplomatic missions, deploying preventive military forces, or conducting private mediation efforts. At the same time, durable prevention of conflict often requires additional measures based on a longer-term perspective. Long-term preventive diplomacy aims at addressing the root causes of latent conflicts through such actions as assisting democratization, establishing the rule of law, building civil society, and monitoring human rights violations.

New and emerging conflicts in the post–cold war era have taken on an increasingly ethnic character, raising the question, "Can we prevent ethnic conflicts?" Many conventional explanations of ethnic conflict stress long-standing mutual hatreds between ethnic communities. These deep-seated animosities had been dormant, held in check for years by authoritarian rule. The collapse of authoritarian rule took the lid off these ancient, implacable rivalries, allowing long-suppressed grievances to come to the surface and thus leading to violent ethnic conflicts. This argument holds that ethnic conflicts are historical and inevitable, and that accordingly there is no leeway for the international community to conduct preventive diplomacy.

Yet even a cursory examination of recent violent ethnic conflicts reveals their political character: They are forged from strategic and political motivations and are not inevitable. In the face of economic crises, political leaders find it relatively easy to mobilize populations by stimulating a sense of collective ethnic identity. The rallying cry of, and international pressure for, democratization has resulted in something other than effective pluralism; the by-products include upsurges in rampant ethnopopulism and the shattering of fragile democratic institutions. Appeals to ethnicity or nationalism, in fact, have been crucial in ousting certain entrenched elites.[1] In addition, the international environment can strongly affect the escalation of ethnic conflicts. In particular, signals from major powers regarding the possibility of international recognition of the independence of seceding national minorities or ethnic nations, and the concomitant expectation of such recognition, can encourage political elites to mobilize populations, leading eventually to unilateral independence. Naturally, these secession movements often meet outright rejection by the respective central governments, thus leading to civil war.

Given that these political aspects do exist in the emergence and escalation of ethnic conflicts, is there any scope for intervention by the international community or major powers to support and develop a preventive diplomacy capacity? If so, how should preventive diplomacy be conducted?

If preventive diplomacy addresses only the immediate triggers of a conflict, the deeper causes may simply reemerge in a new and different configuration of violent conflict. Post-ethnic conflict situations are potentially volatile. While the general image of the post-conflict phase is that peace will be achieved once the conflicting parties have been disarmed, it is in fact extremely difficult to tackle conflict prevention in a country that has experienced violent ethnic fighting. The lingering animosity generated by ethnic violence creates underlying tensions that can erupt at any time. In addition, there are deeper structural changes in society as a result of ethnic cleansing that will shape violent events, since it is not likely that a democratic and stable multiethnic society can be built in the short run. In this context, long-term preventive diplomacy is crucial during the post–ethnic conflict phase. But what sort of preventive diplomacy is effective for building and maintaining a multiethnic society?

The armed ethnic conflicts in the former Yugoslavia provide a tragic example of the failure of short-term preventive diplomacy. Similarly, the long-term preventive diplomacy by the international community toward seceding countries—Bosnia and Macedonia in particular, as well as the current Yugoslavia (the Federal Republic of Yugoslavia)— has not achieved the expected results. This chapter will examine the efforts of the international community, and particularly of European countries, to prevent the ethnic conflicts in the former Yugoslavia and will try to identify the causes of their failure. In addition, I will examine the long-term preventive diplomacy efforts of the international community to prevent a resurgence of ethnic conflict in the post-conflict phase in this region. I will first attempt to develop an understanding of how the belated and uncoordinated preventive diplomacy of the international community in fact triggered internal ethnic conflicts in the former Yugoslavia. I contend that signals from certain major powers that they would recognize the self-determination of seceding ethnic nations in fact served as a triggering factor of the conflicts. Second, I will demonstrate that the international community changed the very character of the self-determination principle so that they could apply it to their recognition of the independence of seceding ethnic nations. Third, I will argue that efforts at post-conflict peacebuilding, as a form of long-term preventive diplomacy, are faced with an unrealistic mission in Bosnia and Kosovo in particular, where compromise is impossible between warring ethnic groups. I suggest that the separation and partition of the warring populations is the best possible solution rather than maintaining multiethnic societies under these circumstances.

An Anticipated War

Mobilized Nationalism

Yugoslavia provides a dramatic and tragic example of the failure to prevent ethnic conflict. The immediate causes of the breakup of Yugoslavia were a decline in the economy and the rise of virulent and aggressive nationalism—especially in Serbia—in the late 1980s and early 1990s.[2] Economic problems during the 1980s provided the context in which the political crisis developed at the end of the decade. Slovenia and Croatia in particular, where the economy was relatively better off, had pursued economic autarky and had come to resent the flow of resources southward to Serbia, Macedonia, and Montenegro, where the economy was impoverished. While Yugoslavia was falling into economic crisis, Slobodan Milosevic, the leader of the Socialist Party of Serbia, rapidly established his credentials as a Serbian nationalist during his visit to Kosovo in 1987, when he openly supported Kosovo Serbs against the Albanians. Through amendments to the Serbian Constitution, introduced just prior to his assumption of the Serbian presidency in 1989, the autonomous status of Kosovo was scrapped, to the outrage of the Kosovar Albanians.

The economic decline and political conflict helped produce growing uncertainty and insecurity among the population of Yugoslavia, thus laying the foundation for ethnic scapegoating and nationalist appeals. Nationalism was discovered to be a powerful political tool, to be used by unscrupulous political leaders to retain their power. These political leaders, who felt that their hold on power was being threatened by the collapse of communism in Eastern Europe, and who were incapable of meeting the pressing needs of the people, skillfully exploited the appeal to nationalism in order to maintain their power. Amid the upheaval in Eastern Europe in 1990, the communists abandoned their monopoly on power in the six republics of Yugoslavia and introduced multiparty elections. Nationalist parties won all of those elections.

The original aims of Serbian nationalism, it should be noted, were to reverse Yugoslavia's fragmentation by recentralizing power in Belgrade. Serbian nationalism, however, provoked a powerful nationalist reaction in other ethnic nations, and rekindled similar sentiments among the Croats and Slovenes in particular, where equally unscrupulous political leaders followed the Serb example and used nationalist appeals for their own political ends.

Self-determination provided the legal tools for establishing the demands of the seceding ethnic nations for independent statehood. The Slovenian Parliament formally proclaimed Slovenian sovereignty in July 1990, and in the same month, the Croatian Assembly promulgated that republic's new constitution, including the assertion of Croatia's sovereignty and right to secede. In December of that year, Slovenia and Croatia declared that they would secede unilaterally within six months unless a more acceptable federal arrangement was negotiated.

It is striking that referendums were held in the seceding republics in order to confirm the will of the populations concerned. A referendum was held in Slovenia in December 1990, with a turnout of approximately 85 percent, of which 88 percent voted for independence (Meier 1999, 161). A referendum was also held in Croatia in May 1991, with a turnout of 83 percent, of which 94 percent voted in support of independence (East and Pontin 1997, 261). As Antonio Cassese points out, this clearly demonstrates that the republics sought a form of legitimization for their movements through the general legal principle of self-determination. Because they lacked any legal claim to secession or independence under international law, they had to resort to the practice of referendums, which undoubtedly constitutes a fair and widely used application of that principle (1995, 266).

Internal and International Implications of Independence

The Socialist Federal Republic of Yugoslavia was one of the most ethnically heterogeneous countries in Europe, and efforts to break it up by declaring independence unilaterally—thereby foreclosing any possibility of negotiating the split peacefully—raised the specter of war. The immediate escalatory potential of the unilateral independence of Slovenia and Croatia from Federal Yugoslavia was twofold. First, there was a real possibility that their declared independence be rejected outright by Federal Yugoslavia, which was under the control of Serbian nationalists. Second, the material and rhetorical measures used in particular by the Croats, the dominant ethnic group in Croatia, to mobilize for independence posed an offensive threat to the Serbs residing in that republic, creating a security dilemma in which neither group could provide for its own security without threatening the security of the other. The intensity of this security dilemma was in part a function of demography; the more intermixed the patterns of settlement of the ethnic groups, the greater the opportunities for offense by either side. It therefore became more difficult to design effective measures for community defense, except by going on the offensive preemptively to "cleanse" mixed areas of members of the enemy group and create ethnically reliable, defensible enclaves. In this context, ethnic conflicts seemed inevitable.

It was apparent from the outset that if Croatia declared independence, the 600,000 Serbs residing there (about 14 percent of the population) would not stay in Croatia. In fact, the first president of the Serbian Democratic Party of Croatia is said to have stated clearly before the conflict erupted, "For every step that [Croatian President Franjo] Tudjman's government takes to separate itself from Yugoslavia, we will take a step to separate ourselves from Croatia" (Goldstein 1999, 217). When the nationalist movement came to prevail in Croatia in the summer of 1990, the Serbs in Croatia organized a referendum. Allegedly, 99 percent of the voters supported unifying with Serbia (Goldstein 1999, 222), and they eventually declared independence with the intention of later merging with Serbia. The intractability of the conflict was evident as soon as the nationalist leaders of Bosnia, Serbia, and Croatia had mobilized their constituents into positions that threatened the other communities. Having failed to recentralize Yugoslavia, Milosevic embarked on the creation of "Greater Serbia" from early 1991.[3] Serb communities living outside Serbia, particularly in Croatia and Bosnia, became increasingly radicalized, partly because of Belgrade's propaganda and partly because of the security dilemma between ethnic groups. There was a real possibility that Bosnia and Macedonia, the most ethnically inter-mixed republics, would be split along ethnic lines, although there were no borders dividing the ethnic groups within those republics. Bosnia, in which none of the three major ethnic groups had an over-whelming majority, also faced the possibility of being partitioned by Croatia and Serbia. In fact, Tudjman and Milosevic met secretly in March 1991 to discuss precisely such a division.

The international implication of unilateral independence was the possibility that war could spread throughout the Balkans. This threat was not putative, but was based on lessons from Balkan history. For both historical and ethnic reasons, nearly all neighboring states had a direct interest in the developments taking place in Yugoslavia, and particularly the status of ethnic minorities within each republic of Yugoslavia, many of whom had ethnic brethren in neighboring re-publics. The breakup would provide the occasion for reviving old territorial demands that had been settled, and there was a real danger that if one neighboring state sought to intervene in or exploit the consequences of the conflict for its own gain, others might follow suit.

Response of the International Community

Preventing the impending war was the primary concern of the inter-national community. A violent breakup of Yugoslavia posed a threat to regional stability, with the possibility that the conflict might spread beyond Yugoslavia's borders to involve neighboring states. The vio-lence that would accompany the breakup was also likely to create a humanitarian crisis, with millions of refugees and hundreds of thousands of casualties anticipated. The international community also had a strategic interest in countering the breakup. If Croatia and Slovenia could demonstrate that they could achieve their aims unilaterally through forceful means, assertive nationalists in other parts of the world would be more likely to conclude that they could implement their own aggressive designs with impunity.

What could be done by intermediaries to avert the ensuing vio-lence? External actors had few instruments at their disposal to mod-erate the behavior of the parties seeking independence. The emerging nationalism and resulting ethnic tension were internal political disputes, and external actors did not have legitimate means with which to intervene. However, both Croatia and Slovenia needed assurances that their declarations of independence would not meet outright hostility among the international community. Both republics craved legitimacy in the West. Therefore, withholding recognition was regarded as one of the key leverage points over the secessionist drives and perhaps the only powerful diplomatic tool available to prevent ethnic conflicts.

In retrospect, however, mixed and uncoordinated signals from the international community regarding the recognition of the independence of the breakaway republics seem to have been among the most crucial factors in producing the ethnic conflicts.[4] Most of the European countries in the phase preceding the outbreak of the armed conflicts aimed at maintaining a unified Yugoslav state. In the late spring of 1991, with the deadline for the declaration of unilateral secession drawing close and the political situation in the former Yugoslavia fast deteriorating, the response of the major powers and international organizations to the proposed secession was negative. For example, the Conference for Security and Cooperation in Europe (CSCE), which was looked upon as the most suitable institution at the time for dealing with the Yugoslav crisis, held a Berlin Council Meeting of Foreign Ministers on June 19–20, at which the members adopted a political declaration, the "Statement on the Situation in Yugoslavia." The message of this declaration was clearly aimed at convincing Croatia and Slovenia not to threaten the territorial integrity of Yugoslavia: "The Ministers expressed their friendly concern and their support for [the] democratic development, unity and territorial integrity of Yugoslavia, based on economic reforms [and the] full application of human rights in all parts of Yugoslavia, including the rights of minorities" (Conference for Security and Co-operation in Europe [CSCE] 1991a).

The European Community (EC) repeatedly expressed its position that the Yugoslav federation had to stay united (Zucconi 1996). Many of the EC member-states themselves had separatist movements that the governments were trying to keep under control, and given the possible impact of Yugoslavia's dissolution on their own situations, they were unwilling to allow it to break up. Shortly before Slovenia and Croatia declared independence, the EC even offered Yugoslavia

US$4 billion of economic aid if the country would stay together. The offer was never seriously considered. Nationalist hysteria is not usually susceptible to economic or any other kind of inducements or penalties.

The U.S. position was that self-determination cannot be unilateral and must be pursued through dialogue and peaceful means, and it would therefore not recognize unilateral secession. Warren Zimmermann, then the U.S. ambassador to Yugoslavia, expressed his concern to President Tudjman that Croatia's secession would have a catastrophic effect. Zimmermann also urged Slovenia to seek its future within Yugoslavia (1996, 132). U.S. Secretary of State James Baker visited Belgrade on June 21, 1991, and expressed his government's opposition to secession as well. He met with Milosevic, the leaders of all six republics, and Albanian leaders from Kosovo. He warned the representatives of Croatia and Slovenia even more clearly that the United States would not support their aspiration for independence. At that time, Kiro Gligorov, the president of Macedonia, and Alija Izetbegovic, the president of Bosnia, were trying valiantly to bring the Yugoslav republics back together in a confederal framework. Izetbegovic focused on Tudjman's reckless strategy and he warned Baker that if Croatia seceded, violence would be unleashed in Bosnia (Zimmermann 1996, 136). Baker reported back to President George Bush, citing the "need to work with the Europeans to maintain a collective non-recognition policy against any republic that unilaterally declared independence, as a lever to moderate behavior" (1995, 483).

RECOGNITION OF INDEPENDENCE
FOR PREVENTING CONFLICTS

Preventive Recognition

Slovenia and Croatia craved assurances that their independence would be recognized by at least some of the major powers in the international community. While most major European powers focused their strategies on maintaining a unified Yugoslavia, the policy of nonrecognition was not well coordinated among international actors. Signs of support for the secessionist positions were coming from both sides of the Atlantic. Actions taken by the U.S. Congress generally reflected a growing preoccupation with the violation of human rights. And even before the declarations of Slovenian and Croatian independence, the European Parliament went so far as to indicate its possible recognition of a change in internal borders within Yugoslavia. A resolution passed in the spring of 1991 stated, "The constituent Republics and autonomous provinces must have the right freely to determine their future in a peaceful and democratic manner and on the basis of recognized institutional and internal borders" (European Parliament 1991).

Moreover, some European governments were approaching Slovenia and Croatia through back channels, urging them to go ahead and secede. According to one account, Slovenian politicians claimed at the time that certain countries—primarily Austria, but also Germany and Switzerland—had promised a "benevolent" reception (Meier 1999, 175). Reacting to the flare-up of violence in Croatia in early May, Austrian Foreign Minister Alois Mock spoke publicly in support of a drive for independence by the two republics. The Germans also expressed their fear that the EC policy to preserve the unity of Yugoslavia would only aggravate the crisis. Throughout the initial stages of the political crisis, Germany indicated a willingness to recognize Croatian and Slovenian independence, reflecting rising domestic pressure in favor of those countries' right to self-determination (Lucarelli 1997, 37–38).[5] German Chancellor Helmut Kohl was quoted as saying in early July 1991: "The people of Yugoslavia must be free to choose their own future. Free Europe must remain loyal to them. . . . The importance of the principle of self-determination is that much more evident for Germans because by the means of self-determination our nation was able to regain its unity" (Edwards 1992, 178).

On June 25, 1991, four days after Baker's visit to Belgrade, the Croatian and Slovenian parliaments voted for independence. The war in Yugoslavia began in earnest the next day, with the Slovenes battling the Yugoslav National Army (JNA). In Croatia, as was fully expected, the decision on unilateral independence set off a chain reaction of self-determination movements. Croatia had a large Serb population, about half of which lived in the region along the Croatian border with Bosnia and in parts of eastern Croatia. Croatia's declaration of independence based on self-determination posed a perceived danger to Croatian Serbs, since it took no account of the rights or aspirations of the Serb minority. Spurred by a demand for their own ethnic identity, and with backing from Belgrade, Croatian Serbs launched an all-out effort to deny Croatian sovereignty over Serb-inhabited territories. The Croatian Serbs' move for self-determination, supported by the JNA, was swift and brutal.

From July 1991, German Foreign Minister Hans-Dietrich Genscher repeatedly used the threat of a German unilateral move to pressure Germany's allies and as a means to deter Serbian aggression. As other attempts to stem the violence failed, it was increasingly argued that the strategy of internationalizing the conflict by "preventive recognition" was the only political lever that Western Europe could still use to preserve the peace. If Slovenia and Croatia were to be internationally recognized, this would transform the internal Yugoslav conflict into an international one, thereby opening the way for the greater involvement of the international community without the permission of Yugoslavia. It was thus expected that the internationalization of the Yugoslav conflict through the recognition of independence could ultimately bring it to an end. Genscher repeatedly stated that Germany would recognize Slovenia and Croatia if the violence were to continue. However, at an emergency meeting of EC foreign ministers held on July 5, his counterparts backed away from recognizing the breakaway republics (Rummel 1992, 167).

Unilateral Independence and Its Aftermath

Throughout the second half of 1991, the EC played an almost exclusive role in dealing with the Yugoslav crisis. At the beginning of September 1991, the EC created the Badinter Commission, whose assignment was to set down the presuppositions for the recognition of those Yugoslav republics seeking independence. For much of that time, however, the Community's strategy remained that of maintaining some form of unified Yugoslav framework. The Troika of EC foreign ministers mediated and persuaded Slovenia and Croatia to freeze the implementation of their independence. A cease-fire was declared on July 4, 1991, and the agreement was formalized in the "Common Declaration for a Peaceful Solution of the Yugoslav Crisis," signed on the island of Brioni on July 7. Slovenia and Croatia agreed to suspend their independence for three months. An EC-sponsored Peace Conference opened at The Hague on September 7, chaired by Lord Carrington, a former British foreign secretary and former secretary-general of the North Atlantic Treaty Organization (NATO). At the conference, the EC mediators advanced a specific constitutional solution that would replace the federal state with a confederation of sovereign states. As an inducement, the EC offered association status to the individual republics. Milosevic, however, refused the EC's proposal on confederation and the conference failed.

The cease-fire did not last long. The Croats violated the cease-fire in the expectation that the country would be recognized if the violence continued. A massive offensive was then launched by the JNA against Dubrovnik in Croatia (the main tourist city). The eastern Croatian city of Vukovar fell after weeks of artillery fire in late November. Self-determination in the intermixed areas of the population led to ethnic cleansing. The Croatian Serbs, with the support of the JNA, captured nearly one-third of Croatia's territory and expelled non-Serbs from much of that area.

In the fall of 1991, the move to support recognition of Slovenian and Croatian independence began to gain strength within the international community. Germany was no longer completely isolated in its position. Italy started to support the preventive recognition cause more openly. The Parliamentary Assembly of the Council of Europe, held on September 21, 1991, issued its resolution "on the crisis in Yugoslavia" and called upon the Council's member-states to consider recognizing the breakaway republics of Yugoslavia that had already declared independence. However, Milosevic had hinted already that military action would take place if Croatia and Slovenia were recognized, and it was clear that this could well be the spark that would set Bosnia alight. The president of Bosnia, Alija Izetbegovic, had made his deep concern known. In Western capitals, then, there still prevailed in December the view that the ethnic tensions could worsen as a result of Germany's campaign to extend diplomatic recognition to Croatia and Slovenia.

It was fully anticipated that the self-determination of Croatia and Slovenia would cause a chain reaction of national minority independence in Bosnia, Macedonia, and Serbia. The Serbian Democratic Party in Bosnia, representing the majority of the Serbs in that republic, had already voiced repeatedly that they would not accept Bosnian independence. If Bosnia became independent, then the Serbs in Bosnia would be a minority—a situation they would consider unbearable. In November, the Bosnian Serbs stated their desire that Bosnia remain within the Federal Republic and warned that, in case of its secession, they would declare an independent Serbian Republic of Bosnia.

Although Bosnia's president had been trying to keep Yugoslavia together within a loose federation, once it became clear that Croatia and Slovenia would be internationally recognized, Bosnia had no choice but to seek its own independence. Both Bosnia and Macedonia concluded that they had little choice but to follow Croatia and Slovenia, lest they be subjugated within a Yugoslavia dominated by the Serbs. Bosnian President Izetbegovic and Macedonian President Gligorov are reported to have warned the United States that they would be destabilized if the Americans recognized other republics but not theirs, and the Bosnian foreign minister similarly told Secretary of State Baker that stability could be best promoted by Western recognition (Baker 1995, 642–640). Macedonia declared independence in September 1991, and the Bosnian parliament declared sovereignty in October and began to seek independence as well.

A last-minute effort to derail German recognition was made in early December. Lord Carrington, chairman of the EC Peace Conference, wrote to the then president of the Community, Foreign Minister Hans van den Broek of the Netherlands, on December 2, warning that a separate initiative by Germany would undoubtedly mean the breakup of the conference, and that "[t]here is also a real danger, perhaps even a probability, that Bosnia-Herzegovina would also ask for independence and recognition, which would be wholly unacceptable to the Serbs in that republic in which there are something like 100,000 JNA troops, some of whom had withdrawn there from Croatia" (Owen 1996, 376). United Nations Secretary-General Javier Pérez de Cuéllar similarly warned that selective recognition could widen the present conflict and fuel an explosive situation, especially in Bosnia-Herzegovina and Macedonia (Owen 1996, 376; Zucconi 1996, 246–247).

In the end, however, the images of violence swayed the international community. The foreign ministers of the 12 European

Community states met on December 16, 1991, to establish a common stand on the seceding republics of the Soviet Union and Yugoslavia. The need to keep some semblance of unity a few days after the signature of the Maastricht Treaty made the meeting a tense and difficult one. As a compromise, they accepted the German position, but they established a set of "Guidelines on the Recognition of New States in Eastern Europe and in the Soviet Union" (European Community [EC] 1991). Under these guidelines, they invited all Yugoslav republics to submit their applications for recognition by December 23, 1991. Slovenia, Croatia, Bosnia, Macedonia, Kosovo, and Krajina applied for recognition. Interestingly, Germany unilaterally recognized Slovenia and Croatia on December 23. The EC and its member states announced their recognition of those same republics on January 15, 1992. The applications from Kosovo and Krajina, on the other hand, were rejected. The recognition of Bosnia was postponed until March 1992 for reasons that will be discussed below, and the recognition of Macedonia was also delayed until April 1993 as a result of Greek concerns that the intended use of the historic Greek name of "Macedonia" implied that they had designs on Greek territory across the border.

Another Failure of Preventive Recognition

Selective recognition of Slovenia and Croatia had fateful consequences for Bosnia and Kosovo. It was clear that intercommunal violence could erupt in Bosnia at any time. In rejecting the recognition of Bosnian independence, the Bandinter Commission of the EC implied that the holding of an internationally monitored referendum to confirm the will of the whole population about its independence would be a precondition for Bosnia to be recognized. The EC thus elevated the status of referendums, making them a basic requirement for the legitimation of self-determination. In this environment of ethnic tension, however, there could be no unified will representing the majority of the Bosnian population. No one of the three major ethnic groups in Bosnia had an overwhelming majority. According to a 1991 census, Muslims constituted 43.7 percent of the population, Serbs 31.3 percent, and Croats 17.3 percent. The Serbs had already made it clear that they would not stay in an independent Bosnia. In

preparation for the imminent Bosnian secession from Federal Yugoslavia, Milosevic and Radovan Karadzic, the leader of the Serbian
Democratic Party in Bosnia, decided in early 1992 to station troops
of Bosnian Serb extraction in Bosnia for use in the coming conflict
(Meier 1999, 210). It was generally assumed that if a Bosnian referendum were held, the hard-line Bosnian Serbs would use the vote as a
pretext for instigating violence and calling for help from their fellow
Serbs in Belgrade. When a referendum was held on March 1, 1992,
roughly 64 percent of the electorate voted, with 99.4 percent of them
choosing independence. The vast majority of the Serbs boycotted the
referendum (East and Pontin 1997, 276; Malcolm 1999, 231). In the
immediate aftermath of that vote, Bosnia declared independence.

As in Croatia, self-determination of the majority induced another
move for self-determination of the ethnic minority in the intermixed
area of the population. Shortly after the referendum, the Bosnian
Serbs proclaimed their own "Serbian Republic of Bosnia-Herzegovina" on March 27, with its capital in Pale, near Sarajevo. Eventually,
the EC states and the United States came to the conclusion that the
collective Western recognition of Bosnia could best contribute to its
stability, thereby warning against efforts from within or without to
undermine its integrity. The EC states recognized Bosnia on April 6,
1992, and the United States followed suit the next day. It was meant
to be another case of preventive recognition.

In fact, however, the formal recognition of Bosnia provided Serbia
with an excuse to contest Bosnia's territorial integrity openly, thus
triggering large-scale ethnic violence in Bosnia. The Serbs (supported
by Serbia), the Croats (supported by Croatia), and the Muslims began to fight to hold onto their respective territory, although there
were no clear ethnic borders. Backed by the JNA, the Bosnian Serbs
instantly secured the two-thirds of Bosnian territory that they had
already occupied by force.

This process of ethnic conflict would follow a similar trajectory
during the Kosovo war of 1998–1999. As Slovenia, Croatia, and Bosnia
became independent, Yugoslavia dwindled away to a nearly unitary
Serbian state, and Albanians in Kosovo province rejected the idea of
staying under the same roof with the Serbs. Albanians began to despair of international help and to turn away from the patient policy
of nonviolence to a more militant solution, resorting to violence to

win self-determination. The Kosovo Liberation Army (KLA) managed to win widespread support among the Kosovo Albanian population, and by 1998, the KLA had managed to seize a large part of rural Kosovo. However, a strong force of Serbian military and police units dislodged the KLA from most of the areas they held late in 1998 and early in 1999, causing the Albanian population to flee from their homes.

It is noteworthy that Macedonia was the exceptional case in which preventive recognition and successive preventive measures contributed to the prevention of armed conflict. Macedonia was admitted to the United Nations in April 1993, and subsequently the EC countries extended recognition to Macedonia later that year. The CSCE acted to forestall the spread of conflicts to other parts of Yugoslavia by sending a long-term mission to monitor any symptoms of embryonic ethnic disputes in Macedonia. The UN also deployed a preventive military force (UNPROFOR) in Macedonia—the first attempt by the UN to deploy military force to prevent ethnic conflicts—and the United States sent a small military force as well. This international diplomatic and military presence served to reassure Macedonia and to deter its neighbors from intervening.[6]

The Missed Timing of Preventive Diplomacy

Why did ethnic conflicts erupt when the policy switch by the major powers became apparent? Why did preventive recognition by the international community fail to prevent an escalation of the conflicts? Was there any range of time when preventive diplomacy could have been effective in avoiding the violent breakup of Yugoslavia?

As Michel Lund points out, mediation and other forms of third-party conflict intervention are likely to be more effective when many of the conditions of advanced conflicts are absent: the issues in dispute are fewer and less complex; conflicting parties are not highly mobilized, polarized, and armed; significant bloodshed has not occurred, and thus a sense of victimization and a desire for vengeance are not intense; the parties have not begun to demonize and stereotype each other; moderate leaders still maintain control over extremist tendencies; and the parties are not so committed that compromise involves a significant loss of face (1996, 15, 94). In addition, effective preventive diplomacy requires not just a strong enough combination of carrots and sticks, but also the use of a variety of actions and instruments to address the many facets of a dispute. Learning from the experience of failed preventive diplomacy, it is also evident that these actions must be closely coordinated among the third parties participating in the preventive effort.

It was already clear in 1990 that conflict was brewing in Yugoslavia after the first free elections that year had given victories to nationalist leaders. Tensions were rising in both Slovenia and Croatia, on the one hand, which favored a confederal association between the republics based on the EC model and a rapid transition to a market society, and Serbia, Montenegro, and the JNA, on the other hand, which favored maintaining the federal constitution.

By the time of the elections in December 1990, Milosevic had not yet adopted the Greater Serbia line. The first priority for the political leaders of both Croatia and Slovenia was to reconstruct Yugoslavia as a confederation (Meier 1999, 143–157). Intensive negotiations were taking place among the leaders of various republics even in the first half of 1991 on a possible confederal arrangement in Yugoslavia. However, once Croatia and Slovenia abandoned the idea of maintaining a unified Yugoslavia and became determined to seek national self-determination, compromise was no longer possible. Throughout the second half of 1991, Croatia and Slovenia sought nothing less than full independence for all territory within each republic, while Belgrade insisted that all the Serbs should live in one state. The claims of Serbs, Croats, and Muslims were incompatible. Resolved to achieve self-determination even if it meant resorting to violence, the Croatian and Slovenian governments had begun to arm themselves already in the first half of 1991.

One point that stands out in this context is the absence of serious organized violent conflict during the period when the international community was believed to be committed to the territorial integrity of Federal Yugoslavia. Ethnic conflicts erupted only when it became apparent that the seceding republics were going to declare independence and that major foreign governments were about to reverse their commitment to the territorial integrity of Yugoslavia and recognize those republics' independence. In fact, as we have seen above, organized ethnic conflicts first erupted in Croatia and Slovenia in the summer of 1991, right after their declarations of independence, and in Bosnia in the spring of 1992, right after its recognition by major Western states. We can therefore conclude that the most significant single factor in producing the perceived threat that eventually threw ethnic groups into a security dilemma was the prospect of the recognition of the breakaway republics by major powers. Psychological factors were primarily responsible for the eruption of conflict, not ancient ethnic differences or the end of authoritarian rule as such. The creation of a unitary—that is, nonfederal—state dominated by a major ethnic nation is often perceived by ethnically distinct sections of the population to pose a threat. Serb inhabitants in Croatia, and Serb and Croat inhabitants in Bosnia perceived that as minorities in unitary states they would be repressed or would become second-class citizens. It was against this background that the Serbs in these newly recognized republics declared their own independence.

Looking back on his experience as a mediator, Warren Zimmermann asked himself in his memoir if it was possible to manage that breakup in a way that would have avoided violence. Tudjman, encouraged by Germany and by supporters in the U.S. Congress, dismissed any concerns that the West might act against him. Similarly, Milosevic and his army, reading between the lines of the Baker visit, were convinced that the United States had no intention of stopping them by force. Zimmermann concludes that Baker's message came too late: "If a mistake was made, it was that the Secretary of State hadn't come six months earlier, before the action-reaction spiral of nationalist threats had spun out of control. We should have chosen an earlier time to express our preference for a loosely confederated Yugoslavia" (1996, 136–139).

The best possible timing for the international community to have conducted preventive diplomacy by showing its strong will not to recognize self-determination achieved by violence would have been in late 1990 or in early 1991, before the unilateral proclamations of independence by Croatia and Slovenia. At that time, Yugoslav Prime Minister Ante Markovic was trying desperately to hold Yugoslavia together and bring about economic reform, but he did not receive sufficient support either from the international community or from within Yugoslavia.

THE SELF-DETERMINATION PRINCIPLE

Whether or not the tragedy could have been avoided, the West's policies, both before and during the conflict, were quickly seen as a failure. The timing of the preventive diplomacy by the major powers and the EC was too late. Moreover, the international community failed to act firmly or to coordinate its approach to conflict prevention. In this regard, the steady and determined German support for the preventive recognition of Croatia and Slovenia proved to be a crucial factor in the eruption of organized armed conflicts. Moreover, the EC's belated commitment to Yugoslavia made a difficult situation worse by first insisting on Yugoslavia's territorial integrity and then abruptly changing direction after the Croatian and Slovenian secessions, supporting them against Serbia. In June 1991, when EC representatives requested that Slovenia and Croatia suspend their decisions on independence for three months, this was taken to mean that they were being asked to buy time and that their independence would sooner or later be internationally recognized. All the same, both the Croatian and Slovenian governments knew that they would have to defend themselves militarily until this goal could be achieved because of the Serbian claims of a Greater Serbia. They knew that the longer they fought, the more they would appear to be victims of Serbia, and the more likely it would be that the international community would support their independence. Thus some 12 cease-fires were signed among the warring parties, each being broken one after another. Although the Yugoslav crisis presented a good opportunity for preventing violent conflict, the ability of the international community to bind together the will of its members into a common approach to Yugoslavia seems to have been insufficient for the task.

While no one knows for certain whether a credible threat of military force at an early stage in the conflict might have deterred Milosevic and his regional allies from resorting to violence, its absence can only have encouraged them to continue forcefully acquiring large swaths of territory. Particularly in the case of Bosnia, a clear message that international actors such as the UN and NATO would deploy preventive forces might have pushed the republics to reach a political solution. Once the newly independent republic was recognized and granted membership in the UN, the international community—and the UN in particular—could have deployed troops to

40

Bosnia as a preventive measure, as they actually did later in Macedonia.[7] In fact, President Izetbegovic repeatedly asked for the deployment
of UN troops to Bosnia, but the UN rejected his requests.

THE CHANGING CONCEPT OF SELF-DETERMINATION
AND ITS IMPACT ON SECESSION

From National Self-Determination
to Peoples' Self-Determination

As Mario Zucconi argues, most commentators do not seem to ap-
preciate adequately the decisive value attributed by the contending
parties to Western European actions—in particular to their recognition of statehood—and therefore the impact of those actions on the
evolution of the conflict. Because of the controversial nature of secessionist action under international law, the recognition of Croatia
and Slovenia, and later of Bosnia, had and was intended to have what
is called a "constitutive" effect. It formalized the existence of these
states for the purposes of international law (Zucconi 1996, 261). As
noted previously, in order to formalize the independence of these
ethnic nations, the self-determination principle was invoked. Ethnic
nations resorted to self-determination by force and the international
community accepted their claim as a legitimate right for an ethnic
nation to become independent.

Cases of self-determination in nations that were previously under
communist regimes have attracted favorable responses, leading to
the recognition of secessionist ethnic nations and to their subsequent
membership in the CSCE/OSCE and the UN. In fact, the admission
of new, post-communist states into the UN has been swift, undertaken without debate or dissenting votes. The admission of each new
state constituted the legal recognition of that entity as a state and its
concomitant right to self-determination (Blay 1994, 292). Here, a
question arises as to the international practice and custom regarding the principle of self-determination. Had the international community previously accepted the secession and creation of new states
as acts of self-determination? Should self-determination be understood as the right of independence of an ethnic nation?

Since the creation of the League of Nations minority regime,[8] it has been regarded that the principle of self-determination might well jeopardize the sanctity of the sovereign state. Modern states have tried to create communities of citizens rather than communities of nationals, and have ensured the primacy of common citizenship over privileges based on ethnicity or religious divisions. After World War II, the UN was reluctant to adopt the interwar rhetoric of national self-determination and its attendant language of minority rights. National self-determination—and the secession and irredentism it could provoke—was viewed as a serious political threat to the new international order (Preece 1999, 183). Consequently, the UN Charter incorporated the vague phrase "self-determination of peoples," as distinct from the more familiar term "national self-determination." Self-determination was accepted only insofar as it implied the right to the self-government of peoples.

Socialist countries, however, understood self-determination essentially as a principle to liberate non-self-governing peoples from colonial domination (Cassese 1977, 85). In fact, as the process of decolonization proceeded, self-determination came to be recognized as a legal norm confined to the cases of people under colonial rule. In other words, the principle of self-determination came to mean the right of people under colonial rule to be independent—i.e., "external self-determination." Self-determination as "internal self-determination" also came to be commonly defined as the right of a people to "freely determine their political status and freely pursue their economic, social and cultural development," as described in the International Covenant on Civil and Political Rights (UN Treaty Series 1976, Art. 1). In the Helsinki Final Act of the CSCE, the "self-determination of people" is defined as the right "to determine, when and as they wish, their internal and external political status, without external interference, and to pursue as they wish their political, economic, social and cultural development" (CSCE 1990, para. 8).

A cursory survey of relevant international conventions does not indicate any positive recognition for the right of post-colonial self-determination. To the contrary, there was a deliberate move in cases prior to the breakaway Yugoslav republics to discredit the idea of self-determination as understood in ethnonational terms (Preece 1999, 183). The principle of self-determination has in fact never been used as a principle to legitimize the independence of any constituent ethnic nation or national minority. The international community has rejected post-colonial self-determination through a commitment to the maintenance of the principle of territorial integrity. The territorial integrity of states has been held as paramount. This was specifically expressed and affirmed in the 1960 UN Declaration on the Granting of Independence to Colonial Territories and Countries, which states, "Any attempt aimed at the partial or total disruption of the national unity and the territorial integrity of a country is incompatible with the purposes and principles of the Charter of the United Nations" (United Nations General Assembly 1960, para. 6). By severely limiting the justifiable application of self-determination and by raising territorial integrity to the level of nearly an absolute principle, the international community has rejected any sort of secession (Bartkus 1999). And when faced with a declaration of independence in 1960 by the Katanga province from what is now known as the Democratic Republic of the Congo, or that of Biafra from Nigeria in 1967, for example, the international community made its implicit condemnation of secession explicit (Bartkus 1999, 68–78; Blay 1994, 283). The determination of the international community to preclude secession and irredentism was largely successful until the breakup of the Soviet Union and the former Yugoslavia.

Self-Determination of National Minorities

Under international law, then, the six Yugoslav republics had no right to external self-determination. In addition, no such right was proclaimed in the Yugoslav constitution. Nevertheless, the international community granted the right of "self-determination of people" to the secessionist ethnic nations. It must be stressed again that this was not the application of self-determination as assumed in the conventional interpretation of that principle.

In the post-communist context, modern states are being jeopardized by a trend toward subnational and ethnic re-territorialization. This is partly a reflection of the new political trend that has seen democracy and minority rights becoming the *sine qua non* for validating governance. The Paris Charter, agreed to at the CSCE Paris summit meeting held on November 11–21, 1990, declared the end of the cold war, saying, "The era of confrontation and division of Europe has ended." It also urged states to "undertake to build, consolidate and strengthen democracy as the only system of government of our nations." Interestingly, as one of the "guidelines for the future" in the Paris Charter, special emphasis was put on national minorities: "Determined to foster the rich contribution of national minorities to the life of our societies, we undertake further to improve their situation. We declare that questions related to national minorities can only be satisfactorily resolved in a democratic political framework" (CSCE 1990).

If minority rights are to be extended and minority groups decide to seek their self-determination, what are the implications for the territorial integrity of a state? In the immediate post–cold war period, ethnic conflicts hitherto suppressed by authoritarian rule did indeed come to the foreground, particularly in the Soviet Union and Yugoslavia, challenging the territorial integrity of those respective states. Former UN Secretary-General Boutros Boutros-Ghali explicitly expressed this concern in his 1992 report, *Agenda for Peace* (para. 18–19):

> The time of absolute and exclusive sovereignty, however, has passed; its theory was never matched by reality. It is the task of leaders of States today to understand this and to find a balance between the needs of good internal governance and the requirements of an ever more interdependent world. . . . Yet if every ethnic, religious or linguistic group claimed statehood, there would be no limit to fragmentation, and peace, security and economic well-being for all would become ever more difficult to achieve. . . . The sovereignty, territorial integrity and independence of States within the established international system, and the principle of self-determination for peoples, both of great value and importance, must not be permitted to work against each other in the period ahead.

The critical issue for the international community is whether to recognize the independence of subnational ethnic groups. The Yugoslav constitution did not include specific provisions for the secession of Yugoslav republics from the federation. In July 1991, just before Slovenia and Croatia were about to declare independence, a CSCE Meeting of Experts on National Minorities took place in Geneva to discuss this delicate issue. It is noteworthy that they could not reach an agreement on the question raised by the Yugoslav delegates as to whether "national minorities" should be granted collective rights. Despite the fact that for a number of CSCE states such recognition would have implied a danger of secession by their own minorities, the meeting could not reach a consensus on how to define the actor of self-determination. At the end of the meeting, the Yugoslav delegation issued an "interpretative statement," regretting that the concluding document did not reflect "a very important issue raised in the debate," namely, "the separatist behavior of national minorities [and] their claim to the right of self-determination." The statement continues, saying that the only objective of the Yugoslav proposal was "to reaffirm the crystal-clear principle of the Helsinki Final Act stating that only peoples, and not national minorities, have the right to self-determination. In failing to do this, the Meeting did not meet its responsibility, and hence it contributed to the defining of a dangerous precedent, whose boomerang may tomorrow hit other participating states, threatening their territorial integrity, stability and peace" (CSCE 1991b).

Yugoslavia was right. The CSCE states could not reconfirm the "crystal-clear principle" of self-determination. To the contrary, the European states changed the traditional interpretation of the principle shortly thereafter and recognized the secession of ethnic nations. As was fully anticipated, a chain reaction of violent secessionist conflicts ensued, as the recognition of the breakaway republics triggered a geopolitical catastrophe. Once the principle of self-determination was applied to the secession of ethnic-based nations within a federal state, the minorities in nascent nation-states in former communist countries started to crave their own self-determination. By the end of 1992, seven secessionist movements had successfully demonstrated their ability to defend their self-determination militarily in Yugoslavia and the Soviet Union.[9]

Self-Determination with Minority Rights

Another noticeable change in the concept of self-determination at the time of the Yugoslav crisis was that it had come to contain human rights and minority protection. Deciding on conditional recognition, as we have seen above, the EC announced its Guidelines on the Recognition of New States in Eastern Europe and the Soviet Union, and formally proclaimed a certain political conditionality for breakaway states to be recognized under the self-determination principle. The EC's guidelines start off with the following words: "The community and its member States confirm their attachment to the principles of the Helsinki Act and the Charter of Paris, in particular the principle of self-determination" (EC 1991). With these words, the EC intended to emphasize that it regarded the secession of the republics from Yugoslavia as the realization of the principle of self-determination. In addition, among the various requirements the nascent states were to meet in order to obtain recognition, the EC included respect for the "rule of law, democracy and human rights," as well as the establishment of "guarantees for the rights of ethnic and national groups and minorities" in accordance with the commitment subscribed to in the framework of the CSCE. Recognition, in other words, was contingent upon internal self-determination.

According to one account, this approach was in some respects "profoundly innovative," so much so that one could even term it "revolutionary." By making their recognition of secessionist republics conditional on respect for democracy and minority rights, the 12 European Community states forcefully affirmed the close link existing between external and internal self-determination. They made it clear that they were prepared to endorse the achievement of independent statehood—i.e., external self-determination—only on the condition that the breakaway republics fully respect the principle of representative democracy—internal self-determination. For the first time in the world community, the inextricable connection and interdependence between the two dimensions of self-determination were brought to the fore (Cassese 1995, 268).

Yet this was not as innovative or revolutionary as it may seem. After World War I, the victorious allies used international law to rearrange the European landscape. The settlement of 1919 made minority rights a prerequisite for international recognition of new states in Central and Eastern Europe. Although the nascent principle of self-determination insisted that these newly created states be ethnically homogeneous, there were 20 million to 25 million people who remained outside of their nation-state, and who were placed under the protection of the League of Nations to enable them to live side by side with the majority ethnic group where they were residing. In this way, Europe tried to establish a minority protection regime as a way of preserving international peace and security (Mertus 1999, 269; Krasner 1999, 90–96).

The regional human rights and minority protection regime under the OSCE's direction that was introduced by the European international community after the breakup of Yugoslavia was redolent of this interwar minority rights protection regime. The OSCE participating states agreed on common norms and principles with regard to human rights and minority protection and provided a mechanism for monitoring and promoting those norms. It should be noted that the establishment of both regimes reflected international perceptions at those respective times that minority issues could threaten international security.

THE DILEMMA OF
POST-CONFLICT CONFLICT PREVENTION

Long-Term Preventive Diplomacy
in the Post-Conflict Phase

The "peace agreement" was not the end of the conflicts in the region. Nor can the "post-conflict phase" be in any way characterized as conflict-free. The root causes of the ethnic fighting have only been frozen, not solved. While peace agreements may represent the point at which conflicts are formally terminated, if root causes are not addressed in the post-settlement phase, conflicts can erupt again during the peacebuilding process. There remain many Central and Eastern European countries whose jurisdiction encompasses regionally concentrated ethnonational minorities that might demand self-determination at any time in the future. The ethnic animosity between these groups has become deeper and increasingly implacable as a result of violent ethnic conflicts. The dividing boundaries between ethnic groups have become more apparent both psychologically and demographically as a result of ethnic conflicts, ethnic cleansing, and population transfers. War in Bosnia and Kosovo in particular remains a possibility. Thus the post-conflict phase in Bosnia and Kosovo requires long-term preventive diplomacy by the international community.

There is a near consensus among policymakers and scholars that the objective of long-term preventive diplomacy in the post-conflict phase should be to recreate and preserve integrated, multiethnic societies. Current efforts by the international community aim to restore multiethnic civil society in Bosnia and Serbia by such means as institution building, power sharing, and identity reconstruction. It is assumed that most of those who have become refugees because of ethnic conflict can return to their pre-conflict places of domicile and enjoy reasonable economic, political, and cultural freedom. The bottom line of this thinking is that working to reintegrate ethnic groups that were once at war with each other is morally preferable and, in the long run, more practical than acquiescing to a partition.

Intermixed population settlement patterns, however, can contribute to maintaining the potential for ethnic conflict. Is the rebuilding or introduction of participatory electoral democracy a feasible means for peacebuilding? There is little likelihood that the Croatian Serbs will accept minority status in Croatia, that Albanians in Kosovo will accept minority status in Serbia, or that Bosnian Serbs will accept minority status in Bosnia. In the post-conflict phase, with ethnic divisions being more distinct than ever, the holding of free elections as a step toward democracy and good governance can actually become another tool through which the parties hope to resolve the unfinished business of war. In the national and local elections held in Croatia and Bosnia, for example, it has become a life or death matter for new ethnic-oriented political parties to win the election. If we look at the post-conflict settlement and the instability in Bosnia and Kosovo in particular, which is barely being maintained with an international presence and forces, it becomes clear that the current approach to peacebuilding is neither feasible nor realistic.

Internal Peace with an International Military Presence

The difficulty of restoring a multiethnic democratic society in the post-conflict phase is shown by the tardy progress of refugees in returning to their homes. The termination of most secessionist conflicts in Europe since 1995 has not brought a significant reduction in the European refugee population so far because the further ethnic divide that resulted from ethnic cleansing and ethnic transfers is standing in the way of the return of the refugees. More than a half million people were forced to flee their homes during the course of the 1991–1995 armed conflict in Croatia. While the majority of the Croat displaced persons and refugees have returned to their places of domicile, the return of the Croatian Serbs has not been easy. It is estimated that around 280,000 Croatian Serbs became refugees or were displaced internally during this period. Even after the Eastern Slavonian region of Croatia, the site of heavy ethnic fighting, was placed under the United Nations Transitional Administration (UNTAES), many Serbs faced continuing harassment and the fear of living in Croatia induced large numbers of them to cross into Serb-held territory. Some 47,000 Croatian Serbs are reported to have fled to Yugoslavia from 1995 on, leaving 12,900 displaced Serbs still in Croatia in early 1998 (Organization for Security and Co-operation in Europe [OSCE] 2000). In addition, after Eastern Slavonia was transferred from UNTAES administration back to the Croatian government in 1998, thousands more Serbs left the area. According to the United Nations High Commissioner for Refugees, by early 2000, there were an estimated 300,000 Croatian Serb refugees still in the Federal Republic of Yugoslavia, and another 30,000–40,000 in Bosnia (United Nations High Commissioner for Refugees [UNHCR] 2000b). Only a small percentage of Croatian Serb refugees have returned to their prewar places of domicile. Between the end of 1995 and October 1999, a total of just under 35,000 Croatian Serbs had returned from abroad (OSCE 2000). As a result of this population transfer, Croatia has become an increasingly homogeneous country.

The situations in Bosnia and Kosovo are even more complex and perilous. The aftermath of the wars in Bosnia and Kosovo reflects a contradiction between the explicit rejection of ethnic cleansing in the settlements and the actual implementation of practices that endorse the principle of ethnic homogeneity. In the Dayton Peace Accords, the affirmation of the territorial integrity of the internationally recognized state of Bosnia accorded respect for the state's earlier act of self-determination. The peace settlement divided Bosnia into two political entities, allotting 51 percent of the republic's territory to the Muslim-Croat federation (the Federation of Bosnia and Herzegovina), and 49 percent to the Bosnian Serbs (the Serb Republic) who had controlled over 70 percent of the territory before the peace agreement. The political entities of Bosnia are de facto two states, each possessing its own army, and thus the agreement accorded Serbs their national self-determination. The Bosnian Serbs obtained what they wanted all along: a semiautonomous state.

Although the Dayton Peace Accords contained clear and unconditional provisions for the return of refugees and displaced persons, and despite numerous political pledges not to accept the results of ethnic cleansing, the reality of postwar Bosnia contradicts those statements. There were 550,000 Muslims in 1991 who were living in the area that later came to be the "Serb Republic"; as a result of ethnic cleansing, that number dwindled to just a few thousand. By the end of 1997, of the 2.3 million displaced during the war and the 80,000 displaced since, an estimated 660,000 people have returned to Bosnia. However, the return of people to their original homes where they would now be part of an ethnic minority has been particularly slow. Five years after the Dayton Peace Accords, Bosnia still had over 809,000 internally displaced persons (UNHCR 2000a). War precipitated ethnic segregation, and the Dayton Peace Accords cemented the national divide by creating a system of ethnicity-based government.

It is now impossible for Bosnia to maintain the facade of a unified state without an international military presence, since the Bosnian Serbs still have strong aspirations for the secession and independence of Bosnia. In the Dayton Peace Accords, the mandate of the Implementation Force (IFOR), mainly composed of NATO forces, was limited to one year, but it has become impossible for IFOR to withdraw since stability in that country is clearly dependent upon the deterrent capability of the international military presence. As of 1998, NATO had decided to continue its operations indefinitely with about 30,000 troops.

In Kosovo, after heavy fighting and the ensuing ethnic cleansing of ethnic Albanians by the Yugoslav army, and later of Serbs by Albanians in return, NATO's intervention in Yugoslavia resulted in the return of over 850,0000 Albanian refugees and internally displaced persons to Kosovo. At the same time, 210,000 Serbs, Roma, and other non-Albanians fled Kosovo (UNHCR 2000a). The number of remaining Kosovar Serbs has dwindled to about 100,000, making Kosovo an ever more homogeneous province. It is not likely that the Serbs will return to Kosovo in the future, as long as the situation of the remaining minority is precarious. Fearful of Albanian retaliation, the Serbs as a minority group in Kosovo cannot survive without an international military presence. Moreover, because of its volatile relationship with Yugoslavia (FRY, the Federal Republic of Yugoslavia), Kosovo also cannot survive without an international presence. In addition to the United Nations Interim Administration Mission in Kosovo (UNMIK) and the OSCE permanent mission (which, with 2,100 staff, is the largest OSCE field presence for peacebuilding), the international community agreed to deploy yet another international military presence, the 60,000-person NATO-led Kosovo Force (KFOR). In essence, Kosovo is now a NATO/UN/OSCE protectorate, although its constitutional and legal status makes it still a part of Yugoslavia (FRY). The relationship between Yugoslavia and Kosovo is therefore yet to be resolved, but it is likely that the international military presence will continue to be needed for the foreseeable future—almost indefinitely—to maintain the semblance of one sovereign state.

The post-conflict policy of refugee return cannot be implemented in the immediate aftermath of wars, and attempts to encourage refugees and displaced people to return to their homes are likely to cost the lives of some of the very people they are supposed to save. It is almost impossible to restore intermixed population settlement. Neither is it feasible to restore a unified sovereign state in Bosnia and Yugoslavia (Kosovo). By deploying an international military presence in Bosnia and Kosovo with the goal of imposing intermixed population settlement, the international community is helping to ensure that Bosnia and Kosovo will have a much more troubled and uncertain future.

Partition as a Means of Conflict Prevention?

Healing the wounds of war will take time, but there is nothing in Balkan history to suggest that these wounds can be healed in ways that will satisfy the distinctive political desires of different ethnic groups in one political entity. Nonetheless, separating populations remains deeply controversial and seems immoral to many in the international community. Even when carried out safely, population transfers inflict enormous suffering, including the loss of homes and livelihoods and the disruption of social, religious, and cultural ties. Thus they can be justified only if they save the lives of people who would otherwise be killed in ethnic violence.

In recent years, however, the idea that separating the warring populations may be the best solution for many areas that have come through intense ethnic conflicts has been gaining ground. In fact, there have been a number of seemingly radical measures such as population transfers applied during the 20th century as post-conflict conflict-prevention measures.[10] Separating populations can reduce interethnic violence, thus contributing to internal stability. After investigating the partitions of Ireland, India, Palestine, and Cyprus, Chaim Kaufmann concludes that when warring populations were separated—either by planned transfers or by ethnic cleansing—violence subsequently declined. If the logic of demographic separation is correct, then why have the partitions in Northern Ireland, Kashmir, Palestine, and Cyprus been so violent? Kaufmann asserts that the continuation of resurgent intergroup violence in limited regions within some of these cases has resulted not from partition or from separation, but rather from the incompleteness of separation of the hostile groups in those specific areas (1998). In keeping with this line of argument, while Croatia has become peaceful and stable because it has become increasingly homogeneous as a result of ethnic cleansing and demographic transfers, the political situations in Bosnia and Kosovo have been tense since the warring groups within those areas have been forced to live side by side under the facade of a nation-state. As long as conflicting parties know that the best security strategy for each is to engage in offense against the other ethnic group and even in ethnic cleansing, neither can base its security strategy on hopes for the other's restraint.

The policy implications of this examination of preventive diplomacy efforts in the former Yugoslavia are clear: the international community should endorse the de facto self-determination of the two entities of Bosnia—i.e., the Muslim-Croat republic and the Serb Republic—as well as the separation of Kosovo from Yugoslavia (FRY), with the condition of minority protection. If not, the international community may have to remain committed to these states almost indefinitely, or the process of war may separate the populations anyway at a much higher human cost.

CONCLUSION

Belated and uncoordinated preventive diplomacy could not forestall the escalation of the Yugoslav crisis into violent conflict. If historical second-guessing is allowed as we reconsider this case of failed preventive diplomacy, the crucial catalyst in this escalation clearly appears to have been the international recognition of the seceding ethnic nations' right of self-determination. The secessionist drives counted on the principle of self-determination as a tool to legitimize their claims. Such an assertion of the principle, however, inexorably has led to the breakup of multiethnic states, given its lack of respect for the territorial integrity of existing states. Self-determination, in fact, has rekindled and enhanced ethnic identity and led to loathsome bloodshed.

It was a mistake to have recognized the unilateral independence of ethnic nations. The creation of new states has led to the creation of new minorities that are seeking their own independence. Although the breakup of Yugoslavia might have been inevitable, it is unlikely that the country would have suffered such a violent collapse if the international community had taken a more coordinated and determined approach to self-determination, based on a policy of non-recognition of unilateral independence by violent means.

The cases of Croatia, Bosnia, and Kosovo show how incompatible it can be to realize both self-determination and international peace and security. Article 1 of the United Nations Charter sets forth the purposes of the United Nations as being to "maintain international peace and security" and to ensure "friendly relations among nations based on respect for the principles of equal rights and self-determination. . . ." Daniel Moynihan correctly notes that the fact that it might not be possible to do both things at one time seems hardly to have occurred to the drafters of the Charter (1993, 66). The idea of self-determination also serves to undermine multiethnic societies, whose very creation is idealized in the melting pot phenomenon (a phenomenon experienced to some extent in the United States but rarely emulated elsewhere).

Looking back at the process through which the seceding ethnic nations of Yugoslavia received international recognition, there was clearly a double standard in the way in which the self-determination principle was interpreted. First, the response of the international community to the Yugoslav cases differed markedly from the past practice in other parts of the world. The principle was never meant to be a norm to legitimize the independence of any constituent ethnic nation, much less national minorities. In fact, it had never been applied to secession drives, even when they involved major conflicts that threatened international security.

In addition, while the self-determination of decolonized states was unconditional, the recognition of the seceding republics of Yugoslavia was conditional upon the respect of human rights and minority rights. The difference may derive from geopolitical and security concerns. Many European countries had good reason to perceive the conflicts in the Balkans as sources of instability in Europe, directly threatening their security interests through possible spillover effects.

Finally, the recognition of external self-determination in the post-communist phase by the international community has been selective. As discussed above, not only the republics of Slovenia, Croatia, Macedonia, and Bosnia, but also Krajina (a Serb region in Croatia) and Kosovo (a largely Albanian autonomous province attached to Serbia) appealed to the EC for recognition. However, the EC eventually rejected the independence of Krajina and Kosovo for fear of further fragmentation and the additional political instability that it would unleash. Does this imply that the international community will recognize the independence of ethnic nations that are constituent parts of a federation, such as Chechnya is of Russia and Montenegro of Yugoslavia? Does this mean that ethnic minorities which are not guaranteed the status of federal republic but are a semi-autonomous executive unit instead, such as Kosovo or Aceh of Indonesia, are not qualified to be independent?

The increasingly interconnected world today is faced with the fragmentation of sovereign and territorial states due to these new approaches to the principle of self-determination. The application of the principle of self-determination to the Yugoslav secession movements shows that the principle has become so central in international law and politics that it has fully encompassed the principle of territorial integrity. Self-determination has come to mean a tool to prove democratic entitlement over the territory inhabited by a people who may wish to exercise their right to democratic government within a separate state entity. The implications of this are staggering if we consider that, as Walker Connor found, of 132 states he examined, only 12 were "essentially homogeneous from an ethnic viewpoint" (1972). According to some estimates, there are over 5,000 minorities and approximately 80 ethnically oriented, protracted conflicts around the globe. Approximately 35 internal wars were under way in 1994 (Carment and James 1997, 2). There is a legitimate fear that international recognition of secession might inspire the unrealizable aspirations of other ethnic communities. When secessionist movements that are likely to threaten the security and peace of Europe proclaim independence with the premise of the respect of human rights and minority rights, how will the international community—and the European community in particular—respond? How can the international community contribute to peaceful independence?

There are several lessons to be drawn from this example of failed diplomacy. First, a few words should be added on the political impact of supporting or even organizing referendums on the question of self-determination. Referendums are found to be a persuasive means to assess the democratic character of self-determination. Holding a referendum is also found to be a handy and persuasive way of mobilizing nationalism for independence. But referendums held in seceding ethnic nations were nothing but a means to realize an ethnic majoritarian rule, and these actions are a prelude to throwing multiethnic society into a security dilemma. For the international community to help and even organize referendums regarding independence is consequently tantamount to helping produce ethnic conflicts. The international community must refrain from supporting referendums in ethnically intermixed areas.

Second, the lessons of the failure of preventive diplomacy in the former Yugoslavia indicate that violence, and any international actors helping violence, must not be condoned. Looking back on the Yugoslav war, we find that it was too late for the international community to conduct effective short-term preventive diplomacy after secessionist movements came to be organized and they began to arm themselves. In that respect, the Macedonian case has been a good example of successful preventive diplomacy by the international community since the timing of the international involvement, including preventive deployment of United Nations forces and the OSCE's active role in short-term and long-term preventive diplomacy, came early enough—well before the society became organized along ethnic lines.

A related lesson to be drawn here is that the international community, with the active and leading role of the United Nations, should establish a global early-warning system and methods of preventive diplomacy that can lead to the peaceful settlement of ethnic disputes. The international community must agree to make the domestic root causes of conflicts a matter of international concern so the international community, and the United Nations in particular, can play a more effective role in preventive diplomacy.

And finally, the experience of the former Yugoslavia vividly demonstrates the urgent need for the international community to establish an international standard for the recognition of independence. This is critical from the viewpoint of preventive diplomacy, considering the emerging drives for self-determination among national minorities around the world. The standard should explicitly show the clear-cut and determined will of the international community that any movements for secession or self-determination that resort to violence will not be recognized. It should also make clear that negotiations for secession or independence are to be conducted peacefully under the auspices of the United Nations, and that minorities should be protected. Finally, in order to ensure that such protections are effective in newly independent countries, the United Nations, as the representative of the international community, should take the initiative in establishing a worldwide minority protection regime.

NOTES

1. For an explanation of ethnic conflicts in the post–cold war era, see Kozhemiakin (1998), Carment and James (1997), and Brown (1996).

2. See Daalder (1996), Goldstein (1999), and East and Pontin (1997). I have

relied heavily on these accounts in my review of the crisis and the process of the breakup of Yugoslavia.

3. "Greater Serbia" is an idea that implies the creation of a monoethnic and contiguous state that would include Serbia proper and all predominantly Serbian areas outside its boundaries—primarily Slavonia and Krajina in Croatia and the Serb regions of Bosnia and Herzegovina, Macedonia, and Montenegro.

4. For an overview of the involvement of the international community in the Yugoslav conflict, see Baker (1995), Zimmermann (1996), Zucconi (1996), and Miall, Ramsbotham, and Woodhouse (1999).

5. In the spring of 1991, there were at least four countries leaning toward support for Slovenian and Croatian independence: Hungary, Denmark, Germany, and Austria. Although in late June, Vienna moved to the collective EC stance, Italy at times reflected domestic pressures favoring Slovenian and Croatian independence (Zucconi 1996, 241).

6. Since I initially wrote this chapter, there has been a fair amount of sporadic conflict and further diplomatic efforts to prevent the escalation of conflict in Macedonia. From February 2001, the Albanian rebels known as the National Liberation Army (NLA) began limited fighting in areas around Tetovo and Kumanovo, the ethnic Albanian region in the northern part of Macedonia. The tensions between the Macedonian majority and the Albanian minority in the country mounted, resulting in the demand by Albanians for a new constitution, greater rights for Albanians, and international mediation in the dispute.

Representing the international community, the EU, the North Atlantic Treaty Organization (NATO), and the OSCE mediated between the Macedonian government and the rebels, and both sides agreed in August 2001 to a peace accord that paved the way for NATO's deployment to demilitarize the rebels. It also promised a series of measures to satisfy the demands of the Albanians. Under the terms of the peace accord, NLA fighters handed in their weapons to NATO and disbanded. Under the pressure of the international community, Macedonia's parliament adopted constitutional changes in November 2001 granting greater rights to Albanians, including the recognition of Albanian as an official language and increasing access for ethnic Albanians to public sector jobs.

The country has succeeded to date in avoiding the escalation of conflict, and peace appears to have returned. However, since the potential for ethnic conflict still exists, the international community decided to step up its commitment to Macedonia by strengthening the OSCE long-term mission there, the mandate of which is to monitor the implementation of the peace accord and to prevent conflict. In addition, NATO has deployed a small force of around 1,000 soldiers to protect the OSCE mission. Although Macedonia has not experienced a large-scale, nationwide ethnic conflict like those in Bosnia and Kosovo, it has become another country that requires an international presence for its stability and conflict prevention.

7. The CSCE sent a mission to Skopje in September 1992, and the UN Security Council authorized the first preventive deployment of UN peacekeepers to Macedonia on December 11, 1992 (UN Resolution 795). This initiative was triggered by concerns that the Yugoslav war would spill over from Bosnia to Macedonia, and by a request from Macedonian President Gligorov for a peacekeeping force.

8. After World War I, minority rights were set in peace treaties with the new states of East and Central Europe, granting full rights to ethnic and religious minorities. In addition, monitoring and enforcement mechanisms were established through the League of Nations and the International Court of Justice.

9. The seven secessionist movements that had proven their ability to establish de facto independence militarily by the end of 1992 were Nagorno-Karabakh from Azerbaijan, Abkhazia and South Ossetia from Georgia, Chechnya from Russia, Transdniestria from Moldova, Krajina/Slavonia from Croatia, and the Serb Republic from Bosnia.

10. For example, after World War I, Greece and Turkey agreed to an exchange of populations, with 400,000 Turks being sent to Turkey in exchange for 1.3 million Greeks. The victorious Allies in 1945 opted for changing populations to fit the borders rather than the other way around, and this was achieved through the expulsion and resettlement of some 15 million people, including the expulsion of 7 million-10 million Germans from East Prussia, Silesia, and Sudetenland, providing a final settlement of what had been lasting territorial conflicts. An exchange of population was also agreed upon between Hungary and Czechoslovakia, as a result of which up to 100,000 Slovaks could choose to transfer to Czechoslovakia and the same number of Magyars could choose to transfer to Hungary. Eventually, some 60,000 persons were exchanged on each side. Germany, Poland, Hungary, and Czechoslovakia became for the first time in their histories nearly homogeneous entities, but in the rest of Eastern Europe the problem was suppressed rather than solved (Baev 1999, 25, 29; Preece 1999, 190).

BIBLIOGRAPHY

Baev, Pavel K. 1999. "External Interventions in Secessionist Conflicts in Europe in the 1990s." *European Security* 8(2): 22–51.

Baker, James A. 1995. *The Politics of Diplomacy: Revolution, War and Peace, 1989–1992*. New York: Putnam.

Bartkus, Viva Ona. 1999. *The Dynamic of Secession*. Cambridge, U.K.: Cambridge University Press.

Birmingham, Katherine. 1995. *The OSCE and Minority Issues*. The Hague: Foundation on Inter-Ethnic Relations.

Blay, Sam. 1994. "Self-determination: A Reassessment in the Post-Communist Era." *Denver Journal of International Law and Policy* 22 (2-3): 275-315.

Boutros-Ghali, Boutros. 1992. *An Agenda for Peace: Preventive Diplomacy, Peacemaking and Peace-keeping*. New York: United Nations Department of Public Information.

Brown, Michael E., ed. 1996. *The International Dimensions of Internal Conflicts*. Cambridge, Mass.: MIT Press.

Carment, David, and Patrick James. 1997. *Wars in the Midst of Peace: The International Politics of Ethnic Conflict*. Pittsburgh, Pa.: University of Pittsburgh Press.

Cassese, Antonio. 1995. *Self-determination of Peoples: A Legal Reappraisal*. Cambridge, U.K.: Cambridge University Press.

——. 1977. "The Helsinki Declaration and Self-determination." In Thomas Buergenthal, ed. *Human Rights, International Law and the Helsinki Accord*. Montclair, N.J.: Allanheld, Osmun/Universe Books.

Chayes, Abram, and Antonia Handler Chayes, eds. 1996. *Preventing Conflict in the Post-Communist World: Mobilizing International and Regional Organizations*. Washington, D.C.: The Brookings Institution.

Conference for Security and Co-operation in Europe. 1975. "Declaration on Principles Guiding Relations between Participating States." *Helsinki Final Act* (1 August).

——. 1990. *Charter of Paris for a New Europe* (21 November).

——. 1991a. "Statement on the Situation in Yugoslavia." Permanent Council Journal No. 2 (Berlin, 19 June).

——. 1991b. "Interpretative Statement by Yugoslavia." Permanent Council Journal No. 15 (Geneva, 19 July).

Connor, Walker. 1972. "Nation-Building or Nation-Destroying?" *World Politics* 24(3): 319-355.

Cumper, Peter, and Steven Wheatley. 1999. *Minority Rights in the "New" Europe*. The Hague: Martinus Nijhoff Publishers.

Daalder, Ivo H. 1996. "Fear and Loathing in the Former Yugoslavia." In Michael E. Brown, ed. *The International Dimensions of Internal Conflicts*. Cambridge, Mass.: MIT Press.

East, Roger, and Jolyon Pontin. 1997. *Revolution and Change in Central and Eastern Europe*. London: Pinter Publishers.

Edwards, Geoffrey. 1992. "European Responses to the Yugoslav Crisis: An Interim Assessment." In Rummel Reinhardt, ed. *Toward Political Union: Planning a Common Foreign and Security Policy in the European Community*. Boulder, Colo.: Westview Press.

European Community. 1991. "Guidelines on the Recognition of New States in Eastern Europe and the Soviet Union" (16 December). 31 International Legal Materials (ILM) 1486 (1992).

European Parliament. 1991. Parliament Resolution on Yugoslavia. (15 March).

Goldstein, Ivo. 1999. *Croatia: A History*. London: Hurst & Company.

Hippel, Karin von. 1994. "The Resurgence of Nationalism and Its International Implications." *The Washington Quarterly* 17(4): 185-200.

Kaufmann, Chaim D. 1998. "When All Else Fails: Ethnic Population Transfers and Partitions in the Twentieth Century." *International Security* 23(2): 120-156.

Kozhemiakin, Alexander V. 1998. *Expanding the Zone of Peace?: Democratization and International Security*. London: Macmillan.

Krasner, Stephen D. 1999. *Sovereignty: Organized Hypocrisy*. Princeton, N.J.: Princeton University Press.

Lucarelli, Sonia. 1997. "Europe's Response to the Yugoslav Imbroglio." In Knud Erik Jorgensen, ed. *European Approaches to Crisis Management*. The Hague: Kluwer Law International.

Lund, Michael S. 1996. *Preventing Violent Conflicts: A Strategy for Preventive Diplomacy*. Washington, D.C.: United States Institute of Peace.

Malcolm, Noel. 1999. *Bosnia: A Short History*. London: Papermac.

Meier, Viktor. 1999. *Yugoslavia: A History of Its Demise*. Translated by Sabrina P. Ramet. London: Routledge.

Mertus, Julie. 1999. "The Dayton Peace Accords: Lessons from the Past and for the Future." In Peter Cumper and Steven Wheatley, eds. *Minority Rights in the "New" Europe*. The Hague: Kluwer Law International.

Miall, Hugh, Oliver Ramsbotham, and Tom Woodhouse. 1999. *Contemporary Conflict Resolution: The Prevention, Management and Transformation of Deadly Conflicts*. Malden, Mass.: Polity Press.

Moynihan, Daniel Patrick. 1993. *Pandemonium: Ethnicity in International Politics*. Oxford, U.K.: Oxford University Press.

Organization for Security and Co-operation in Europe. 2000. "Mission to Croatia: Return and Integration."<http://www.osce.org/croatia/return/return.htm> (11 February).

Owen, David. 1996. *Balkan Odyssey*. London: Harcourt.

Parliamentary Assembly of the Council of Europe. 1991. *On the Crisis in Yugoslavia*. Resolution 969 (1991).

Preece, Jennifer Jackson. 1999. "Self-determination and Minority Rights." In Ho-won Jeong, ed. *The New Agenda for Peace Research*. Aldershot: Ashgate Publishing.

Foundation on Inter-Ethnic Relations. 1997. *The Role of the High Commissioner on National Minorities in OSCE Conflict Prevention: An Introduction*. The Hague: Foundation on Inter-Ethnic Relations.

Ronen, Dov. 1997. *The Challenge of Ethnic Conflict, Democracy and Self-determination in Central Europe*. London: Frank Cass.

Rummel, Reinhardt, ed. 1992. *Toward Political Union: Planning a Common Foreign and Security Policy in the European Community*. Boulder, Colo.: Westview Press.

United Nations General Assembly. 1960. Fifteenth Session, Official Records, Supplement 16. *Declaration on Granting Independence to Colonial Territories and Countries* (14 December). General Assembly Res. 1514 (XV), A/4684 (1961).

United Nations High Commissioner for Refugees. 2000a. "The World—South East Europe/ Bosnia and Herzegovina." <http://www.unhcr.ch/world/euro/ seo/bosnia.htm> (28 July 2001).

——. 2000b. "The World: South-East Europe/ Croatia." <http://www.unhcr .ch/world/euro/seo/croatia.htm> (28 July 2001).

United Nations Treaty Series. 1976. International Covenant on Civil and Political Rights (23 March). *Treaties and International Agreements Registered or Filed or Reported with the Secretariat of the United Nations*, 999(1976), no. 14668.

Zaagman, Rob. 1996. "Some Reflections on OSCE Conflict Prevention and the Code of Conduct." *Helsinki Monitor* 7(2): 29–39.

Zimmermann, Warren. 1996. *Origins of a Catastrophe: Yugoslavia and Its Destroyers—America's Last Ambassador Tells What Happened and Why.* New York: Random House.

Zucconi, Mario. 1996. "The European Union in the Former Yugoslavia." In Abram Chayes and Antonia Handler Chayes, eds. *Preventing Conflict in the Post-Communist World: Mobilizing International and Regional Organizations.* Washington, D.C.: Brookings Institution Press.

CHAPTER TWO

Security Communities, Power-Sharing, and Preventive Diplomacy

Hoshino Toshiya

UST as no two individuals can agree on everything, so too must the international community inevitably live with disputes. One would have thought that by now mankind would have learned its lesson—particularly through the history of war and peace in the 20th century—and been able to come to an agreement on a simple but enduring dictum: the desirability of settling disputes by peaceful means. But over the past decade, the post-cold war period, we have been shocked to witness yet more human tragedies on a massive scale: genocide in Africa, ethnic cleansing in Europe, religious intolerance in Asia, and most recently, the devastating terrorist attacks in the United States. In every case, violence superseded peaceful means even before any serious efforts were made to bridge the differences of ideas and interests.

The international community did not stand idly by while all of these disputes among parties careened out of control. In fact, multi-faceted steps were taken in many cases to diffuse the violent conflicts. However, not all cases have been given the international attention necessary to deal with them preventively, effectively, or holistically. In this regard, the turn of the 20th century will be remembered as a time of greatly missed opportunities in our modern world history— opportunities lost to reconstruct a new international consensus, structure, and order.

It is true that these were turbulent years of unprecedentedly rapid political transformation, coupled with ever-expanding economic globalization and an information technology revolution. A number of old states and regimes disappeared, first and foremost of which was the Soviet Union. At the same time, many new governments emerged after the thaw and, as a consequence, our once familiar map of the world has been revised considerably.

Certainly, the end of the cold war was a rare case of a peaceful closure to a chapter in history; it did not entail a "hot" war on a global scale. (The outbreak of the Gulf Crisis/War in 1990–1991 can be considered an exception to this statement, but even that was as much a catalyst for further change as it was a major breakdown of peace.) Equally remarkable, however, was the lack of any consistent effort on the part of the international community to put these myriad changes into clear perspective in order to chart a new direction for the next chapter of history. Unlike past watershed periods, the world was unbearably slow and reluctant to institutionalize specific initiatives in the 1990s. No new Peace of Westphalia was signed, nor was a new United Nations established. Quite the contrary, the dilemma of the Westphalian state system resurfaced in the turmoil, and the United Nations, which itself was created over half a century ago, was summoned to counter newly emerging challenges.

But while conflict on a global scale was averted, conflicts on a smaller scale began to proliferate. From East Asia to West Africa and from Northern Europe to the South Pacific, multitudes of deadly conflicts and humanitarian catastrophes broke out—mainly within national borders—overwhelming our short-lived euphoria. Most of these conflicts no longer stemmed from opposing ideologies, but rather from ethnic, religious, and cultural underpinnings. Surely the world was not standing still, but when the international community did undertake peacemaking efforts, it seemed to be constantly frustrated by the gap between the anticipated and actual results. Despite efforts to control events by various means from diplomacy to military options, and from massive humanitarian relief operations to coercive "humanitarian interventions," frequently the negative forces prevailed, resulting in the severest forms of violence, despair, and confusion.

The renewed attention to "preventive diplomacy" in the early 1990s was one reflection of the world's genuine pursuit of a practical way out. The concept was first underscored in that new context in a widely read 1992 report by United Nations Secretary-General Boutros Boutros-Ghali, *An Agenda for Peace: Preventive Diplomacy, Peacemaking and Peace-Keeping.* The proliferation of fierce civil wars during the years that followed, however, was a clear indication of the failures of international endeavors, or lack thereof, to prevent them from happening.

Many reasons can be identified for the absence of progress during the last decade. At the outset, we should not forget that the peaceful resolution of conflicts is ultimately the responsibility of the parties directly concerned. However powerful they may be in physical terms, third parties cannot completely control situations that are created by local parties. But the international community, as the external party, does have the potential to influence the life history of a conflict.[1] And this potential can work both ways: the collective will of the international community can certainly pressure the warring parties to retreat to their corners, while the lack of it can adversely affect local situations. Therefore, we have to realize the degree to which the absence of attention, action, and consensus on the part of international actors at certain crucial points has a significant impact on the course of events leading up to violence.

Likewise, a false consensus and wrong signals on the part of the international community can easily undermine effective action to prevent and contain violent situations. In fact, what has frequently been observed during these critical years when international actors intervened in local situations has been not so much a lack of international consensus on the need for conflict transformation, if not its resolution, but rather a one-sided and repeated application of two ideas—democratic governance and strategic stability. These are hardly new ideas. What was seen as the lack of a "new" consensus indeed reflected not merely the inability of the international community to devise new guiding principles, but its benign belief that the conventional ideas of liberal democracy and stability would provide the most promising way for conflicting parties to cease their acts of hostility while preventing domestic troubles from spreading to a broader region. The West's victory over the East's system solidified that belief. But each of these two orientations is controversial in its own right, and more often than not, the two are incompatible.

First, in spite of the overall consensus on the desirability of democratic governance, few concepts are more controversial when it comes to actual application (Snyder 2000). The resultant debate is a clash of two worldviews. One strand of thought stipulates that it is the lack of democracy that causes violent conflict, so proponents prescribe democratic governance or democratization as the key to conflict prevention and resolution. The so-called democratic peace theory clearly reveals this preference. No, the other school would respond. While they do not deny the importance of democracy's legitimating role (as evidenced by all those "Democratic People's Republics" of the world that are in fact no different from single-party, often militaristic, authoritarian regimes), they tend to stress that its untimely introduction to divided societies can produce more harm than good. The message is that ballots should be held, but bullets should not be totally excluded.

Second is the international community's frequent reliance on a myopic sense of stability, through which it demonstrates its inclination to avoid radical changes in local situations for fear of the wider spread of instability. This is an overarching factor that has inspired many of the recent debates on the wisdom of maintaining the status quo of territorial integrity versus the demand for more revisionist national self-determination.

These two preoccupations are often contradictory in the sense that the former demands radical change while the latter seeks to avoid it. The combination of the two strategies, when not coordinated, will make the actions of the international community most inconsistent and ineffective. They are obviously not easy concepts to reconcile. But there is no way for us to escape from this dilemma. We are compelled to step up to the hard choices between the sanctity of national sovereignty and the necessity of international intervention, and between order within national borders and transnational justice across state boundaries. These questions can be translated as a dichotomy between "national security" and "human security," or between "two concepts of sovereignty," as Kofi Annan has put it (1999, 49–50).

Our challenges are daunting. But considering the magnitude of the present challenges, and in order to avoid missing any more opportunities, we need to undertake a structural analysis of both the sources of and solutions to each respective conflict, as it is these structural factors that have created chasms between the interests of "state" and "society" in many nations. Therefore, our interest here does not lie in taking the side of either "humanitarian interventionism" or "sovereignty absolutism." Rather, we will be looking at the option of reconceptualizing "security communities" in the state-society relationship, through which more peaceful power-sharing and toleration mechanisms can be practiced.

With this as background, we will start by reviewing some of the structural causes related to the present state-sovereignty system. First, we will look at the structural rifts at the international level (i.e., the incongruity between the "nation" and the "state" of a "nation-state") and at the domestic level (i.e., the disparity between "state" and "society" within a country) that underlie the recent cycle of civil strife in many states around the world in the 20th century. Then, we will explore the structural remedies under the broad concept of "power-sharing"—as opposed to "democracy"—that can bridge these structural discrepancies. This chapter will argue that, while we do not discount the time-tested values of democratic principles and the demand for regional stability, the critical importance of locally generated initiatives should not be dismissed as long as they are in line with (or within the framework) of broadly accepted international practices. If democratization is usually a preferred choice for both local and international actors, we need to explore the terms and tempo of democratization so that it can be rigorous enough to pursue necessary changes but still open enough to respect endogenously acceptable solutions—what this author calls an "endogenous democratization" process. In these analyses, the implications for preventive diplomacy will be given particular attention. Finally, the chapter will briefly review cases in Asia—most notably those in Cambodia and Myanmar—to demonstrate the empirical significance for the international community of finding the nexus between external pressure and "endogenous democratization" impulses.

STRUCTURAL CAUSES OF CONFLICTS

One of the lessons we have learned from the profusion of internal warfare in the past decade is that contrary to conventional wisdom divisions based on group identity (as defined by ethnic, religious, cultural, linguistic, or other distinctions), while they are indeed key triggers of many conflicts, are rarely the exclusive factors in and of themselves. The causes of conflict are multifaceted. The conclusion of a comprehensive analysis by the European Union, for example, lists four sets of root causes of violent conflict: (1) an imbalance of political, socioeconomic, or cultural opportunities among different identity groups; (2) a lack of democratic legitimacy and effective governance; (3) an absence of opportunities for the peaceful conciliation of group interests and for bridging dividing lines between different identity groups; and (4) a lack of an active and organized civil society (Council of the European Union 1998). Similarly, Peter Harris and Ben Reilly point out that it is the "combination of potent identity-based factors with wider perceptions of economic and social injustice" that often fuel what they call "deep-rooted conflict" (1998, 9). These and other studies properly highlight the question of identity groups or identity-based factors, examining the correlation between the composition of identity groups in a state and the disparity of opportunities among them as the background to conflict escalation.

While these characterizations are useful, however, it should be stressed that the politics of group identity formation—rather than a more common primordial understanding of group identity—has been a key factor in violent conflicts. Indeed, today more than ever before, group identity has become a strong political force. Frequently "imagined" (to use Benedict Anderson's famous expression which stressed the artificial nature of nationhood in many states), group identity has often been manipulated by political leaders.² In order to understand why these group-based identities can easily become subject to political manipulation, however, we need to take a step back and scrutinize the structural problems embedded in the process of interaction between local and international authorities. This analysis of structural rifts—both at the international and domestic levels—will be useful for identifying structural remedies, most conspicuously in the form of power-sharing.

First, in terms of the international political structure, in which sovereign nation-states interact as independent units, the problem lies in the rift between "nation" and "state" in many of what we generally call "nation-states." The oft-mentioned legacy of artificial borders may exemplify this ambivalence. It is true, as Marina Ot-taway points out, that "all borders, except perhaps those of small island states, are artificial," and that it is not the artificiality of borders but the artificiality of states that makes post-colonial societies unstable, especially in Africa. Indeed, states in Africa, and many colonial states in other regions as well for that matter, were granted independence "through agreements with the former colonial powers, not through the emergence of strong leaders and governments that could establish effective control over territory and extract the resources necessary to sustain an independent state" (1999, 13). Nonetheless, the artificiality of borders does have an enduring effect, perpetuating the existing divisions among differing groups that happen to be within the jurisdiction of a particular state.

The much-celebrated process of decolonization of Third World countries did not ameliorate the situation. Under the tense cold war environment, those states could not escape the bipolar competition of powers even when they chose to be "nonaligned." For example, changing colonial borders was not permitted because a modus vivendi was generally employed that limited "self-determination claims for political independence to those situations that did not involve the dismemberment of any existing state" (Falk 1999, 372–374).[3] As a result, the opportunities were missed to modify colonial or other artificial borders once and for all at the time of a country's independence. In Asia, for example, East Timor was a victim of this unilateral colonial handoff, as its original attempt at independence was denied and it was overrun by the neighboring Indonesian military. In so many instances, the logic of power-balancing and stability-seeking among nation-states has largely taken precedence over the wishes of the people within a country. This was one of the primary rules of the game during the period of East-West rivalry, but the trend has not changed in the aftermath of the cold war either.

The second level we need to examine concerns the domestic political structure, in which the nature of governance of each state actor (i.e., the structure of state-society relations) is at stake. As has been alluded to in the preceding paragraphs, by stressing their "territorial integrity," states are not so much "national-sovereign" as they are "territorial-sovereign" units.[4] Thus, the maintenance of the state's territoriality—that is its physical expanse—is often given precedence over the composition of its peoples. As a result, battles over territories can easily be expected.

As discussed above, there are a number of nation-states that are made up of divergent and conflicting identity groups with complex territorial claims, but certainly not all multigroup nation-states have had to experience internal rebellions and violent conflicts. And conversely, even a purely homogeneous state, including presumably democratic ones, can be faced with division and confrontation for reasons other than a "territory-identity complex." What, then, are the alternative factors that make one state more prone to internal armed conflicts than others?

One recent study conducted under the auspices of the World Bank is useful for understanding the generalized background of civil wars. In that work, Paul Collier and Anke Hoeffler (2000) compared two contrasting motivations for rebellion: greed and grievance. A grievance-rebellion model looks at situations in which intergroup hatred (for example, ethnic or religious hatred), political exclusion (such as inequality and oppression), and historical vengeance motivate people to rise up. In contrast, a model of greed-rebellion tries to highlight an "economic calculus" in initiating civil wars, especially for the purpose of controlling primary commodity exports (e.g., diamonds in Angola and Sierra Leone, drugs in Columbia, and timber in Cambodia). The striking aspect of this research is that, somewhat contrary to the general perception, the authors stress the primacy of greed over grievance motivations, although when the two imperatives were integrated, the explanatory power was significantly improved.

However enlightening it may be, this economic analysis based on a common rational choice model runs the risk of losing sight of the significance of noneconomic factors. But on the other hand, if we consider "greed" as a manifestation of not just the control of resources in economic and financial terms but also the dominance of power (i.e., the structure of political authority), then we are able to paint a fuller picture of the interaction in which "the state" (usually authoritarian) tries to control "the society" by depriving it of political rights, while the dissatisfied part of "the society" attempts to revolt against "the state" because of this deprivation. Ethnic, religious, and cultural factors will be employed in this process, but they are symbolic rather than exclusive causes. Again, a peaceful power-sharing mechanism (and particularly the lack of it) is the key.

Having briefly looked at the two levels of structural rifts—the international incongruity between nation and state and the domestic discrepancy between state and society—we realize that these are in essence nothing new. But today they are confronting the world with a new urgency. And to prevent and transform intractable conflicts, we need to go back to the basic question of statehood and the application of democratic considerations in the state-formation process. What stance should external parties take in the face of choices that affect the integration or disintegration of a state?

ON STATEHOOD, DEMOCRACY, AND STRATEGIC STABILITY

Notwithstanding its many limitations and deficiencies, statehood has been one of the strongest aspirations of—and manifestations of the desire for—people's social identity. For "stateless" people or for those who are under what they perceive to be "foreign" rule, the attainment of their own state constitutes a powerful symbolic drive. For citizens of any state, "nationality" is a central part of their identity, although usually it is taken for granted. The state is a concrete physical existence, attributed with populace, territory, and government. Needless to say, it is an actor with both domestic and international bearings: domestic autonomy and international recognition are its principal qualities, on which the state bases its legitimacy. And the idea of respect for state sovereignty, with its internal and external functions, is considered to be one of the most fundamental principles in our international life.

Aside from this common sanctity of sovereign rights, however, individual states are quite divergent. Their physical power is highly asymmetrical. In this regard, "sovereign equality"—an ideal that holds the world's only superpower (the United States), the most populated state (the People's Republic of China), and one of the smallest states (Fiji, for instance) to be equal in qualifications—is largely a fictitious concept. In fact, as Stephen Krasner has eloquently demonstrated in his work, *Sovereignty: Organized Hypocrisy*, "There has never been

some ideal time during which all, or even most, political entities con-
formed with all of the characteristics that have been associated with
sovereignty—territory, control, recognition, and autonomy" (1999,
238). He contends that the norm of sovereignty itself is best characterized by the concept of "organized hypocrisy" because of its du-
rability despite so frequent a compromise. Certainly, the impact of
economic globalization, instant communication, and transnational
civil society movements may be tremendous, but state sovereignty
will not evaporate.

We will continue to be faced with this fascinating contradiction
between the pervasiveness of the demand for sovereignty on the one
hand and the fragility of many sovereign states on the other. The end
of the cold war advanced both the forces of integration and disintegration, one manifested by the reunification of Germany and the
other by the dissolution of the former Soviet Union. These are examples of relatively peaceful transformations, but most others have
been quite different stories.

Adding to the complication is that, as discussed previously, we
cannot attribute the recent increase of wars and violent conflicts to
the end of the cold war alone, although the parsimony of this explanation is highly attractive. While the demise of the bipolar confrontation certainly altered the world at large and made it less predictable,
we need to pierce through to the core question. We must examine
the politics surrounding "state-formation," or "nation-building," the
fundamental matters of nationalism and statehood that often pre-
date the cold war and have largely characterized much of the history
of the 20th century. By delineating the question of nationalism and
its political manipulation as one principal underlying factor of per-
ennial wars, we will be able to shed light on new prescriptions to
transform, if not resolve, violent conflicts. And given the desirability
of preventing rather than responding to the severe human suffering,
this study will introduce some key approaches for effectively pursuing preventive diplomacy in the face of imminent conflicts.

The study of nationalism is no easy task. But it would be useful
to revisit this question primarily in the context of the juxtaposition
between two supposedly clashing ideas of "state sovereignty" and
"national self-determination." The former intrinsically defends the
territorial status quo—the perspective of "stabilitarians," to use

Michael Lind's expression (1994, 89)—while the latter demands more revisionist solutions. Disagreements on how to reconcile these two motivations have occurred frequently, first in the context of post–World War II decolonization, and then in the cold war–motivated struggle between national liberation movements (i.e., those seeking liberation from alleged "imperialist" regimes) on the one hand and political liberalization thrusts (i.e., from "communist" dominos) on the other. Regardless of which side you are on, those in power would expect a continuation of their advantageous status quo, while those out of power would take every opportunity to challenge it.

These issues have gained renewed attention today, first and foremost in dealing with movements to secede from existing states (and resistance to them). The question is also relevant in the process of reconstructing so-called failed states. The secession option is a manifestation of international power-sharing among competing parties in one state. The reconstruction of "failed states" requires a governance mechanism. In both cases, it is believed that democracy, or democratic governance, can provide the best solution. Just as the concept of sovereignty is considered a case of organized hypocrisy, however, the very idea of "democracy" can take many forms. Robert Dahl is certainly aware of "the enormous and often impenetrable thicket of ideas of democracy," but advises that it is still "possible to identify some criteria that a process for governing an association would have to meet in order to satisfy the requirement that all the members are equally entitled to participate in the association's decisions about its policies." Dahl then identifies the following five criteria for a democratic process: effective participation, voting equality, enlightened understanding, control of the agenda, and inclusive adult suffrage (1998, 37–38). But even these criteria may vary in practice. This seems to be the very reason why the concept of democracy, while it is cherished as a goal to pursue, is frequently employed in contradictory ways in the course of legitimating (or "illegitimating") certain states' practices.

One example of this is the theory of democratic peace, which generally denotes that because democratic states do not fight each other, the diffusion of democratic governance throughout the world will reduce the probability of war,[5] but does not rule out the necessity of war itself. When democracy is widely accepted as an ideal to pursue, it is considered highly justifiable to wage wars against those who oppose democracy for the sake of democracy. This was the rationale for the two world wars in the 20th century. The cold war, from the Western industrial democracies' point of view, was also a fight for freedom by containing and reversing the communists' domino-like expansionism.

But at the same time, we must recognize that two sets of "structural" compromises were evident, as a result of which strategic stability among major powers was given precedence over the true pursuit of democracy. The first was the result of so many abuses of democratic rationalization on the part of the West in their maneuver to support barely democratic regimes (or antigovernment rebels), only to support the larger objective of stopping the spread of communist takeovers of states around the world. The other was the idea that greater emphasis should be placed on the maintenance of the United States–Soviet Union strategic balance (i.e., stability) than on the resolution of fundamental problems. The frustrating numbers game in the U.S.-Soviet arms control negotiations ("disarmament" was not discussed until the closing years of the cold war) was one such example, as was the arbitrary application of "the right of self-determination" in the post–World War II decolonization process. As discussed previously, the unresolved issues of artificial borders and multiethnic societies that resulted from the limited implementation of the "self-determination" principle during the decolonization process resurfaced in the closing years of the 20th century. But this second chance was largely missed, as the principle was given inconsistent treatment again by the international community.

As Adam Roberts bluntly argues, "All too often (the self-determination principle) seems to be part of the problem, not part of the solution. The central weakness of the principle is that it appears to assume that each specific 'people' or 'nation' is neatly arranged on the map, and only awaits liberation from outside control in order to assume its rightful place in a peaceful and democratic international order." Roberts continues, "The vision is attractive, seductive and misleading" (1999, 83). With the oft-professed fear of "balkanization," or secessionist "dominos" to use another metaphor, the idea of (national) self-determination has recently been put into practice much more reluctantly than it was during the period of decolonization or during the cold war. For example, former UN Secretary-General Boutros Boutros-Ghali remarked in his widely read report, *An Agenda for Peace*, "If every ethnic, religious or linguistic group claimed statehood, there would be no limit to fragmentation, and peace, security and economic well-being for all would become ever more difficult to achieve" (1992, para. 17). Indeed, wars that demand adjustments of territorial demarcation lines have become numerous, although paradoxically, as Juan Enriquez observes, "Today, the goal of most wars is to make countries smaller rather than larger" (1999, 36).

Cautiously but inevitably, the world has had to take up these self-determination challenges directly since the beginning of the 1990s. But what is unfortunate is that numerous misjudgments by international actors, who took the wrong side at the wrong time, helped to throw these situations into even deeper turmoil. Again, the world's preference for strategic stability took precedence over the resolution of root causes of conflicts.

There were exceptions. If we look at the West's arch rival, the former Soviet Union, for instance, the world welcomed democratic reforms in that society. Most were totally caught off guard by the subsequent collapse of the Moscow government. Indeed it was a surprise because, being preoccupied with the idea of strategic stability, the world did not anticipate a situation in which one of the superpowers would ever implode. A short while later, when faced with the possible disintegration of the Balkans, a number of European neighbors (Germany, among others) reversed the original preference of the international community—most strongly advocated by the United States—to keep the former Yugoslavia's territorial integrity intact. Instead, they rushed to recognize the self-determination movements of Slovenia and Croatia, this time quite prematurely, before those republics had declared that they would meet the European Commission's conditions for protecting national minorities. Soon, Bosnia followed suit, and all three were engulfed by severe ethnic-based conflicts in exchange for independence.

Subsequently, the actions of the international community became ambivalent. In the case of Kosovo, it adamantly opposed the idea of an independent Kosovar state by making the maintenance of Yugo-slavia's territorial integrity a key provision of the peace agreement (Hoshino 2000). More recently, in East Timor, the world correctly endorsed the irreversible wave of separatism (as represented by the result of a referendum calling for full independence from Indo-nesia), but only after the island was subjected to mass killings and destruction by violent pro-integration militia members.

Granted, each individual case is unique, but clearly the interna-tional community has applied a double standard. Ted Gurr, for ex-ample, observes, "In most recent wars of self-determination, fighting usually began with demands for complete independence and ended with negotiated or de facto autonomy within the state" (2000, 57). This is based on the view that peaceful settlement—or at least a po-litical accommodation—of separatist conflicts is possible, whereas nationalist movements that demand nothing short of total independ-ence, as seen in Chechnya and East Timor, are quite rare and excep-tional. Richard Falk's analysis is more ominous in believing that there has been "no support for claims of self-determination that would shatter an existing state unless a 'people' was being victimized either by genocidal behavior or through repeated crimes against humanity, and in exceptional cases, as a result of severe abuses of basic human rights targeted at a given ethnic community and sustained over a period of years" (1999, 374–375). If the latter view is correct, it is nec-essary for the international community to have compelling evidence of mass killings and significant deprivation of human rights before it considers granting recognition of the option for independence. Otherwise, political compromises will be encouraged so as not to radically change the status quo.

Why is the international community so shy about changing the present look of the world? Are there better ways to manage group identity-based conflicts? And can we effectively prevent these con-flicts from escalating into violence? To break out of this tendency toward structural compromise, as Lind states, neither "indiscrimi-nate support for national self-determination" nor "reflexive defense of the territorial status quo around the world" is the correct approach (1994, 97). We need a better strategy, preferably a preventive one, that takes into consideration the structural remedies that go beyond our hitherto piecemeal, rather erratic reactions.

STRUCTURAL REMEDIES AND
PREVENTIVE DIPLOMACY

As discussed above, many of the issues we face today are intractable because they reflect not just conflicts on the surface but deep structural rifts among the parties directly involved. Moreover, we have seen that there are many cases in which problems are exacerbated by external parties who have repeatedly demonstrated their preference for tentative strategic stability over a more permanent resolution of issues. The world after the end of the cold war was emboldened by the perceived "triumph" of democracy over communism, but this emphasis on democratic governance represented a lack of any strategy other than simply enlarging the zone of democracy. Misjudgments and the lack of timely attention and action on the part of international actors have added up to a frustrating inability to bring conflicts to a conclusion. Nonetheless, with adequate preparation, useful preventive measures can be employed. And while conflicts are primarily the matters of those parties directly involved, it is clear that the international community also has many opportunities to influence the course of those conflicts.

In order to deal with the structural issues, our remedial approaches should also encompass a structural equation. The choices that local conflicting parties and the international community must reconsider are twofold: (1) the promotion of power-sharing mechanisms in a state—either maintaining the status quo of its borders or altering the status quo by exploring secessionist proposals (i.e., separation of the warring populations directly as a practical form of conflict management), or (2) the contemplation of a new political community—a "security community"—as an alternative to the traditional form of a state. Certainly these options are challenging, but they hold great promise as being rewarding options for preventive diplomacy.

The first option is concerned with promoting power-sharing by instituting certain mechanisms among the conflicting parties. Two approaches can be contemplated here. One envisions domestic power-sharing within an existing state boundary, which could be termed "power-sharing democracy," as it constitutes a part of the overall domestic process toward democratization. (It should be made clear that this is a scheme for peaceful power-sharing, whereas power-sharing in the general sense of the term can at times be brought about violently in our international life.) This can be considered a conservative approach in that it does not foresee any change of the state's basic borders or political system. Note that the term "power-sharing" or "power-sharing democracy" is used here instead of the more common concept of "democratic governance."

The idea of power-sharing democracy can be contrasted with "'regular' or majoritarian, winner-take-all democracy in which the losers of elections must wait out-of-power in loyal opposition for a later chance to replace the government of the day" (Harris and Reilly 1998, 139 and ch. 4). In essence, power-sharing systems are generally more "transitional" in character than a permanent structure of democratic governance. During that transitional stage, a certain artificiality of formulas to divide the political power would be devised (as represented in the size of autonomous territories, quotas for cabinet members, proportionality in parliamentary seats, etc.). It is always recommended, however, that the goal of democratic governance be kept clearly in sight. Thus, the power-sharing mechanism would be best viewed as a tool in the process of democratization as opposed to an attempt to impose a prefabricated model of democracy all at once. And if peace agreements are tools to formally acknowledge the terms among conflicting parties, they can be the vehicle for this kind of transitional power-sharing mechanism.

One recent study (Harris and Reilly 1998, 145) introduces the following five options as samples for these power-sharing mechanisms:

1. Creating a mixed, or nonethnic, federal structure, with boundaries drawn on other criteria such as natural features or economic development zones;
2. Establishing an inclusive, centralized unitary state without further subdividing territory;
3. Adopting winner-take-all but ethnically diverse executive, legislative, and administrative decision-making bodies (e.g., a purposefully diverse language board to set policies on language use);
4. Adopting an electoral system that encourages the formation of pre-election coalition (vote pooling) across ethnic divides; and
5. Devising "ethnicity-blind" public policies and laws to ensure non-discrimination on the basis of identity or religious affiliation.

Of course, there is no guarantee that these agreements for peace will be acceptable to those who are engaged in long, violent conflicts. Furthermore, whether they are workable is another question.

One painful reminder is the case of Bosnia. We know that the Dayton Peace Accords were concluded in the fall of 1995 under the severest pressure of North Atlantic Treaty Organization (NATO) military power. Reflecting the reality of the power balance on the battleground, the agreement meticulously sorted out a system of power-sharing among the three ethnic-based groups. But the subsequent picture of this ill-fated state is far from the multiethnic democracy the Accords intended to produce. Rather, the prolongation of what might be called a "one country, three systems" framework is evident, even though the formula was backed by the heavy oversight of the NATO-led Implementation Force (IFOR, which was followed by the Stabilization Force, or SFOR). This episode eloquently demonstrates the limits of military power to enforce peace, as well as the difficulty of devising a power-sharing mechanism that can achieve an integrated state among divided societies.

Having said that, however, the failure of the Bosnian case should not be taken as an indictment of the power-sharing option as a whole. It was not the power-sharing option per se but its implementation that failed in Bosnia. In fact, the Bosnian power-sharing mechanisms could have been implemented more effectively if the international community had not been so preoccupied with stressing the balance between the various ethnic groups, each with its own strong residual nationalistic tendencies. While important by all means, in a war-torn society it is both necessary and inevitable that the conflicting parities be separated while assuring their respective rights to participate in the political decision-making process. But once the overall goal of the international community was to keep Bosnia intact—in other words, not to allow it to disintegrate along ethnic lines—a strong centralized power to promote the integration process was needed. In Bosnia, the Office of the High Representative, an international third-party organ created under the Dayton Peace Accords, was supposed to play this integrative role during the transitional period. But in actuality, the Office's authority and power were often undermined by the three separate ethnic voices. If it had exerted its authority in a more assertive fashion, although it may not have looked democratic, it would have been better able to navigate the artificially divided peoples toward a common direction.

Nonetheless, we can conclude that at a minimum the absence of a recurrence of war in Bosnia speaks to certain advantages of this power-sharing approach. Power-sharing mechanisms are a prerequisite for the democratization process. And it is always encouraging when the process comes from within, as an endogenous initiative by local political parties. But at the same time, we have to admit that most local situations do not allow for such endogenous options, particularly if the society has experienced the severest of conflicts. In those cases, a "transitional authority" type of United Nations peacekeeping operation would prove to be of particular significance as an avenue for endogenous processes to develop into a fully functioning state. Under this option, the international community assumes the administrative power during a transition period until the local parties are ready to govern themselves. The delicate void created by structural change in the host states can thus be filled with the presence of an international authority. The UN has undertaken such activities in Namibia (UNTAG), Cambodia (UNTAC), El Salvador (ONUSAL), and Eastern Slavonia in Croatia (UNTAES), as well as in the ongoing missions in Kosovo (UNMIK) and East Timor (UNTAET).

The expertise gained from these efforts can be utilized to reconstruct so-called failed states. Particularly important is the role of external parties in providing political authority, when necessary, under the legitimacy of the United Nations—"peace-maintenance" operations, to use Jarat Chopra's term (1998). More study and practical application is needed of the political roles of the United Nations, its officials, and its member-states in supporting the reconstruction of weak states in transition—whether a transition from colonial rule to independence, from war-torn society to postwar government, or from "failed" state to functioning state.

The second option within the power-sharing approach addresses the question of secessionist ideas more directly and gives serious consideration to international recognition of proposals to separate the warring populations in an existing state. In a sense, this separation option is indeed a result of power-sharing ideas, in which parties choose to share the power by drawing demarcation lines externally rather than maintaining the existing state boundaries. As Chaim

Kaufmann points out, whereas there has been "a near consensus among policymakers and scholars that the objective of ethnic conflict management should be to support and preserve integrated, multi-ethnic societies," separating populations may be the best solution "when all else fails" (1998, 120). Kaufmann supports his controversial claim for separation and partition through ethnic population transfers by examining four famous 20th-century partitions—Ireland, India, Palestine, and Cyprus. At first glance, the history of these four cases does not seem to support his conclusion, given the substantial violence that has accompanied each case. But with detailed scrutiny of the course of events in each situation, he concludes that in all four cases "separation of the warring did reduce subsequent violence" and that "continuing or resurgent intergroup violence in limited regions within some of the cases has resulted not from partition or from separation but rather from the incompleteness of separation of the hostile groups in those specific areas" (1998, 121).

One of the key elements of the logic behind supporting a separation/partition option is its highly realistic consideration of the security dilemma among different ethnic communities where, absent an impartial central authority, a group's pursuit of self-defense threatens the security of others. Kaufmann relies on Barry Posen's analysis on this point, which reveals that "the more intermixed the pattern of settlement of the hostile populations, the greater the opportunities for offense by either side; and it becomes more difficult to design effective measures for community defense except by going on the offensive preemptively to 'cleanse' mixed areas of members of the enemy group and create ethnically reliable, defensible enclaves" (Kaufmann 1998, 122). To prevent potential conflicts from getting out of control, and certainly to prevent one party from taking aggressive preemptive measures, international support for the idea of separation should be given more thought. The current stance, as described previously, that self-determination—which is indeed a form of separation—can be endorsed *only* after evidence of mass killings and human deprivation is presented should be abandoned. Certainly, it is important to take full account of the timing, as well as the threshold beyond which the international community should resort to separation and partition (Kaufmann 1998).[6] In this respect, the diplomatic recognition given to the former Yugoslav republics of

Slovenia, Croatia, and Bosnia was too hasty, while international support for East Timor independence was too late, and the continuing efforts to maintain integrative solutions in Kosovo, and in Bosnia in a similar vein, are rather ineffectual.

The world has been too shy about endorsing "disintegration" options. "Assertions that successful secession by one or a few nations will produce runaway disintegration, thanks to the demonstration effect," Lind observes, "deserve to be greeted with the same skepticism that should be directed at other straight-line extrapolations" (1994, 90–92). In fact, how many states are too many? Has the world been having trouble managing the increasing number of states? Lind's answer on these questions is "no," stressing, "While there are thousands of ethnic nations in the world, there are at most only dozens of national groups numerous, unified and compact enough conceivably to serve as the nuclei of sovereign nation states. . . . Even if the number of nation-states were to increase by a dozen or two in the next few decades, through the peaceful or violent partition of several multinational countries, the very inequality of power among states would *prevent* too great a degree of disorder" (1994, 90; emphasis added).

One caveat to this line of thought, however, is its heavy emphasis on pure ethnic cause in many civil wars across the globe. Ethnic rivalries are indeed intractable. But as seen in the previous section of this study, there are multifaceted factors involved that fuel the ethnic hatred.

The second set of options, which will be explored more fully in the following section, is to go beyond the hitherto dominant discussion of nation-states as the principal unit of analysis and to explore the validity of alternative political units—security communities—and their internal workings for conflict prevention and transformation purposes.

RECONCEPTUALIZING INTERSTATE AND STATE-BASED SECURITY COMMUNITIES

The "security community" is a concept that was put forward in the late 1950s by Karl Deutsch (1957).[7] Deutsch observed that a high level of noninstitutionalized collaboration between states results in the settlement of disputes by compromise rather than by force.[8] The idea was certainly thought-provoking at a time when the ontology of intellectual debate on international politics was largely dominated by realist theory, which stresses the "security dilemma" (as opposed to a "security community") among states in an anarchical international system. In today's post-cold war environment, as Adler and Barnett detect, even "many seasoned policy makers and hardened defense officials [are] marrying security to community in new and unanticipated ways: they identify the existence of common values as the wellspring for close security cooperation, and, conversely, anticipate that security cooperation will deepen those shared values and transnational linkages" (1998, 4). Certainly, the recent awareness of new conceptions of security, transcending its more traditional military sense, has contributed to this trend.

Our interest in security communities for this study is twofold. The first aspect of interest is the possibility of reconceptualizing security communities among potentially conflicting actors as a prescriptive policy goal—not as a given phenomenon—for conflict prevention and transformation. In this context, actors can be nation-states, as Deutsch's school is primarily concerned with, but they can also include subnational, intrastate groups and individuals. This modification may sound irrelevant, but in fact the intrastate perspective is increasingly relevant given that most of the hostile wars in recent years have been within national borders instead of between state actors as they used to be. This requires a rethinking of the concept because, as we discussed earlier, it is those structural rifts (the state-nation rift on one hand and the state-society rift on the other) that complicate conflicts. In other words, it is becoming increasingly important today to reconceptualize the nation-state as a security community in and of itself, a community composed of all the substate groups, rather than conceiving of a security community solely as one composed of sovereign states.

The second area of interest relates to the guiding principles required for sustaining a security community. Particularly relevant from our perspective is the institutionalization of "toleration" in community building. As Michael Waltzer points out, toleration is the *practice* of tolerance, and thus is more institution-driven than simply the *attitude* of tolerance (1997, xi–xii). In this regard, the questions of what mechanisms are necessary for toleration and how they can be institutionalized and sustained are important policy issues.[9]

To prevent violent conflicts from breaking out or from recurring among different identity groups, initiatives at both the national and international levels to organize security communities with toleration mechanisms should be promoted instead of openly allowing the expression of each identity group's exclusive sentiment of competing nationalism, which would make it difficult to hold the country together. *Interstate-based* security communities—the groups of state actors among whom an assurance is shared to settle their differences without force—will exogenously constrain member-states' behavior. Examples can be found in a number of formal and informal intergovernmental arrangements, including the Association of Southeast Asian Nations (ASEAN), as will be discussed below. Here, a delicate but important balance of state sovereignty and international engagement (if not straightforward intervention in domestic affairs) has to be pursued, however contentious it may be. Similarly, *intrastate-based* security communities—those among subnational identity groups—would be useful vehicles to promote a habit of coexistence within states, based on the understanding that disputes will only be settled by peaceful means. Actually, these intrastate-based security communities can be equated with regular states that have a tradition of democratic governance, where all the disputes among their members (groups and/or individuals) are deemed to be settled peacefully. But for a state that has lacked both the recent history or the practice of peaceful settlement of disputes, conscious efforts toward community building are required to achieve common security interests for the people in that state. Here, the balance to be struck will be between group interests and individual human rights.

How, then, should these two layers of security-community consciousness be linked and developed? Internationally, our diplomats will negotiate the terms of peace. Domestically, more meticulous systems of governance and coexistence have to be devised. Comparing this with the other two options we discussed above, it is an integrative approach in contrast to the separation approach, but is closely related to the power-sharing option.

Indeed, successful power-sharing is a necessary condition of building an intrastate-based security community. While the hasty imposition of strict democratic conditionality based on a prefabricated model of democracy may not be appropriate, the introduction of fundamental principles of what is generally considered to be good democratic governance is necessary. These include a transparent political process, a government that is highly accountable, the peaceful transition of political power, the empowerment of the people, the rule of law, an independent judiciary, and civilian-controlled, responsible state apparatuses (e.g., police and military), among others. These principles are very much in line with many rules and procedures to ensure inter-group/individual systems of toleration. In order to enhance toleration, education—including education that is mindful of minority rights[10]—plays an exceptionally important role by "reproducing" the social institution of toleration.[11]

In this way, conscious efforts to turn a nation-state faced with identity-based strife into a tolerant security community provide an important avenue for reinventing it as a nation-state less prone to violence. The implementation of such a strategy, however, is far from easy. The experience of Western democracies may not be directly transplanted, as they have evolved into their present form through centuries of struggle. The critical challenge is to change the mindset of potentially conflicting parties so they do not exploit a "security dilemma" through confrontation among identity groups, but rather explore "security community" consciousness through coexistence and the transcendence of narrow group-oriented consciousness. For pursuing "security communities" internationally or internally, it is vitally important to take various steps to reduce fear and to build confidence among parties in an inclusive setting. In this regard, "the mutual reinforcements of community and individuality," as Waltzer reminds us, is a challenge "to serve a common interest," but it is going to be a continuing goal (1997, 111–112).

Nation-states are the products of history. But history is not made by itself. It is built on the actions of human beings, who lead a complex existence comprising ambition, fear, and brutality, as well as compassion, trust, and sincerity. People make mistakes. But they must correct their wrongs or history will simply repeat itself. The two sets of options discussed above—instituting "power-sharing" mechanisms in a transitional stage, and building "security community" consciousness based on the idea of toleration—are, in fact, nothing new. But the problem is not so much the availability of options as the timely and effective use of, or combination of, each option based on the reality on the ground. We need to learn lessons from past failures and successes. Accordingly, let us look next in some detail at two actual cases in Asia that highlight the problems and potential of conflict prevention and transformation: Cambodia and Myanmar.

TWO CASES OF CONFLICT PREVENTION IN ASIA: CAMBODIA AND MYANMAR

So far, we have analyzed the deep structural rifts that divide many conflict-prone societies, most conspicuously prompted by colonialism and the cold war. In many cases, the international community declines to get involved in conflicts. But in other cases, such conflicts are exacerbated by external actors' flawed interventions, and particularly by their zeal for democratic governance on the one hand and for overall strategic stability on the other. We then looked at two sets of options for structural remedies: power-sharing and security communities.

In Asia, the legacies of colonialism and the cold war are evident. If prevention requires proper predictions, we have no shortage of knowledge about the potential areas of conflict in Asia, most of which are internal to individual states. Here, the old rivalries within Southeast Asia have gradually been superseded by the expansion of ASEAN membership to include four new members from the Indochina peninsula—Cambodia, Laos, Myanmar, and Vietnam—which have very different political, economic, and ideological backgrounds than the founding members. And in Northeast Asia, we see the ongoing separation of North and South Korea, as well as China and Taiwan, with little hope in the near future for breakthroughs with regard to their respective bilateral relationships or to their future reunification. Schisms in national societies have created separatist movements and demands for self-determination within a number of Asian states, including China, India, Indonesia, and Sri Lanka, to name just a few. The independence of East Timor was one such example, and additional struggles have been witnessed in Indonesia, most notably in the provinces of Aceh and Irian Jaya. In Cambodia first, and currently in East Timor, the "stateless" situations that arose in the wake of severe internal conflict required large-scale international support activities in the form of a United Nations "transitional authority."

We must realize that the seeds of civil conflict, matters that were put off or left unsettled during the last century, were carried with us as we crossed the threshold of a new century, and so we continue to face daunting challenges worldwide. Warning signals abound, and the international community cannot afford to be simple onlookers. Asia is no exception.

The cases of Cambodia and Myanmar, two Southeast Asian states which have experienced constant periods of actual or imminent conflict, are instructive for considering what the world can do to prevent local parties from crossing the line between control and chaos. Within both countries, there are now domestic forces that are working to bring about changes in their political systems, and the developments in Phnom Penh and Yangon are under close scrutiny from the international community.

Regionally, ASEAN, as an example of an interstate security community, is taking pains to improve the domestic situation within member-states, as well as supporting regional stability.[12] But this is a region where members are exceptionally sensitive about "intervention" in their internal affairs, and the dilemma between their demands for external assistance and for maintaining the nonintervention norm has made international action very difficult. By examining the cases of Cambodia and Myanmar, we will seek to answer such basic questions as: What have been the responses of the international community to the crises that have repeatedly besieged the peoples of these two countries? Have those responses been effective? Why was prevention not possible? And can further crises be prevented by employing the two options we have discussed in this study, namely, power-sharing and security community building?

In Cambodia, beginning in 1970, people were engulfed by more than two decades of civil war among various factions—the communist Pol Pot/Khmer Rouge faction, a faction led by Prince (later King) Sihanouk, another supported by neighboring Vietnam (the one-time occupier of Cambodia), and others—conducted under the shadow of cold war rivalries. Its society was tormented by factional competition for power, mass killings, and other human rights violations.

The case in Cambodia may not fully represent a typical ethnic conflict characterized by a divided nation and state in one country, as the conflict was primarily among the Khmer people in Cambodia, the main dividing lines being more political and ideological than ethnic in nature. Nonetheless, the issue required structural remedies. The problem in successive conflict-ridden regimes in Cambodia was deeply associated with their fundamental lack of a democratic tradition. Indeed, during this most recent round of civil war, five political regimes came and went with no real prospects for peace until the Paris Peace Accord of October 1991, which proved to be the first serious attempt to introduce democratic governance to the Khmer state.

The international community made strenuous diplomatic efforts to conclude that agreement and bring peace to this war-torn country. One of the largest UN peacekeeping forces in history, the United Nations Transitional Authority in Cambodia (UNTAC), was then deployed to implement the accord. With a national election in 1993, held under UN supervision, a process of post-conflict peacebuilding began under the first coalition government of Cambodian factions. That effort, however, collapsed in a violent military clash in July 1997 between the two main political forces. It was only after the July 1998 general election that a fragile but more stable peace arrived for the Cambodian people, which was again the result of the renewed international efforts to bring the rival parties to the negotiating table. Cambodia's admission to ASEAN—which was delayed in the aftermath of the July 1997 incident and because of a lack of consensus among existing ASEAN members—was finally achieved in April 1999.

If we look at the roles played by external actors in this process, the performance of the international community, including the United Nations and ASEAN, was not perfect in the sense that the United Nations was not successful in involving the most violent faction, that of Pol Pot, into the peace mechanism, while ASEAN was never able to form a truly united front on this question because of its traditional adherence to the principle of nonintervention. But without international pressure and support, which are aimed at addressing the issues from the structural level, political accommodation among the conflicting parties in Cambodia would not have been possible.

For Cambodia, it can be said that both the "power-sharing democracy" option and an attempt to form a "security community" have been employed in essence to prevent the civil wars from reoccurring and to consolidate a lasting peace. In fact, the power-sharing democracy option was employed in two distinct stages: first, under the UN peacekeeping mission in 1992, as agreed upon in the Paris Peace Accord, and second, under the new constitution in 1993. During the UN transitional administration, the Cambodian government was administered by Akashi Yasushi, the UN Special Representative, in consultation with the Supreme National Council (SNC), composed of local political leaders (excluding the Khmer Rouge faction). It was a preparatory period during which many steps were taken to gradually give political authority to local leaders. The process culminated with the election of a constituent assembly in May 1993. This assembly was the first product of the newly established constitution, which made King Sihanouk the constitutional monarch, and placed two prime ministers under him who were appointed by the Cambodian people to lead the new government. These arrangements could hardly be viewed as a model of full-fledged democracy as we usually conceive of it. But they did play a key role in uniting the Cambodians to reconstruct their country in an environment that is free from the fear of war.

Given its artificial nature, this power-sharing scheme could not be totally sustained. The political turmoil of 1997 demonstrated the volatile state of power competition in the country, as represented by the tensions between the two prime ministers. Nonetheless, there is no doubt that "endogenous democratization" is under way in this formerly war-torn country. Notwithstanding the often frustratingly slow progress, the endogenous habit of resolving disputes through the law and democratic processes is indeed taking root, implying that the process of building a security community in Cambodia based on toleration principles is making progress.

As Thun Saray, a Cambodian lawyer and human rights advocate, rightly reminds us, "Democracy is a non-violent form of internal conflict management, improving and strengthening the democratization process is [an] important factor for conflict prevention. Separation of power and democratic institutions must be strengthened and

developed" (2000). Thun, who was jailed twice for political opposition during the years of turmoil in Phnom Penh, holds a strong personal conviction regarding the need to bring about good democratic
governance, mechanisms for peaceful power-sharing, and the rule of
law (particularly with regard to the prosecution of the Khmer Rouge,
who instigated the genocidal rule in Cambodia).

But how soon this process of democratization can gain a solid
foundation will depend on the efforts of Cambodians themselves.
The growth of NGOs and civil society in this country, and increasing
instances of government–civil society collaboration, are opening a
new path to the future for the people of Cambodia. Now, as one of the
newest members of ASEAN (which itself is becoming a model of an
interstate security community), and with the continuous attention
and support of the international community, Cambodia's future is
no longer totally pessimistic.

Whereas the opportunities are relatively open for Cambodian
people to express their views on various matters, however, the situation is much murkier for the people of Myanmar. Having gained independence from British colonial rule in 1948, Burma (as it was known
until the present military regime changed the name to Myanmar in
1989) enjoyed a short-lived period of democracy up until a military
coup by General Ne Win in March 1962 (The Economist Intelligent
Unit 1999). The rest of the history of this multiethnic state has been
one of successive military regimes with authoritarian and isolation-
ist ideologies. A glimmer of hope was seen in the multiparty election
of 1990, when the main opposition National League for Democracy
(NLD) overwhelmingly defeated the party of the ruling military
council, the State Law and Order Restoration Council (SLORC). But
SLORC, which subsequently renamed itself the State Peace and Development Council (SPDC) in 1997, refused to accept the election
results and kept the opposition leader, Nobel laureate Aung San Suu
Kyi, under house arrest for the next six years. In spite of a series of
cease-fire agreements concluded by the mid-1990s with key ethnic
groups, the military regime's confrontation with larger minority
groups who claim autonomy, such as the Karens and Shans, has continued. As Ted Robert Gurr correctly observes, the "settlement" of
ethnic conflicts "in the traditional way—by overwhelming force"—
did not produce an enduring result (2000, 62). The international

community remains deeply troubled by the lack of progress in Myanmar, particularly in terms of the human rights situation under the rule of the military council.

In many ways, Myanmar can serve as a test case of the possibilities and limitations of preventive diplomacy. The country is embedded with serious sources of conflict, ethnic and otherwise, most notably in the domestic context. The ruling military council is highly repressive. But protest movements remain widespread and international attention is high (largely as a result of the plight of Suu Kyi). The real test will be whether the international community can in fact help prevent the local situation from deteriorating by taking the necessary measures in a timely manner.

The prospects for success, however, are at best mixed. One apparent indication can be found in the serious gap in approaches between the Western democracies and their Asian counterparts. While the former have shown a predominant interest in the early introduction of democracy to this troubled land, the latter's policies, while not fully congruent, are generally more reserved. Also, the mixture of structural causes of societal rifts must be taken into consideration in devising structural remedies. The lack of the tradition of democratic governance is unquestionably a part of the problem, but other structural causes—e.g., the animosity toward former colonialist Western states, an ethnically divided society, and power struggles among the political leadership—also make the untangling of the country's problems quite a difficult job. In other words, it is wrong to attribute the problems of Myanmar solely to the lack of democracy. As a result, prescribing stringent democracy and human rights standards alone will not resolve the problems. More balanced, multidimensional responses are required.

The two options laid out in the previous sections could again be usefully applied here. First, with regard to the power-sharing options, the situation in Myanmar is reaching a critical juncture as the United Nations–mediated "dialogue" between the ruling SPDC and Suu Kyi's NLD, which started in October 2000, seems to be on track. Various indications, including those obtained during this author's field research in Yangon in early 2001, lead to the conclusion that both parties are serious in their attempts to strike a deal in which both will have a role to play in the future conduct of Myanmar's national

affairs. One important agenda of their dialogue is the future composition of a People's Assembly, since the results of the 1990 election
were nullified by the SLORC government. The ongoing dialogue may
enable both parties to come up with a formula to secure their representation—a potential formula for power-sharing in the form of legislative seats, for example. It will take some time for these efforts to
move beyond the confidence-building stage under the present delicate situation. But the stakes are high, and although the process may
be highly anomalous, as it does not seem to bring us back to the 1990
election result but rather attempts to reinstate the Assembly through
negotiation, the direct contact (an endogenous attempt by the parties directly involved, with the timely and discrete facilitation of the
United Nations) is expected to bring about a pragmatic outcome.
Again, it is likely that it will require a power-sharing arrangement—not
necessarily a pure form of democracy in the Western sense—to move
forward.

Second, with regard to the security community option, through
its 1997 accedence to ASEAN (a form of interstate-based security
community in Southeast Asia), Myanmar is now expected to behave
according to the common rules and procedures of fellow ASEAN
members. The inclusion of this state in ASEAN itself can be considered as a preventive or preemptive move on the part of its neighboring states. Domestically, it is certainly not easy for a country like
Myanmar, which has been tormented by authoritarian rule together
with ethnic rivalries, to build a security community among groups
or individuals within its state boundaries. But surely this is an indis-
pensable direction that all domestic identity groups should explore
if there is to be any hope (or will) to pursue coexistence. Of course,
considering that no state is truly homogeneous or unitary, building
an intrastate-based security community is in many senses synonymous with creating a "normal" democratic state that is equipped with
various mechanisms for the peaceful settlement of disputes.

The separation option is often contemplated when the dominant
force in power is repressive. In contrast, when those in the dominant position shift their policies to more democratic ones, the prospects for the coexistence option among different identity groups
are heightened. Having said this, however, a prefabricated model of
democracy and human rights would not be effective if imposed on

Myanmar society; rather, more nuanced steps should be taken. The applicable toleration mechanisms are critical for this multiethnic nation given that the separation option, although attractive to some identity groups, would be neither sustainable nor realistic.

This brief examination of Cambodia and Myanmar serves to remind us of the unique political background of each case. But at the same time, we see that in both cases endogenous efforts toward democratization, however slow they may be, are taking shape. In these contexts, the external parties can play a useful role by providing a respite when local parties are facing a tense situation or pressure when they are losing sight of the eventual goal of peaceful coexistence.

This study has looked at power-sharing democracy and security-community building as two main options for preventing potential conflicts from escalating or recurring. These two options cannot materialize without having an endogenous effort toward democratization and exogenous support to promote it. Having seen the rocky paths that both Cambodia and Myanmar have traveled, we cannot be too optimistic about quick reform and change. But by recognizing the utility of a transitional phase that allows time for community-consciousness building without asserting too much pressure for strict democratic conditionalities, it is not unrealistic for societies that have experienced severe conflicts to start a new chapter in their history. And as seen in this study, Cambodia and Myanmar, two Indochinese states with difficult pasts, have the potential to structurally rebuild their societies to be more resistant to triggers of violent civil conflicts.

CONCLUSION

Conflicts are part of human life. To some extent, they are inevitable when our interests contradict those of others. And while not all conflicts are violent or irreconcilable, the unfortunate fact of life is that in so many instances, in so many locations around the world, people turn to firearms to fulfill rather parochial interests. Moreover, the international community has not been effective, either by inaction or overreaction, in containing the sources of conflicts. Those sources are by no means easy to cope with. In particular, their structural nature—both in terms of the international state-nation gap and of the domestic state-society gap—make conflicts more complicated.

During the past decade, the world has been challenged by the fundamental question of statehood. New states have been created and more groups have begun claiming their legitimate right of political independence and self-determination. The responses of the international community have been mixed and uncoordinated. Nothing speaks more eloquently to the failure of preventive efforts than the sheer number of conflicts that we have witnessed.

Prevention requires precise predictions of how local situations will evolve. Prevention also calls for continuous efforts. There is no room for complacency. Thus, the investment of sustainable resources is needed. By nature, hypothetical arguments to prevent would-be events from happening cannot be proven. This has made prevention a greatly abused concept. History is full of examples in which political leaders took advantage of this lack of counterfactual evidence to justify preemptive actions in the name of "preventive" self-defense or for "humanitarian" pretexts.

Prevention is difficult. But the world cannot afford to overlook human tragedies across the globe. During the past decade, we have created many failures primarily because of our two main preoccupations: our confidence in the immediate introduction of democratic governance and our concern for maintaining strategic balance. These two opposing forces frequently send confusing signals to the parties involved in conflicts. Certainly, no single formula is available or possible that can be applied to all conflicts.

Having said that, however, it is both necessary and useful to single out some basic approaches to prevent, transform, and possibly resolve violent conflicts. As outlined above, there are two alternatives to the norms of democratic governance and strategic stability: first, devising certain power-sharing mechanisms, and giving serious thought to the secession option if that is deemed to be the only option; and second, encouraging the formation of security communities, both at the interstate and state-based levels, that incorporate the practice of institutionalizing "toleration" mechanisms. Also to be stressed is the importance of "transitional stages," during which the international community would give a respite to the local conflicting parties to move away from violently resolving differences, and would provide opportunities to settle their disputes by peaceful means. The ultimate goal of these steps would converge with the principles of democratic governance. But this must be undertaken through endogenous democratization efforts rather than by the imposition of a democratic template from outside. We need to recognize that this encouragement of endogenous democratization efforts, though it will certainly take a longer time, will have a more lasting effect on local societies.

If the past decade was one of lost opportunities, we urgently need to learn the lessons from those failures to avoid repeating the same mistakes again. More nuanced and consistent efforts on the part of the international community can constitute a major step toward preventing deadly conflicts.

Notes

1. "Life history of conflict" is a term used by Michael Lund to describe the stages of peace or conflict, starting from "stable peace" to "unstable peace," followed by "crisis" that can escalate into "war," although as Lund admits, the course of actual conflicts "can exhibit many different long and short life-history trajectories, thresholds, reversals, and durations" (1996, 37–40).

2. For a good collection of contemporary debates on the relationship between ethnicity, nationalism, and state sovereignty, see Mortimer (1999) and Smith (1993). The original idea of a nation as an "imagined community" is discussed in Anderson (1991).

3. This formula of limited application of the right of self-determination was subsequently endorsed in the 1970 Declaration of Principles of International Law Concerning Friendly Relations among States, adopted by the UN General Assembly.

4. Hall (1999) analyzes the transition of the international system since the 16th century, from the "Dynastic-Sovereign" (Augsburg, 1555) system composed of kingdoms and realms, to the "Territorial-Sovereign" system (Westphalian, 1648) constituted by territorial-states, through to the "National-Sovereign" (the first post-Westphalian) system.

5. A summarized definition is offered by Kegley and Wittkopf (1999, 567).

6. Kaufmann (1998, 155) stresses that "we need to identify the threshold of intergroup violence and mutual security threats beyond which we must resort to separation and partition, and we should set the threshold conservatively—no one wants to dissolve diverse societies, even deeply troubled ones, that have any hope of avoiding massive violence and attaining civil peace."

7. For a collection of studies that employ Deutsch's pioneering idea of

security communities in the more contemporary regional context, see Adler and Barnett (1998).

8. This condensed definition of the concept is from Kegley and Wittkopf (1999, 579).

9. In this connection, note that Waltzer (1997, 14–36) introduces five ideal-typical models, or "regimes," of a tolerant society, ranging from the international to domestic levels: multinational empires, international society, consociations, nation-states, and immigrant societies.

10. For theoretical and empirical analyses of politics of minority rights protection, see Krasner (1999, chap. 3).

11. For a discussion of the role of education for "the reproduction of the regime of toleration," see Waltzer (1997, 71–76).

12. For a study of ASEAN that treats it as a security community in a non-Atlantic area, see Acharya (1998). See also Satō (1998, 21–22).

BIBLIOGRAPHY

Acharya, Amitav. 1998. "Collective Identity and Conflict Management in Southeast Asia." In Emanuel Adler and Michael Barnett, eds. *Security Communities.* Cambridge, U.K.: Cambridge University Press.

Adler, Emanuel, and Michael Barnett, eds. 1998. *Security Communities.* Cambridge, U.K.: Cambridge University Press.

Anderson, Benedict. 1991. *Imagined Community* (ed. and trans. by Peter Connor, et al) Minneapolis, Minn.: University of Minnesota Press.

Annan, Kofi A. 1999. "Two Concepts of Sovereignty." *The Economist* (18 September): 49–50.

Boutros-Ghali, Boutros. 1992. *An Agenda for Peace: Preventive Diplomacy, Peacemaking and Peace-Keeping.* New York: United Nations Department of Public Information.

Chopra, Jarat. 1998. "Introducing Peace-Maintenance." *Global Governance* 4(1): 1–18.

Collier, Paul, and Anke Hoeffler. 2000. *Greed and Grievance in Civil War.* Policy Research Working Paper 2355. Washington, D.C.: The World Bank Development Research Group.

Council of the European Union. 1998. Conclusion on "The Role of Development Co-operation in Strengthening Peace-Building, Conflict Prevention and Resolution." (28 November).

Dahl, Robert A. 1998. *On Democracy.* New Haven: Yale University Press.

Deutsch, Karl. 1957. *Political Community and the North Atlantic Area.* Princeton, N.J.: Princeton University Press.

The Economist Intelligence Unit. 1999. *Country Profile: Myanmar (Burma) 1999–2000.* London: The Economist Intelligence Unit.

Enriquez, Juan. 1999. "Too Many Flags?" *Foreign Policy*, no. 116: 30–49.

Falk, Richard. 1999. "The New Interventionism and the Third World." *Current History* 98(631): 370–375.

Gurr, Ted Robert. 2000. "Ethnic Warfare on the Wane." *Foreign Affairs* 79(3): 52–64.

Hall, Rodney Bruce. 1999. *National Collective Identity: Social Constructs and International System*. New York: Columbia University Press.

Harris, Peter, and Ben Reilly, eds. 1998. *Democracy and Deep-Rooted Conflict: Options for Negotiators*. Stockholm: International IDEA.

Hoshino Toshiya. 2000. "Beikoku no Kosobo funsō kainyū: Sono dōgisei, gōhōsei, seitōsei (U.S. intervention in the Kosovo conflict: Its morality, legality, legitimacy). *Kokusai Mondai*, no. 479: 17–29.

Kao, Kim Hourn, and Jeffrey A. Kaplan. 1999. *Principles Under Pressure: Cambodia and ASEAN's Non-Interference Policy*. Phnom Penh: Cambodian Institute for Cooperation and Peace.

Kaufmann, Chaim D. 1998. "When All Else Fails: Ethnic Population Transfers and Partitions in the Twentieth Century." *International Security* 23(2): 120–156.

Kegley, Charles W., Jr., and Eugene R. Wittkopf. 1999. *World Politics: Trend and Transformation*, 7th ed. Boston: Bradford/St. Martin.

Krasner, Stephen D. 1999. *Sovereignty: Organized Hypocrisy*. Princeton: Princeton University Press.

Langford, Tonya. 1999. "Things Fall Apart: State Failure and the Politics of Intervention." *International Studies Review* 1: 59–79.

Lind, Michael. 1994. "In Defense of Liberal Nationalism." *Foreign Affairs* 73(3): 87–99.

Lund, Michael. 1996. *Preventing Violent Conflicts*. Washington, D.C.: United States Institute for Peace.

Mortimer, Edward, ed. 1999. *People, Nation and State: The Meaning of Ethnicity and Nationalism*. London: I.B. Tauris.

Ottaway, Marina. 1999. "Africa: Think Again." *Foreign Policy*, no. 114: 13–25.

Posen, Barry R. 1993. "Security Dilemma and Ethnic Conflict." In Michael E. Brown, ed. *Ethnic Conflict and International Security*. Princeton: Princeton University Press.

Roberts, Adam. 1999. "Beyond the Flawed Principle of National Self-Determination." In Edward Mortimer, ed. *People, Nation and State: The Meaning of Ethnicity and Nationalism*. London: I.B. Tauris.

Satō Hideo. 1998. "Japan's China Perceptions and Its Policies in the Alliance with the United States." Asia/Pacific Research Center Discussion Papers (September 1998). Palo Alto, Calif.: Stanford University, Institute for International Studies.

Smith, Anthony D. 1993. "The Nation: Invented, Imagined, Reconstructed?" In Marjorie Ringrose and Adam J. Lerner, eds. *Reimagining the Nation*. Buckingham: Open University Press.

Snyder, Jack. 2000. *From Voting to Violence: Democratization and Nationalist Conflict*. New York: W.W. Norton & Co.

Thun Saray. 2000. "The Role of NGOs in Conflict Prevention: Cambodian Experience." Paper presented at a symposium on "The Role of NGOs in Conflict Prevention," June 9–10, in Tokyo, Japan.

Waltzer, Michael. 1997. *On Toleration*. New Haven, Conn.: Yale University Press.

CHAPTER THREE

Human Rights, Democratization, and Preventive Diplomacy: The OSCE in Belarus

Miyawaki Noboru

HE linkage between the use of preventive diplomacy and the pursuit of such goals as human rights and democratization has become increasingly evident in the post–cold war era. By seeking to avert armed conflicts, preventive diplomacy can be a means to protect human rights and reinforce the rule of law in crisis situations. Conversely, human rights and democratization efforts can facilitate preventive diplomacy by serving as a barometer of how far down the road toward crisis a society might be.

This linkage was highlighted in a recent report to the Security Council by the secretary-general of the United Nations on "the causes of conflict and the promotion of durable peace and sustainable development in Africa." In that report, Kofi Annan stated, "Respect for human rights and the rule of law are necessary components of any effort to make peace durable. They are cornerstones of good governance." He went on to stress that, "Democratization gives people a stake in society. Its importance cannot be overstated, for unless people feel that they have a true stake in society lasting peace will not be possible and sustainable development will not be achieved" (1998). The rule of law and human rights are also crucial to the concept of

98

"democratic peace," as proposed by Bruce Russett, which seeks to explain why we have seen few conflicts between democratic nations (1993). Democracy and human rights, it can thus be argued, play an important role in preventing both internal conflicts and international conflicts, as well as in the restoration and rebuilding of a post-conflict society.[1]

But while there seems to be a general consensus on the desirability of promoting democracy and human rights, the way in which those targets are promoted and standards are set by the international community, and the appropriate response of the international community when a nation fails to meet those standards, are extremely complex issues. This chapter will focus primarily on European efforts to promote human rights and democracy. These efforts have been carried out primarily through the Council of Europe in the legal dimension and the Organization for Security and Co-operation in Europe (OSCE) in the political dimension. The latter in particular plays a central role, offering a political framework for creating standards of human rights and democracy and then assisting the member-states in implementing those standards.

The OSCE has standards for democracy and requests its participating states to implement those standards. More concretely speaking, in the 1990 Document of the Copenhagen Meeting of the Conference on the Human Dimension of the Conference for Security and Co-operation in Europe (CSCE), the member-states recognized "that pluralistic democracy and the rule of law are essential for ensuring respect for all human rights and fundamental freedoms, the development of human contacts and the resolution of other issues of a related humanitarian character." The document further states, "everyone will have the right to freedom of expression including the right to communication. This right will include freedom to hold opinions and to receive and impart information and ideas without interference by public authority and regardless of frontiers" (Conference on Security and Co-operation in Europe [CSCE] 1990).

The basis for OSCE activities can be found in various declarations of the importance of human rights, democracy, and the road to a market economy, and particularly those included in the Charter of Paris for a New Europe, signed in November 1990. I will refer to this set of values and rules, including the OSCE standards, as the "Paris

Regime" (Miyawaki 1999, 256–262). By contrast, when the CSCE was launched in 1975, these values were suggested only in the context that human rights violations might worsen security situations in Europe. The 1975 Helsinki Final Act of the CSCE mentioned nothing about the norms of "democracy" or the "market economy" because the East-West confrontation at that time made it difficult to apply these words as trans-European norms. In addition, Western states hesitated to add "democracy" to the Helsinki Final Act because Eastern states had also used such terms as "people's democracy" as a socialist concept. I regard the Helsinki Regime, then, as a concept consisting of a narrower range of norms than those embodied in the Paris Regime (Miyawaki 1999, 252–256).

Through the Paris Regime, the OSCE has come to play a role in promoting democracy, as well as monitoring human rights issues as it did before. For example, with pressure from the OSCE, the authoritarian regimes in Slovakia under Vladimir Meciar, Croatia under Franjo Tudjman, and Serbia under Slobodan Milosevic have given way to more democratic governments either through parliamentary elections (in Slovakia in 1998 and Serbia in 2000) or following the death of a leader (in the case of Croatia in 1999). The OSCE, however, has faced difficulties when some of the authoritarian regimes or the so-called transitional regimes have refused to compromise, as seen in the case of the former Soviet regions when they faced setbacks to their progress toward democracy in the 1990s.

In this chapter, I will point out the limitations of the very high "European standards" or "OSCE standards," which are not necessarily conducive to the process of democracy building or to the implementation of human rights norms in undemocratic or human rights violating states. Further, I will argue that not all undemocratic states or human rights violating states show signs of internal or international conflict, thereby calling into question the sometimes reflexive linking of preventive diplomacy with those broader goals.

To illustrate these points, I will examine the case of Belarus, which can be termed an undemocratic state or a transitional state on the path to democracy. Belarus President Aleksandr Lukashenko has been able to maintain enough political power to contain opposition activities by dissidents against his government since 1996. In light of this situation, the OSCE has applied a democratization-support policy toward this country. Despite pressure from the OSCE and Western states, however, the progress made toward democratization has been steadily reversed. The case of Belarus, I will argue, is one in which democracy was once established but subsequently broke down and has still not revived. I will examine why the OSCE lacks the requisite power to resolve the problem in Belarus, and will analyze the alternatives for bringing about change in the future.

Finally, I conclude that the case of Belarus seems to resemble the case of the USSR at the time of the CSCE, adhering more to the character of the Helsinki Regime than the Paris Regime. Fundamentally, through an analysis of the Belarus case, I argue that while it is appropriate for decisionmakers to pay attention to human rights issues, it is not necessarily appropriate that human rights or transitional democracy be the primary goal of preventive diplomacy.

VIEWPOINTS AND ACTORS

The Lukashenko Regime

Aleksandr Lukashenko has ruled Belarus since he was elected president in July 1994. The Lukashenko presidency has been characterized by three fundamental political objectives: integrate with Russia, increase the presidential powers, and oppress members of the opposition.

Lukashenko has formed strong ties with Russia in order to overcome Belarus' economic and social crisis, and the country is heavily dependent on Russia for its energy supply and as a market for its exports. As of 1996, Belarus' cumulative debt to Russia amounted to roughly US$1.3 billion, the equivalent of 6.5 percent of the Belarusian gross domestic product (Heenan and Lamontagne 1999, 58–64). Accordingly, Russia is the key to handling economic issues in Belarus, and Lukashenko has recognized that fact, expanding barter trade with the Russian national and regional governments.

In November 1996, Lukashenko started to reorganize his country's political structure. He proposed the adoption of a new constitution that would broaden his authority and extend his term in office from five years to seven years. It would also dissolve the Chamber of Representatives (Supreme Soviet), creating in its place a bicameral

National Assembly comprised of an Upper House (the Council of the Republic, or Soviet Respubliki) and a Lower House (the new Chamber of Representatives, or Palata Pretsaviteley). The Upper House members were to be appointed by the president or elected by the deputies of local councils; the Lower House members were to be comprised of the members of the former Chamber of Representatives and would be elected by popular vote. The opposition criticized Lukashenko, claiming that his intention was to lead the country backward to the Soviet era. The Belarus parliament started to discuss the impeachment of Lukashenko for trying to create a dictatorship.

This confrontation between the president and the parliament created political instability and so Russia intervened, proposing that the two sides agree to Russian arbitration as a way of backing off from the confrontation. Russia dispatched its mediators—Prime Minister Viktor Chernomyrdin and Russian Duma Chair Gennadii Seleznev—to assist in solving the political crisis in Belarus. The effort failed in the end, however, and Lukashenko instead appealed directly to the Belarus people to accept his plan to change the constitution. Whatever the irregularities of the process, the majority answer (70 percent) from the nation was a "yes" for Lukashenko. The impeachment attempt did not come anywhere near succeeding because the Chamber itself was sharply divided between the president's supporters and his opponents (Heenan and Lamontagne 1999, 58).

After the new Lukashenko regime was in place, politically motivated arrests and detentions of opposition members became a frequent occurrence. In April 1999, former National Bank Chairwoman Tamara Vinnikava disappeared. She later resurfaced in London, where she remains in exile. In May 1999, former Interior Minister Yuri Zakharenko also disappeared and has never been found. And in September 1999, another opposition leader, Victor Gonchar, deputy chairman of the 13th Supreme Soviet of Belarus, disappeared three days before the ratification of a framework for a new Advisory Council. He, like Zakharenko, is presumed dead. These events were apparently triggered by the opposition's suggestion that Lukashenko's presidency had already expired by the summer of 1999.

The Belarusian government has increasingly restricted the freedom of expression. According to a human rights survey conducted by Freedom House, the status of Belarus from 1991 to 1996 was "partly free," but it took a turn for the worse from 1996 to 2000, dropping down to the "not free" category. Similarly, its democratization rating in the Freedom House "Nations in Transit Scores" deteriorated from 5.90 in 1997 to 6.44 in 1999–2000, the worst possible score being a 7 (Freedom House 2000a).

In sum, the current political regime of Belarus might very well be classified as a dictatorship or an authoritarian regime (Heenan and Lamontagne 1999, 58).[2] The OSCE, however, has adopted a different approach, choosing not to apply these types of classifications to Belarus in the diplomatic dimension. This is because the OSCE regards all participating states as either democratic states or states which should become democratic states rather than returning to another political regime. Of course, the Lukashenko government itself denies that its political regime is authoritarian, claiming that "Belarus is on the path to democracy."[3]

The OSCE and the Foreign Policy of Western States toward Belarus

The OSCE took the place of EU leadership (which limited itself to economic sanctions) on Belarus in 1997, and has subsequently become a key player in the region's affairs. Since 1998, the OSCE has been monitoring the human rights situation and trying to help promote democracy in Belarus. The OSCE chairman-in-office, Danish Minister for Foreign Affairs Niels Helveg Petersen, launched a concrete initiative to promote democracy in Belarus by establishing the Advisory and Monitoring Group (AMG) in Belarus. The Belarus government initially resisted ("Die OSZE lobt" 1997), but later reached a compromise with the OSCE that would confine the Group's mission to "advising" and "monitoring." Notably, Russia played a very important role in pressuring Belarus to work toward that compromise. Given its apprehensions about the North Atlantic Treaty Organization (NATO) plans to expand as far as Ukraine, Russia preferred to strengthen the OSCE's ability to deal with security issues in the region.[4]

According to a Memorandum of Understanding between the Government of Belarus and the OSCE, the AMG has two important roles: to "assist the Belarusian authorities in promoting democratic institutions and in complying with other OSCE commitments," and to "monitor and report on this process." The memorandum further states that "the OSCE and its personnel have the right to seek and maintain unimpeded contacts with all national and local authorities, as well as with every person, individually or in association with others, including NGOs, and with the media" (Organization for Security and Co-operation in Europe [OSCE] 1997). These phrases mean that the OSCE can help Belarus' domestic political opposition toward the goal of democratization, but at the same time that it can take actions that in a sense legitimize the Lukashenko regime for the sake of stability. Despite the singular purpose of the AMG in terms of promoting a democratic society in Belarus, there is clearly a contradiction between its two mandates—on the one hand, to assist the Lukashenko regime, and on the other, to promote democratic institutions through which the anti-Lukashenko movement can act. This fundamental contradiction reveals the nature and limits of the OSCE.

The AMG's presence in Minsk has perpetuated that contradiction, as there have been mixed results on human rights and redemocratization. On the positive side, we see that the Belarus government has shown some willingness to compromise with the opposition, although progress has been uneven. A number of detained dissidents have been released, political dialogue between the government and the opposition started (although it later stopped), and the Belarus government agreed to change its penal code and electoral law. Unfortunately, however, there have been as many failures as successes in Belarus.

The Belarus government has shown its authoritarian essence in a number of ways, first and foremost of which is through the violation of its citizens' human rights. Peaceful assemblies have been suppressed by political force. For example, on March 25, 2000, roughly 500 participants in a peaceful demonstration march in Minsk were arrested, including an accredited diplomat who was a member of the AMG (OSCE 2000a). As noted previously, opposition politicians have been under attack. Former Prime Minister Mikhail Chigir, for example, was detained by the government from April to November 1999. Independent newspapers have also been suppressed, as the government issued an order annulling the registration of nine independent papers in September 1999 (International Helsinki Federation for

Human Rights 2000, 69). On October 5, 1999, the opposition news-paper, *Navinje*, had to close down under pressure from the govern-ment (OSCE/Advisory and Monitoring Group in Belarus [AMG] 2000b, 8).

Objectively speaking, however, at least the harassment of inde-pendent newspapers was a frequent occurrence even before the Luka-shenko regime took charge in 1994. Ultimately, then, has the human rights situation in Belarus become worse or better? "Worse" or at least "unchanged" according to those in nongovernmental organi-zation (NGO) circles and opposition parties in Belarus. Tatsiana Pratsko, chair of the Belarusian Helsinki Committee, noted that the "effect of the OSCE is reasonable. Concretely, AMG has proposed le-gal amendments and held seminars. But they lack money."[5] On the other hand, Stanislav Bogdankevich, former chairman of the United Civil Party, felt that the situation had not improved,[6] while Aaron Rhodes, executive director of the International Helsinki Federation for Human Rights (Vienna), holds that the "human rights situation is worse. It is difficult to negotiate. The OSCE mission is limited in its role. The OSCE cannot stop human rights violations."[7]

Another demonstration of the authoritarian nature of the Luka-shenko regime can be seen in its handling of an AMG-initiated po-litical dialogue between the government and the opposition. That dialogue began in the wake of the opposition's failure to field a presi-dential candidate against Lukashenko in May 1999. The OSCE re-sponded by urging all political forces to overcome constitutional conflict through dialogue in preparation for the upcoming 2000 parliamentary election. (It should also be noted that Lukashenko was forced to soften his diplomacy toward the Western powers fol-lowing unsuccessful unification talks with Russia in July 1999.) He received the ambassador from the OSCE, Hans-Georg Wieck, and agreed to hold a free, fair, and recognizable parliamentary election in the year 2000. In response to this agreement, the AMG drafted its proposal for a "tripartite dialogue" in July 1999. Only when the op-position refused to recognize Lukashenko's constitution did Luka-shenko agree to the proposal.

On August 10, 1999, after several meetings, the opposition leaders agreed to establish an Advisory Council in order to facilitate negotiations with the government. On September 3, 1999, the first consultation between the government representatives and their counterparts in the opposition was held, covering such issues as access to state-run media. However, the Gonchar incident and the government's suppression of independent papers made the dialogue increasingly confrontational, eventually interrupting the process. At the urging of the AMG and of OSCE Chairman-in-Office Knut Vollebaek, the negotiation over access to state-run media resumed on October 15, 1999. The so-called confidence-building process between the government and the opposition was often suspended, but they managed to sign a protocol of agreement "on conditions of political opposition access to the state mass media" (OSCE/AMG 2000b, 9). This protocol required that some parts of the newspapers be handed over to the opposition, but Lukashenko quickly revoked the agreement the following month. The AMG tried to talk with both sides after all negotiations were suspended but had little success. Instead, a new negotiation process, this time initiated by Lukashenko and excluding the AMG, started at the end of March 2000. These talks succeeded in instituting some reforms to the electoral system prior to the parliamentary election, but some members of the opposition such as the United Civil Party refused to participate. In the end, the OSCE was able to foster a dialogue, but that dialogue ended in failure.

Before the parliamentary election in October 2000, Lukashenko made one concession to the AMG and to the opposition—he agreed that the Central Electoral Committee would include members of the opposition political parties (Dekret prezidenta 2000). But in the end, the opposition side boycotted the election because other political obstacles still remained.

Another complaint leveled against the Lukashenko regime was that proposals from the OSCE to the government to improve certain laws "had not been taken or had been absorbed into the legislation (i.e., electoral law) in such a way that the preponderance of the presidential administration and the vertical character of the state prevailed" (Wieck 2000, 54). Indeed, the AMG criticized the new electoral code signed by Lukashenko on February 15, 2000, as being insufficient: "[In spite of] substantial democratic changes, substantial issues have not been achieved. Despite some formalistic and minor changes, the provisions of the current Electoral Code do not comply with international democratic standards such as items 7 and 8 of the 1990

Copenhagen Documents" (OSCE/AMG 2000a, 11).[8] The government responded by revising the electoral code in some areas, but we must conclude that the OSCE has had only limited success on this issue. The Belarus government circumvented the bulk of the OSCE's advice. (Of course, another possible evaluation of this code is that it may represent some slight progress for the opposition. One member of the opposition, for example, felt that the code became "milder due to the OSCE."[9])

There is a striking similarity between the Belarus case and the way in which the Soviet Union in the past dodged Western pressure regarding human rights. Belarus has not implemented policies or regulations to uphold universal human rights, in spite of official documents that claim to recognize the importance of those values. In official statements of the Belarus government, one can find such passages as, "Let us not impede progress to the same aims and objectives—democracy, economic prosperity, priority of human rights," but "let everyone achieve these aims in his own way and manner" ("Ural Latypov" 2000, 2). In other words, on the surface Lukashenko has accepted the good advice of the OSCE AMG, but he has not truly implemented it.

Western states have continued to show interest in the situation in Belarus, but their economic ties with the country are too small for them to wield any influence with the Belarus government. According to 1998 statistics, the most important trading partners for Belarus outside the Commonwealth of Independent States (CIS) were Germany (only around 6 percent of total trade) and Poland (3 percent), followed by Austria, the United States, the United Kingdom, Turkey, and China (Heenan and Lamontagne 1999, 65). With such small ties, Western states cannot successfully link trade issues to human rights issues. The EU has criticized Belarus as lacking the rule of law and has lodged diplomatic protests, but in November 1999, the EU Troika (consisting of the past, present, and future EU presidents) visited Minsk and signed the Technical Assistance for CIS (TACIS) agreement, notwithstanding the fact that they "emphasized that negotiations on free elections should commence as soon as possible" (OSCE/AMG 2000b, 10). The budget for the TACIS Program in Belarus for the period 2000–2003 is 10 million euros.[10] Thus it seems that, at least beginning in 1999, Western states have begun

trying to properly combine two approaches—sanctions and assistance—in a way that is more conducive to bringing about improvements in the situation in Belarus.

Another Asymmetrical Regime

Article 33 of the Constitution of the Republic of Belarus states, "Each
person is guaranteed the freedom of thought, belief, and expression"
(Andreeva 1999, 125). But as previously mentioned, the Belarus government has shown little intention of implementing either this
clause of the Constitution or the OSCE norms and principles, despite OSCE activity and Western pressure.

   In the cold war era, the Helsinki Regime featured an "asymmetrical regime" (Miyawaki 1999, 50-76) between East and West. Both
sides agreed to a set of common words on human rights, but broadly
speaking, the Eastern bloc did not change its domestic policies on
these issues. The reason for the Eastern rejection of fundamental
change was that Eastern politicians—and even Western governments
—regarded the Helsinki Accords as a symbolic document and not a
practical one. For example, during the second stage of the CSCE conference, which was the formative process of the Helsinki regime, one
U.K. diplomat expressed in a 1973 brief to his country's delegation
that "we do not expect the Russians and their allies to make radical
changes in their political systems; and it would be unrealistic to
think that as a result of the CSCE 'The Times' will be freely available
in Moscow" (Bennett and Hamilton 1997, 179). But Western opinion
and diplomacy, triggered by President Jimmy Carter's human rights
diplomacy and by the formation of the Helsinki Group by dissidents
in the Eastern bloc, were obliged to pay more and more attention to
the human rights situation, even if it destroyed the air of détente.
The human rights situation in the East did not improve and in fact
it worsened in the first half of the 1980s, as evidenced by Andrei
Sakharov's exile (1980-1986) and the imposition of martial law in
Poland (1981-1983).[11]

   From 1989, the situation improved somewhat, mainly as a result
of citizen movements. Nonetheless, the same asymmetrical regime
that existed in the cold war era prevails again in Europe in the
post–cold war era. This time, the regime is seen in the cases of Belarus

and some of the former Soviet countries in Central Asia. These countries have maintained their authoritarian regimes with "democratic" trimmings. Western states and NGOs cannot accept this situation and the OSCE cannot give up on its goal of fostering democracy in all OSCE areas. But more than a decade after 1989, the asymmetrical regime continues to exist. And if the situation continues on its present course, the Paris Regime of the OSCE will either be forced to adapt its values to reality, or its fundamental significance may be forgotten.

MEASURES OF PREVENTIVE DIPLOMACY TOWARD BELARUS

Having examined how the situation has evolved to date, the next question is what approaches are available for addressing the Belarus issue. In this section, I will outline four options that the relevant actors might adopt to bring about a change.

The First Option: Sanctions with Pressure

This first approach, sanctions with pressure, is represented mainly by Western diplomacy toward Belarus and can be characterized as "linkage diplomacy." Initially, the EU negotiated with the Lukashenko regime on human rights issues, but when they failed to persuade Belarus to turn back to a democratic regime, the EU implemented diplomatic and economic sanctions against Belarus. From 1997 to 1999, the EU states cut some dimensions of their economic cooperation program with Belarus that had been authorized under a Partnership and Cooperation Agreement signed in 1995. The World Bank (International Bank for Reconstruction and Development) similarly stopped its new financial support program from 1994, when Lukashenko halted the shift to a market economy and reintroduced a planned economy in certain areas. In 1997, the Council of Ministers of the EU decided upon a number of sanctions against Belarus—it refused to support Belarus' membership in the Council of Europe, suspended bilateral relations at the ministerial level, and froze EU technical assistance programs in Belarus (European Union 2000b).

The member-states of the EU all recalled their ambassadors during the period from 1998 to 1999. The Parliamentary Assembly of the Council of Europe also suspended the "special guest" status of Belarus in January 1997, and the EU has continuously refused to hold any high-level political dialogues with Belarus.[12]

The United States was another prominent actor that turned to sanctions. The American ambassador was recalled from June 1998 to September 1999—seven months longer in duration than other Western states—due to U.S. insistence that Belarus had violated the Vienna Convention on Diplomatic Relations when it forced Western embassies in Minsk to relocate to sites in the suburbs.

But the AMG suggested that this approach was a failure, stating that "the diplomatic isolation of Belarus does not strengthen the democratic forces" (OSCE/AMG 2000b, 4). Moreover, the fact that it was primarily Western states that imposed these sanctions rendered them ineffective. Lukashenko appears impervious to Western pressure since Belarus is not heavily dependent on Western markets, natural resources, culture, or information. The failure of this approach was confirmed by the decision of the EU itself to extend the TACIS Program to Belarus in 1999.

The Second Option: A Constructive Approach

The AMG has tried to adopt a second, constructive approach. As mentioned previously, the AMG is skeptical about the efficacy of a hard-line policy toward Belarus, and has sought to avoid the one-sided use of any kind of power. Instead, the AMG has tried to play an important role by endorsing democracy and improving the human rights situation. Unfortunately, however, it has not achieved a sufficient level of success, mainly because of the limitations on its power and financial resources.

The AMG faces informal obstruction by the Belarus government on the one hand and the high expectations of the Belarus citizens on the other.[13] The AMG is surrounded by daily criticism from the Belarus government, such as the charge leveled by the new chairman of the State Committee for Security (KGB) of Belarus, Leonid Yerin, that the AMG's mission is "giving aid to radical opposition groups intent on overthrowing the present Soviet-style regime" ("OSCE Slams

Charges" 2000). And yet the OSCE is uniquely positioned to bring about change: it is the only major international organization with a "permanent" presence in Belarus to monitor the human rights situation, with no need to extend its mandate annually as is the case for other OSCE missions (Timmermann 1999). Faced with these dual forces of pressure and anticipation, the AMG must maintain a course between watching calmly and pressing the government to change, adopting a subtle balance between "cooperation" and "confrontation" with the Belarus government.

It is clear that Lukashenko holds the greatest influence and power in Belarus, making outright confrontation difficult. That point was clearly illustrated by the government's suppression of the demonstration in Minsk on March 25, 2000, as noted previously, at which even a member of the AMG was arrested. Nonetheless, Lukashenko's power and options are limited to some extent by the presence of the AMG through the small amount of pressure it creates with its many statements, its activities, and its strong protests. It is also important to note that the presence of international organizations, including the AMG, give the Lukashenko regime legitimacy "from outside." This is particularly noteworthy in light of the continuing constitutional controversy that has split Belarus politically and raised questions about the legitimacy of Lukashenko after July 1999. (The Belarus Constitution was revised in 1996, under Lukashenko's direction. Had it not been revised, the term of Lukashenko's presidency would have expired in 1999, and the opposition has thus been urging that he step down.)

In short, this more patient, constructive approach adopted by the AMG has helped to promote democracy to some extent, but its achievements are limited by the AMG's lack of power to enforce recommendations and its lack of sufficient influence or leverage to significantly affect Lukashenko's policy choices.

The Third Option: Selective Intervention

The third option refers primarily to the possibility of using Russian influence to affect Belarus policy on human rights issues. Certainly Russia pressured Belarus in 1997 to make use of the OSCE human rights regime in order to decrease the possibility of NATO's further eastward expansion. But Russia has used pressure in only one other case, namely its mediation efforts between President Lukashenko and the opposition during the constitutional crisis in November 1996. Generally speaking, while it frequently uses pressure and cooperation in the economic area, Russia has maintained a wait-and-see attitude toward Belarusian human rights issues. Despite the strong ties between the two countries, Russia does not want to risk having Belarus pull away, even in the short term, and it still harbors the fear that democratization could lead to a pro-West government in Belarus.

Nonetheless, Russia is uniquely positioned to be the main actor in dealing with Belarus because it is the sole country that has a strong influence on Belarus in the political, economic, and social dimensions. In the political dimension, for example, Belarus has sought greater interdependence with Russia, signing a treaty that created a confederation between the two countries in December 1999.

In the economic dimension, close cooperation with Russia is all but inevitable for Belarus. Its trade with Russia and the other CIS member-states accounted for more than 60 percent of all its foreign trade in September 1998, and as noted previously, the country's debt to Russia is substantial (Heenan and Lamontagne 1999, 64). Even before the Lukashenko regime, the government of Belarus aligned itself closely with Russia in the economic realm. Under the Lukashenko regime, Belarus further accelerated its economic integration with Russia as a whole, as symbolized by the fact that Russia and Belarus have agreed to introduce the Russian ruble as the two nations' common currency in 2005.

In the social dimension, the population of Belarus has been subject to high levels of linguistic Russification since the Stalin period. As a result, by the mid-1970s, not a single Belarusian school remained in the 95 cities of the republic, and Belarusians in a survey in 1984 were ranked in last place among the 15 Soviet nationalities in terms of the percentage (74.2 percent) of people residing in their national republic who retained the capacity to speak their native language. To be sure, national language is not always necessary for national consciousness, but in the case of Belarus, existing as it does in the long shadows of its neighboring Slavic states, the lack of a linguistic identity makes it virtually impossible for the country to develop a strong ethnic and national consciousness. Even after having achieved independence, 85 percent of Belarusian people watch television programs from Russia, and most of them have relatives in Russia.[14] David Marples uses the term " a denationalized nation" to describe Belarus, pointing to the difficulty of severing its cultural ties with Russia (1999, 50–52). Belarus is thus dependent on Russia in many ways, and this gives the Russians some degree of leverage to influence Belarusian politics.

But this third option has one enormous obstacle. It can easily turn into a means of support for Lukashenko rather than a means of preventing conflict or endorsing democracy. For example, in the Belarusian parliamentary election of October 2000, nearly 200 individuals from 28 states—including CIS states, mainly represented by Russia—who were requested by Lukashenko to serve as election monitors, recognized the validity of the election, contrary to the opinion of most international organizations, including the OSCE and NGOs, which did not recognize its validity.[15] The OSCE's Office for Democratic Institutions and Human Rights (ODIHR), for example, concluded that the "parliamentary elections process in Belarus failed to meet international standards for democratic elections, including those formulated in the 1990 Copenhagen Document of the OSCE" (OSCE 2000c). Western states and NGOs raised a number of problems with the way in which the CIS monitors observed the election. For example, the ODIHR reported that some of the invited observers from these countries, including those from CIS states, "were invited by the CEC (Central Election Committee) with hotel expenses paid. On election day, the CEC provided most of these observers with guided bus tours of selected polling stations. The following day, these observers were invited by the CEC to participate in a press conference where the results of the elections were to be announced." The report concluded that the CEC's coordination of the observers' activities "compromised the credibility of their findings" (OSCE 2000c). In short, these low "CIS standards" for monitoring the election stand in sharp contrast with the "OSCE standards," which have been respected as the international standard for monitoring elections. The frequent usage of "CIS standards" by and in OSCE memberstates jeopardizes the political paradigm that OSCE has constructed in post-cold war Europe.

But despite the drawbacks of this option, the possibility remains that Russia might play an important role in endorsing democracy and improving the human rights situation in Belarus. Essentially, Russia is capable of playing such a role but it currently has no intention to do so. It is possible that Western states could press Russia to take such action, however, and this might be the most effective way to improve the situation in Belarus. A similar case was seen beginning in the early 1990s with human rights and democratization issues in Myanmar. Western states persuaded Japan, which has the most influence over Myanmar through its economic assistance, to apply pressure on that country's military regime. This has subsequently produced some improvements in the human rights situation there in this author's opinion.

The Fourth Option:
Transnational Cooperation with NGOs in Belarus

The AMG and Western NGOs take this fourth, cooperative approach. Here we see the possibility of a bottom-up democratic evolution in Belarus, although at this stage, it is inevitable that the Lukashenko regime will try to suppress it to some extent. With more cooperation between NGOs through technical assistance, training, and daily information exchange, the NGO community could earn the confidence of and gain greater influence among the Belarusian people. In fact, NGO cooperation between the Moscow Helsinki Group and Belarusian human rights NGOs has increased recently, for example in the form of a school program on human rights that is funded with Western financial support.[16] More than the intergovernmental route, it is this kind of nongovernmental link between Moscow and Minsk that can pave the way for more drastic improvements in the human rights situation. The increased interaction between NGOs is given further justification by the fact that they parallel the moves toward Belarusian-Russian unification. And the merit for Western NGOs of this particular route through the Moscow Helsinki Group is that the human rights assistance would gain a "neutral" image instead of being characterized as "Western" in nature. This is one way in which the concept of and support for human rights could gain universality in Belarus.

The influence of human rights NGOs is based on the confidence people have in them. It is very important for NGOs to inform the Belarusian people of the human rights situation in the country because the state control over the mass media usually prevents the truth from being reported. But the effectiveness of this approach is limited in one essential dimension: NGOs are powerless unless people act, cooperate with NGOs, and are sympathetic toward NGO activities. Unfortunately, while there has been some progress in this direction, most people in Belarus are still reluctant to work with NGOs.

Another concern is that if Russian President Vladimir Putin turns against the human rights movement in Russia, in spite of his statement in his inaugural address regarding the need to promote the further progress toward democracy in Russia, the effectiveness of this course will be diminished. Putin would be able to cut off the NGO network between Moscow and Minsk, and thus he holds a strategically important position for the success or failure of this option as well. This shows the vulnerability of relying on this fourth approach.

Additionally, we see another serious limit to this option, at least for now: the effectiveness of this approach depends on the free flow of information. In Belarus, however, the state-run media is powerful enough to control political information and to conduct political campaigns against the opposition. In the case of the parliamentary election on October 15, 2000, according to an investigation by members of the ODIHR Media Monitoring section conducted for about one month prior to the election, on the sole (state-run) TV station in Belarus, 90 percent of the news programs were occupied with reports on the president or the government. Similarly, 73 percent of the articles in the state-run newspapers focused on the president (62 percent) or the government (11 percent), while only 9 percent dealt with independent candidates or groups, and 18 percent covered others (Maiola 2000). These figures clearly show a bias in the state-run media when compared with news from independent newspapers, which devoted 27.1 percent of their articles to the president, 20 percent to the government, 18.7 percent to independent candidates, and 34.2 percent to others including the opposition, according to the same investigation by the ODIHR. This problem is exacerbated by the fact that state-run newspapers are given priority and enjoy a better environment for publishing papers, receiving a great deal of government assistance and enjoying a large daily circulation (for example, *Sovetskaia Belorussiia* has a circulation of around 460,000). Independent newspapers, by contrast, generally lack their own printing house and have a limited circulation of less than 1,000 per paper. Of course, this situation is not peculiar to the Lukashenko regime; even before 1994, most independent papers were "small and poorly funded," and the government "remained the owner and chief financial backer of nine major publications" (U.S. Department of State 1994, 9). But under the Lukashenko regime, the trend of suppressing the free media has become more evident. Regulation of the mass media in Belarus for political reasons is legitimated by the Law of the Republic of Belarus on the Press and Other Mass Media of January 1995. This law prescribes that the mass media cannot be used to disseminate "information defaming the honor and dignity of the President of the Republic of Belarus (or) heads of state bodies whose status is established by the Constitution of the Republic of Belarus" (Art. 5).

These limits make it difficult to circulate information on or among the opposition, including NGO information in Belarus. In the future, we might hope that the building of a nationwide Internet structure in Belarus and increased access to it will offer the possibility for people to obtain and exchange information on the opposition. For the time being, however, a lack of resources has prevented the people of Belarus from having sufficient access to the Internet. On the other hand, it is worth noting that the Open Society Institute and the United Nations Development Programme (UNDP) have been helping to build an Internet network throughout Belarus, known as Unibel. This was one of the first two Internet networks admitted in this country, and it has already connected hundreds of NGOs in Belarus.[17]

If transnational NGOs can gain in power and if information flows continue to improve, then this fourth option might become a realistic means for improving the political situation in Belarus. At the present, however, the NGOs working in this area do not have sufficient influence to have an impact.

POTENTIAL ACTORS IN THE SEARCH FOR A SOLUTION

The OSCE Dilemma Continues

As mentioned previously, the OSCE has two functions in Belarus: advising and monitoring. To a certain extent, the advisory function requires the AMG to take the Belarus government's side, and to maintain its ties with the Lukashenko government. On the other hand, the monitoring function implies an element of taking the Belarus opposition's side by investigating of and commenting on human rights issues. Even though these two functions are not contradictory in the longer term, they are inherently in conflict in the short term, as the OSCE must choose which side to support each time one side presses another side to change its policy, challenges the other's legitimacy, or takes an opposing political stance.

To be certain, the OSCE has another desired function: creating stability. The AMG might contribute to fostering a stable situation between the Belarus government and the opposition, although this function was not effective in the case of the March 2000 collision between the two sides. In that instance, the only role that the AMG could play was to report on that collision. The AMG lacks the power to do more, having only six full members and a relatively limited budget (935,000 euros in the 2000 fiscal year), and receiving relatively little attention from the West. If the OSCE could address these issues and solve its basic dilemma between seeking political stability and promoting democracy, it might be able to play a more powerful role in solving the Belarus situation.

The most serious and fundamental dilemma facing the OSCE, however, is that its "universal values" impose a standard that is too high and too difficult to implement in the ex-Soviet states. These universal values—or even more so, the European values—that the OSCE has agreed upon set too high a threshold for some transitional states or undemocratic states like Belarus. But given that the OSCE prides itself on being not a community of interests but a "community of values," as was stated in the concluding document of the OSCE Ministerial Council in Stockholm in 1992, it cannot be expected to change its stance on promoting these values. And yet, this community of values continues to be challenged by some participating states that have not committed themselves wholeheartedly to the OSCE standards, leading us to conclude that, after all, the Paris Regime of the OSCE is "an inadequate community of values" (Middelkoop 1995, 30–31).

The United States and the European Union: Pressing Russia to be a Catalyst

As described in the options outlined in the previous section, while Russia may have the capacity to act, it is difficult to predict a major Russian role in changing the human rights situation in Belarus. Western states, along with the Council of Europe and other international organizations, have continued to criticize Russian behavior in Chechnya since the Yeltsin era. If Western states want to change Belarus, they must put pressure on Russia first to influence the Belarus government, just as they have pressed Russia, with some degree of success, to modify its own behavior in the Chechnya case.

But we need to assess how pressure might effectively be applied on Russia to convince it to use its influence over Belarus. First of all, it is more difficult for Western states to offer Russia some kind of bargaining chip related to the Belarus issue than it is with military or economic issues in Russia itself. Western states have no justification to bargain on values like human rights issues with Belarus, because Belarus is at most a middle power, and not a major power like Russia. In the case of Western negotiations with Russia, for example, Western states expressed their understanding of Boris Yeltsin's actions when he ordered military commanders to batter down the parliament building with cannons in October 1993, and again when he started the war in Chechnya, in the common "interest" of preventing the reemergence of communism in Russia. Of course, this type of compromise has inherent risks. As Grigory Yablinsky notes, "The danger comes when the West, while promoting the rhetoric of democracy and capitalism, backs Boris Yeltsin, Anatoly Chubais, Viktor Chernomyrdin, Boris Nemtsov, and Yegor Gaidar even when they embark on actions that do not promote democracy or markets" (2000, 256). Nonetheless, in the case of a major power, in order to protect its values, the West might be willing to sacrifice certain interests (e.g., by making trade or arms control concessions). But this trade-off of an "interest" for a "value" is politically more costly than would be a straight "interest" for "interest" exchange, and in the case of Belarus—a country that is hardly even known by many people in the West—there would be little political support for such sacrifices.

What is more, Western states cannot extend any support to Lukashenko in principle, so they cannot make political deals with him on democratization or human rights issues directly. They can do it through Russia, however, even if it is not easy. I call this route the "Russia as a catalyst" strategy. Western states could make a deal with Russia and offer concessions to Russia on certain economic, military, or territorial issues, and in turn Russia would make a deal with Belarus. In exchange for Russian concessions on economic issues (such as the cancellation of its huge debt to Russia) or on the "confederation agenda" between Russia and Belarus, Belarus would make concessions to Russia in terms of improving its human rights record or its efforts at democratization (the beneficiaries of which would be Western states, and even more so, the people of Belarus).

This strategy works effectively only when Russia clearly perceives itself to be a mediator between Western states and Belarus on these issues and only when it is possible for Western states to give Russia what it desires, like allowing it to default on its obligations of over US$48 billion to the 19 creditor nations of the Paris Club, or offering U.S. concessions on the National Missile Defense Program. A good example of this strategy was seen in 1997, when Russia played a role in persuading Belarus to accept the OSCE AMG, while Russia for its part succeeded in preventing NATO's prospective expansion to Romania, the Baltic states, and Ukraine. Learning from this precedent, it is necessary, at least as a temporary option, to create an institution or international regime that can legitimate these dealings between Russia, Belarus, and the Western states.

But there is also a negative side to this strategy. First, there is a bigger political gap between Lukashenko and Putin than there was between Lukashenko and Yeltsin. In contrast with Yeltsin, who was motivated by emotion, Putin's diplomacy is calculated rationally. Given the existence of rumors about the Kremlin preparing to "help" Lukashenko not be reelected in the presidential campaign, it appears that the relationship between Belarus and Russia began to cool substantially in 2000 ("Belarusian President" 2001). That also implies that Lukashenko will be very cautious about being under the

Kremlin's control. The fundamental reshuffling of high officials in November 2000, for example, including the head of the KGB (the State Security Committee of Belarus), Vladimir Matskevich, Prosecutor General Oleg Bozhelko, and KGB Secretary Viktor Sheiman, can be interpreted as a move by Lukashenko to expel pro-Putin members from the government. Moreover, it was quite evident that improving the human rights situation and making progress on democratization issues before the presidential election scheduled for September 2001 would decrease the probability of Lukashenko's reelection, thus making it contrary to his own interests. (That election was held after this chapter was written. Lukashenko was in fact reelected, although the OSCE declared that the election was not in compliance with OSCE election standards.)

Finally, it still remains to be seen whether Western states can provide Russia with what it desires or not. It is difficult to determine what to negotiate, or how to negotiate with Russia, because it could set a precedent that Russia would then try to repeat in its dealings with Western states on other matters (for example, on human rights or democratization issues in Central Asian states, or even in the case of Chechnya). This is why the relevant actors need to create a specific framework or regime to deal with the issue of Belarus.

With Whom Can the Belarus Opposition Collaborate and How Can They Win?

In interviews conducted by this author with NGO representatives engaged in human rights issues in Belarus, all of them are currently putting, or intend to put, pressure not only on Western states but also on Russia to improve human rights and democratization in Belarus. The Russian government has a great deal of interest in Belarus, as do the Russian parliament and people. To be certain, Russia currently shows no inclination to press Lukashenko to improve the human rights situation. But, as Bogdankevich mentioned, "Russia has the potential ability to change the Belarusian situation with economic and political ties."[18] The NGO community regards the democratic Yabloko Party and the Union of Right Forces in the Russian parliament (as well as Polish, Ukraine, and Baltic parliamentarians) as meaningful partners in order to launch an appeal on the human rights situation across the border.[19] And the Russian mass media has a great deal of influence on the Belarusian people as well.

But it is also important for us to assess whether the opposition side would be ready to win the presidential election if it were to be held in accordance with the OSCE standards. In January 2001, the Belarusian opposition was mulling a single presidential candidate from among three possible candidates: Syamyon Domash, Mikhail Chigir, and Uladzimir Hancharyk ("Belarusian Opposition" 2001). However, according to a poll conducted in October 2000 by a non-governmental, Minsk-based association, the Independent Institute for Social-Economic and Political Studies (IISEPS), in a race between Lukashenko and Chigir, the citizens of Belarus would favor the current president over the opposition candidate by a margin of 35.9 percent to 13.5 percent.[20] It is therefore difficult to predict how the opposition might win the next presidential election. In general, it is possible to envision a "Yugoslav scenario" (i.e., a scene similar to the victory of Vojislav Kostunica in Serbia after the election of September 2000 with the support of mass demonstrations) occurring in Belarus in the next election. But this will not easily be realized since it is not expected that the opposition can succeed in mobilizing the Belarus masses. According to the German Embassy in Minsk, a gathering organized by the opposition side to call for a boycott of the parliamentary elections in October 2000 only drew around 3,000 people.[21] Even in April 1996, a demonstration to mark the tenth anniversary of the Chernobyl disaster drew a crowd of only around 50,000–80,000, and that was probably the largest gathering by the opposition side since the country gained its independence in 1991. In the case of Kostunica's win in Serbia, where more than 10 million people reside, an opposition that had for years been divided was finally consolidated, conducted an election campaign over ten months, and mobilized about 100,000 people every day after the election. But in Belarus, which has roughly the same population, it is hard to imagine similar numbers being mobilized in the immediate future.

The primary causes for the lack of political support for the opposition side in Belarus lie in a combination of the vulnerability of the opposition parties themselves and regulations that limit political action by the opposition.[22] At both the local and national levels, most members of the opposition side have boycotted parliamentary elections since 1996.[23] In Belarus, there are 24,000 members of local councils and over 90 percent of them are appointed by professional associations. Only the remaining positions (roughly 600 in number) are elected directly by voters. Out of those elected council members, around 400 are pro-Lukashenko, and the opposition has only 172 members, all of whom belong to the Communist Party of Belarus (the anti-Lukashenko faction).[24] The boycott tactics of the opposition have led to decreased expectations of what the opposition party can achieve. The boycott therefore has had a very limited political impact and is generally deemed to be a "failure."[25] The end result has been that it is difficult for the opposition to take an effective political leadership role in promoting democratization.

CONCLUSION

A Practical Prescription

As indicated above, the West, the OSCE AMG, and domestic NGOs cannot solve Belarusian human rights issues by themselves. They simply do not have enough leverage over the government or influence over the Belarus population to bring about the desired changes. At the moment, the only potential avenue for change is President Putin, who could bring his strong influence to bear on Belarus. Western states must therefore press Putin to do so by offering Russia some kind of incentive. If Russia changes its policy on Belarus, it is possible that Lukashenko will be obliged to shift the political regime back from an authoritarian to a democratic one again.

The OSCE could assist in promoting such a Belarusian redemocratization, but it is not sufficiently powerful at this time to do so. The OSCE is only one actor, and not a major one. In the current environment, it will require a full complement of actors—the OSCE framework, Russian pressure on Belarus, Western pressure on Russia, and an NGO network—to bring about change. This implies a comprehensive approach to conflict prevention in Belarus.

Of course, there are other factors that may play a role in shifting Belarus toward the path of democratization in the future as well. This can be seen in the successes of Slovakia and Serbia in redemocratizing, although it took roughly five to ten years to do so. Of course, these states were aided by their proximity to the center of Europe—particularly as the EU and NATO have been pushing eastward. Belarus is situated farther to the east. But the environment around Belarus is shifting and may change dramatically in the near future. After Polish admittance to NATO in 1999 and also to the EU at some point in the future, Belarus finds itself in increasingly close proximity to areas that are benefiting from European-derived economic prosperity and security, which could ultimately have an impact.

The Problem of Asymmetrical Regimes

The question remains, however, whether the complete democratization of Belarus would actually contribute to the prevention of potential conflicts. This question relates to a more fundamental problem: the idea that an asymmetrical regime could revive in the post–cold war era. Under the Helsinki Regime, the asymmetrical character, in which one side—i.e., the USSR—did not demonstrate sufficient respect for the Helsinki Accords, lasted for at least a decade after the accords were signed in 1975. Similarly, in the case of Belarus, we see a country that has failed to implement the many documents adopted by the CSCE/OSCE, of which Belarus itself is a member. Looking at the history of the USSR's adoption of the Helsinki Accords through a process of sanctions by Western states, cooperation mainly with Western Europe, and transnational cooperation among NGOs in the East as well as in the West, it appears that we might need to adopt the same process in order to succeed in the redemocratization of Belarus.

There are similarities with the type of ideological confrontations we saw in the cold war era. In my interview with a number of high-ranking officials of the Ministry of Foreign Affairs of Belarus, they emphasized, "Democracy becomes another weapon for Western states to put pressure on Belarus. The cold war still exists in many points in the OSCE area due to Western activities."[26] And they referred to the notion of "security through democracy," that "democracy is a solid basis of security only in the case where it is equal and even for everybody."[27]

These arguments represent the idea that democracy must progress and develop in its own way in each nation, and that no one should "import" democracy from another state. This is clearly in conflict with the comprehensive character of Western preventive diplomacy, which seeks to introduce democracy building in the relevant state. As long as Western states persist in their desire to realize democratization in the whole OSCE area, the OSCE will continue to exhibit a clear contradiction between its high standards and low degree of implementation. As one officer of the Belarus Ministry of Foreign Affairs said, speaking on an unofficial basis, we have already seen that "in the OSCE there is one democracy for the West, one democracy for the East. It is not always bad, but always unsatisfactory. If the standards of the OSCE are applied only by some states and not others, it will spell the end of the organization."[28]

Some elements of these arguments expressed by the Belarus government are similar to the ideological controversy over human rights during the cold war era. But the environment surrounding these arguments has decisively changed. Of course, the main differences between now and the cold war era can be found in the distribution of power, the degree of economic cooperation, and the relative lack of ideological struggle. But it is surprising to see that Belarus, given its position as just one middle power among the CIS states, could continue to disregard the OSCE standards for more than five years. After all, in contrast to the USSR during the cold war, Belarus is not a country with a large military, economic power, or ideological influence of its own, but simply a country with strong ties to Russia. This must lead us to conclude that Belarus has been able to sustain its position solely through its economic dependence on Russia.

Another point that we must assess is whether we need a "democracy clause" for conflict prevention everywhere or not. In considering the relationship between democracy and domestic conflict, it is useful to examine the examples of Saudi Arabia and India. Saudi Arabia is not a democratic country, but it has a great degree of domestic stability. By contrast, India is a democratic state, but it has significant internal conflict. In this regard, Belarus can perhaps best be described as an undemocratic "Saudi Arabia" in Europe.

Belarus has little power and probably little intention of instigating military confrontations with its neighbors, at least as a rational choice. For example, Belarus completed its transport of nuclear weapons (a legacy of the Soviet Union) into Russia, ratified the Comprehensive Test Ban Treaty in May 2000, and signed treaties with neighboring

states, including the Baltic states, confirming state borders. And after the Kosovo conflict, Belarus reopened its military relations with
NATO even earlier than did Russia.[29] Certainly, the international
community might feel some unease when viewing Belarus policies
on such issues as its expansion of weapons exports, its establishment
of regular civilian flights between Belarus and Iraq and maintenance
of economic cooperation with Iraq despite the UN sanctions, and its
military consolidation with Russia (particularly in light of NATO's
enlargement and the fact that Belarus now shares a border with
NATO member, Poland). Nonetheless, there is a general consensus
both domestically and internationally that as long as the Lukashenko
regime continues, it is unlikely that interstate conflicts or territorial
disputes will emerge. Even on the domestic front, despite the serious
divide between pro- and anti-Lukashenko forces, there is little chance
of internal military conflict. To the contrary, one Belarusian diplomat has argued that if a conflict were to emerge, there is a greater
likelihood that it would be caused by the emergence of an extreme
nationalistic government in Poland in the future, which could potentially generate some kind of ethnic tension between Poland and Belarus—but in that case, the source of the tension would be Poland.[30]

    In sum, we find a country in which there is a high degree of politi-
cal stability and low security risk despite the repression of human
rights. Given this context, the OSCE Paris Regime appears to be an
asymmetrical regime, and the correlation between traditional security issues and human rights or democratization does not appear to
hold true in Belarus.

The Human Rights Dimension

Similarly, the relationship between human rights and domestic conflict bears rethinking. Generally speaking, although a country's human rights record is one means of assessing whether a conflict is
escalating, we see many exceptions, especially in the case of authoritarian or socialist states. According to human rights surveys conducted by Freedom House from 1972 to 2000, a total of 38 countries
have had both civil liberties and political rights ratings of seven—the
worst rating (table 1).

Table 1. Countries Receiving Freedom House's Lowest Rating for Civil Liberties and
Political Rights, 1972–2000.

Country	Years Received
Afghanistan	1978–1988, 1989–1992, 1993–2000
Albania	1972–1990
Angola	1977–1991, 1993–1995
Benin	1975–1979, 1984–1990
Bhutan	1994–1998
Bulgaria	1972–1990
Burma	1983–2000
Cambodia	1975–1991
Central African Republic	1972–1979
Chad	1972–1977
China	1972–1977, 1989–1998
Congo	1972–1973, 1979–1981
Cuba	1972–1976, 1989–2000
Equatorial Guinea	1977–1979, 1985–1992, 1993–2000
Ethiopia	1977–1987, 1989–1991
East Germany	1972–1978, 1979–1980, 1981–1984
Guinea	1972–1984
Iraq	1972–1978, 1984–2000
North Korea	1972–2000
Laos	1976–1988
Liberia	1990–1991
Libya	1973–1975, 1989–2000
Mali	1975–1979
Mongolia	1972–1990
Mozambique	1976–1983
Nigeria	1995–1996
Romania	1984–1990
Sao Tome and Principe	1983–1988
Saudi Arabia	1992–2000
Somalia	1976–2000
Sudan	1989–2000
Syria	1972–1974, 1989–2000
Tajikistan	1993–1997
Turkmenistan	1993–2000
USSR	1984–1987
Uzbekistan	1993–1996
Vietnam	1972–1987, 1989–2000
South Yemen	1972–1979, 1988–1990

SOURCE: Freedom House 2000b.

Of these states, 19 are or were socialist or pro-socialist states during the period in question. However, only nine countries experienced serious civil wars during the periods that they received those lowest ratings (Afghanistan, Angola, Chad, Liberia, Mozambique, Somalia, Sudan, Tajikistan, and South Yemen). And we see only five countries engaged in prominent and massive external warfare or military intervention during their respective low-ranking periods (Chad, Iraq, Syria, the USSR, and Vietnam). Additionally, we find countries on the list like Saudi Arabia or Syria, which could be deemed quite stable. By contrast, we do not see the names of countries that have experienced serious civil wars in the post–cold war era—Azerbaijan, Bosnia-Herzegovina, Croatia, Serbia, Sri Lanka—or that have undergone political instability or local ethnic conflicts, such as Turkey. The reason why the names of countries known for civil war are not seen on the list is that those military conflicts cannot happen without the intent of the government as long as authoritarian regimes control the people as a whole. As is widely known, the main causes of conflict lie in the struggle for ethnic identity, equal access to economic prosperity, and to political participation, and not just for democracy or human rights per se. In sum, human rights indicators do not necessarily equal signs of conflict.

I agree with those who argue that the building of democratic institutions and respect for human rights are important conditions to make post-conflict society stable in the long run. But before the conflict, indicators of democracy or human rights have not necessarily functioned as an effective early-warning system. As seen in Belarus, the suppression of human rights or democratization does not necessarily lead to conflict.

Preventive diplomacy in the post–cold war era includes a wide range of means to prevent armed conflict, from the support of human rights to confidence-building measures. We see that the means and the goals of preventive diplomacy face daunting obstacles, such as those presented in the Belarus case. We stand at the crossroads of preventive diplomacy. One path would be to pursue a preventive diplomacy approach that includes democratic or human rights values. This policy has higher stakes and will face more obstacles. It will require more years, more resources, and more patience. Another path would be to pursue preventive diplomacy without human rights values, which would have a smaller stake and be less difficult to achieve. This will require that we reexamine why we are preventing conflicts, and design more effective means of contributing to peace, prosperity, and stability among states as well as among individuals.

Notes

1. In this context, the Fund for Peace has developed an analytical model that uses political indicators related to human rights and democracy among its top 12 indicators of internal conflict and state collapse. Among the indicators that would suggest a situation deteriorating toward internal conflict are the "suspension or arbitrary application of the rule of law and widespread violation of human rights." These are taken to consist of the emergence of undemocratic rule, the outbreak of politically inspired violence, a rising number of political prisoners or dissidents, and/or the widespread abuse of legal, political, and social rights. This model also addresses post-conflict issues, and includes among the indicators the establishment of the basic rule of law and the cessation or reduction of human rights abuses (Baker and Weller 1999, 23-26).

2. Interview with Ambassador Hans-Georg Wieck, head of the OSCE Advisory and Monitoring Group in Belarus, in Minsk, on March 30, 2000.

3. Interview with Youri Parfiyanovich, head of the Department of Analysis and Foreign Policy Events Planning of the Ministry of Foreign Affairs of the Republic of Belarus, on December 6, 2000, in Minsk.

4. Interview with Wieck on March 30, 2000.

5. Interview with Tatsiana Pratsko, chair of the Belarusian Helsinki Committee, in Minsk, on March 30, 2000.

6. Interview with Stanislav A. Bogdankevich, chairman of the United Civil Party, on March 31, 2000, in Minsk.

7. Interview with Aaron Rhodes, executive director of the International Helsinki Federation for Human Rights, on March 28, 2000, in Vienna.

8. Item 7 of the Copenhagen Document specifies that the participating states agree "to ensure that the will of the people serves as the basis of the authority of government" by holding free elections at legally defined intervals, with votes cast by secret ballot or by an equivalent free voting procedure, with a "free and fair atmosphere" for political campaigning (i.e., the parties, candidates and voters should not be subjected to intimidation or retribution), with "unimpeded access to the media on a non-discriminatory basis for all political groupings and individuals wishing to participate in the electoral process." Item 8 notes that "the presence of observers, both foreign and domestic, can enhance

the electoral process for States in which elections are taking place." The participating states therefore agreed to invite the participation of observers from any
other CSCE participating states and any appropriate private institutions and
organizations. The AMG pointed out insufficiencies in such areas as the electoral commission, public openness during preparation for and holding of elections, access to state media, election campaign financing, early voting, mobile
polling stations, and the threshold of electors for the validation of elections.

9. Interview with Bogdankevich.

10. From 1991 to 1996, the amount of the TACIS budget was 5.4 million
euros according to two reports, "Belarus Indicative Programme TACIS 2000-
2003" and "The EU's Relations with Belarus," at <http://europa.eu.int/
comm/external_relations/belarus/intro/indexl.htm> (1 December 2000).

11. It should be noted, however, that there was indeed some improvement
after 1975 in certain countries (most notably Poland and East Germany), particularly on issues of migration, reunification of family members, and other humanitarian issues between East and West.

12. But in 2000, the World Bank renewed negotiations with the Belarus
government to restart the financial support. Interview with Sergey Kulyk, Resident Representative of the World Bank in Belarus, on December 7, 2000, in
Minsk.

13. In a public opinion poll conducted in January 2000 by the polling organization Zergara, and sponsored by the independent news agency BelaPAN,
16 percent of Minsk citizens said that they trusted the AMG overall in Belarus;
44 percent of them trusted it to some extent. In Belarus, the UNDP and UNHCR
are active, but they draw attention to humanitarian issues such as Chernobyl.

14. Interviews with Ambassador Andrea Wiktorin and Holger Kraemer, Ref-
erence for Law and Press, on December 6, 2000, in Minsk.

15. Interview with Wieck on December 6, 2000, in Minsk. At the CIS summit
in December 2000 in Minsk, CIS heads approved the parliamentary election in
Belarus, as well as the presidential election in Kyrgystan and the parliamentary
election in Azerbaijan. The OSCE pointed out that, similar to Belarus, neither
the Kyrgystan nor the Azerbaijan elections met OSCE standards. For example,
see "Parliamentary Elections in Azerbaijan" (2000).

16. Interview with Tanya Lokshina, of the Moscow Helsinki Group, on
April 3, 2000, in Moscow.

17. Interview with Bjorn Halvarsson, of the UNDP in Belarus, on December
5, 2000, in Minsk.

18. Interview with Bogdankevich. Despite the fact that Russia has the potential to change the situation, the Russian government currently rejects requests to do so. For example, the Russian embassy in Belarus has refused to
accept documents from the Belarusian opposition requesting its assistance.

19. Interview with Bogdankevich.

20. Other respondents answered as follows: "against both" 16.2 percent,

"would not vote" 5.7 percent, "no answer" 29.5 percent (*Belarus Today* November 28–December 4, 2000).

21. Interviews with Wiktorin and Kraemer.

22. For example, the Lukashenko regime has denied registration to many opposition candidates on highly questionable grounds, detained over 100 individuals advocating a boycott of the elections, and burglarized the headquarters of an opposition party (Smith 2000).

23. Among the opposition, only members of the Social Democratic Party participated in the parliamentary election in October 2000, though as individuals.

24. Interview with Miraslau Kobasa, Fond imia L'va Sapegi (Lev Sapieha Foundation), on December 8, 2000, in Minsk.

25. Interview with Heinz Timmermann of the Federal Institute for Russian, East European and International Studies (BIost), on November 28, 2000, in Cologne. The EU member-states urged the opposition to take part in the parliamentary election.

26. Interview with Youri Parfiyanovich and Vladmir Serpikov of the European Cooperation Department, Ministry of Foreign Affairs of Republic of Belarus, on December 6, 2000, in Minsk.

27. Ibid.

28. Interview with Dmitry Ponomarev, European Cooperation Department of the Ministry of Foreign Affairs of Belarus, on December 6, 2000, in Minsk.

29. Interview with Aleksandr Baichorov, deputy head of mission of the Republic of Belarus to the EU and NATO, on February 20, 2001, in Brussels.

30. Ibid.

BIBLIOGRAPHY

Andreeva, G. N., ed. 1999. Konstituchi Stran SNG I baltii (*Constitution of CIS and Baltic states*) Moskba: Yunosti.

Annan, Kofi. 1998. "The Causes of Conflict and the Promotion of Durable Peace and Sustainable Development in Africa." Secretary-General's Report to the United Nations Security Council (16 April). UN document A/52/871-S/1998/318.

Baker, Pauline, and Angelie E. Weller. 1999. *Conflict Prevention and Recovery Program*. San Francisco: The Fund for Peace.

"Belarusian Opposition Mulls Single Presidential Candidate." 2001. *Russia Today* (19 January). <http://www.russiatoday.com/news> (21 January).

"Belarusian President Happy with Visit, but Moscow May Be Thinking About Replacing Him." 2001. *Russia Today* (19 January). <http://www.russiatoday.com/news> (21 January).

Bennett, G., and K. A. Hamilton, eds. 1997. *The Conference on Security and*

Cooperation in Europe, 1972–75. Documents on British Policy Overseas. Series III, Volume II. London: The Stationery Office.

Conference for Security and Co-operation in Europe. 1990. "Document of the Copenhagen Meeting of the Conference on the Human Dimension of the CSCE." Copenhagen, 29 June.

Dekret prezidenta Respubliki Belarusi (Decree of the president of the Republic of Belarus). 2000. No. 18. September 11. <http://194.226.121.66/webnpa/> (3 January 2001).

"Die OSZE lobt ihre neue Rolle als Konfliktverhueterin" (The OSCE praises its new role of conflict prevention). 1997. *Frankfurter Allgemeine Zeitung* (19 December).

European Union. 2000a. "The EU's Relations with Belarus: An Overview." <http:/europa.eu.int/comm./external_relations/belarus/intro/index.htm> (1 December).

——. 2000b. "Belarus Indicative Programme TACIS 2000–2003." <http:/europa.eu.int/comm./external_relations/belarus/intro/index1.htm> (1 December).

"Finding Austria Upholds 'European Values,' EU Panel Calls for End to Sanctions." 2000. *International Herald Tribune* (9–10 September).

Freedom House 2000a. "Nations in Transit 1999–2000." <http://www.freedomhouse.org /research.nitransit/2000/pdf_docs.htm> (28 December).

——. 2000b. "Freedom House Country Ratings: Annual Survey of Freedom Country Scores 1972–1973 to 1990–2000." <http://www.freedomhouse.org/ratings/index.htm> (22 January 2001).

Hattori, Michitaka. 2000. "Belarus Russia rengō no kyozō to jitsuzō" (Fiction and reality of the Belarus-Russia confederation). In Roshia Tōō Bōekikai, ed. *Country Risk Information Survey.* Tokyo: Roshia Tōō Bōekikai.

Heenan, Patrick, and Monique Lamontagne, eds. 1999. *The CIS Handbook.* London and Chicago: Fitzroy Dearborn Publishers.

International Helsinki Federation for Human Rights. 2000. *Human Rights in the OSCE Region: Report 2000 (Events of 1999).* Vienna: International Helsinki Federation for Human Rights.

Maiola, Dzhobanna. 2000. "Media Monitoring by OSCE in Belarus." Report presented at the International Seminar Belarus: SMI and Elections, held in Minsk on December 8.

Marples, David R. 1999. *Belarus: A Denationalized Nation.* Amsterdam: Harwood Academic Publishers.

Middelkoop, Eimert von. 1995. "The OSCE: An Inadequate Community of Values." *Helsinki Monitor* 5(4): 30–34.

Miyawaki Noboru. 1999. "Anzen-hoshō to jinken no rinkeji" (The linkage between security and human rights). In *Kokusaiteki anzen-hoshō no shintenkai* (New developments in the international security system). Tokyo: Waseda Daigaku Shuppan-bu.

——. 2000. "OSCE, jinken to minshushugi" (The OSCE, human rights, and democracy). In Iwasaki Masahiro et al., eds. *Minshushugi no kokusai hikaku (Democratic viability in politics)*. Tokyo: Ichigei-sha.

Organization for Security and Co-operation in Europe. 1997. "Memorandum of Understanding Between the Government of Belarus and the Organization for Security and Co-operation in Europe on the OSCE Advisory and Monitoring Group in Belarus." Copenhagen (18 December).

——. 2000a. "Press Release" No.100/00.

——. 2000b. "Democratization Programme Begins in Belarus." *OSCE Newsletter* 7(5).

——. 2000c. "Statement of Preliminary Findings and Conclusions," October 16. <http://www.osce.org/odihr/election/bela00-2-prelim.htm> (11 December)

Organization for Security and Co-operation in Europe, Advisory and Monitoring Group in Belarus. 2000a. "Assessment of the Electoral Code." Minsk, March 1.

——. 2000b. "Introducing the Notion of Consultations, Negotiations and Compromise in Belarus: A Chronology of the Dialogue between Government and Opposition in Belarus from May 1999 to March 2000." Minsk: OSCE/AMG.

"OSCE Slams Charges by Belarus KGB, Defends Mandate Rights." 2000. *Russia Today* (December 16). <http://www.russiatoday.com/news> (17 December).

"Parliamentary Elections in Azerbaijan Fall Below International Standards." 2000. *OSCE Newsletter* 7(12). <http://www.osce.org/publications/newsletter/2000-12/nl122000_13.htm> (20 December).

Russett, Bruce M. 1993. *Grasping the Democratic Peace: Principles for a Post–Cold War World*. Princeton, N.J.: Princeton University Press.

Satterthwaite, Margaret. 1998. "Human Rights Monitoring, Elections Monitoring, and Electoral Assistance as Preventive Measures." *International Law and Politics*, no. 30: 709–791.

Smith, Christopher H. 2000. "Flawed Elections in Belarus." Extensions of remarks made by Representative Smith of New Jersey in the House of Representatives, October 12. 106th Cong., 2nd sess. *Congressional Record*, October 13, vol. 146, no. 128.

Timmermann, Heinz. 1999. "The OSCE Representation in Belarus." In Institute for Peace Research and Security Policy at the University Hamburg, ed. *OSCE Yearbook 1998*. Baden-Baden: Nomos Verlagsgesellschaft.

"Ural Latypov, Deputy Prime Minister, Minister on Foreign Affairs Answers Questions of Belarus Magazine." 2000. <http://www.president.gov.by/eng/faq/faq6.htm> (24 June).

United States Department of State. 1994. *Belarus Human Rights Practices, 1993*. <gopher://dosfan.lib.uic.edu/00ftp:DOSFan> (31 January).

Wieck, Hans-Georg. 2000. "The Advisory and Monitoring Group of the OSCE in Belarus." *Helsinki Monitor* 11(1): 48–60.

Yablinsky, Grigory. 2000. "Russia's Phony Capitalism." In Gregory M. Scott, Randall J. Jones, Jr., and Louis S. Furmanski, eds. *21 Debated Issues in World Politics*. Upper Saddle River, N.J: Prentice-Hall, Inc.

CHAPTER FOUR

Forced Displacement and the Prevention of Further Conflicts: Lessons from the African Great Lakes Region and Kosovo

Akizuki Hiroko

THE end of the cold war paved the way within a number of African, Asian, and even European countries for the actualization of latent internal conflicts that had been contained by East-West tensions. As a consequence, millions of people have been forced to flee their homes to escape from fighting and violence. In many cases, these war-induced mass population movements have in turn contributed to the spread of conflicts, as is vividly demonstrated in the case of Central Africa. This interconnection between forced human displacement and conflict implies that not only can the prevention of conflicts contribute to the preclusion of forced displacement, but the prevention of forced displacement can serve to limit further conflicts as well.[1]

This chapter analyzes how forced displacement causes further conflict by examining two cases. The first is that of the Great Lakes region of Africa, focusing on the situation in the Democratic Republic of the Congo (hereafter, referred to as Congo). In this case, the mass influx of refugees from neighboring countries threatened the internal security of the asylum country, Congo, and induced a prolonged internal war there. The second case is that of the Kosovo crisis, focusing on the situation in the former Yugoslav Republic of Macedonia. Here, the possible destabilization of the asylum country, Macedonia, was avoided through the implementation of an extraordinary "transfer program" of refugees. The differing international responses to these crises is perhaps symptomatic of larger issues, when one considers that what is provided to refugees in Africa, including food and other basic survival items, is far less than in other parts of the world (United Nations High Commissioner for Refugees [UNHCR] 2000c), whereas the emergency relief effort in Kosovo has been one of the largest per capita international relief operations ever (UNHCR 2000g).

Through a comparison of these two cases, we will identify the critical issues to be addressed by the international community in considering appropriate methods of intervening for the prevention of further conflicts within asylum countries. The chapter will emphasize the importance of stabilizing the asylum country, propose that refugee problems be considered as a political issue—i.e., an issue of peace and security—rather than a humanitarian issue, and suggest possible institutional reform of the United Nations system.

Because this chapter focuses on the asylum country and ways to prevent further conflicts caused by the very existence of refugees, it will not focus on the root causes of the refugee-producing situations within the countries of origin.[2] Addressing such root causes as human rights violations, social injustice, absolute poverty, and so on, falls within the realm of the more time-consuming search for permanent solutions to conflicts and refugee problems, rather than that of conflict prevention. Preventing the extension and/or escalation of conflicts that are caused by the existence of refugees in an asylum country or in other neighboring countries is more urgently important from the preventive perspective.[3] Accordingly, this chapter also refers mainly to refugees who have left the country of their nationality and does not touch on the issue of internally displaced persons and returnees in the country of origin. This does not imply that those groups are less important factors in conflict prevention, or that their situation is less tragic from a humanitarian point of view, but simply that they are beyond the scope of this inquiry.

THE CASE OF THE GREAT LAKES REGION

Background

In 1994, the genocide of approximately 800,000 Tutsis and moderate Hutus was committed by Hutu extremists in Rwanda. The Rwandan Patriotic Front (RPF) forces in Rwanda, created by Tutsi exiles in Uganda, quickly gained control of the capital city of Kigali, which caused over 2 million refugees (mostly Hutus) to flee to what was then known as Zaire (now Congo), Tanzania, and Burundi (UNHCR 2001, 245). Roughly 160,000 of the refugees returned voluntarily to Rwanda. The repatriation, however, came to a halt when members of the former Rwandan government, the former Rwandan Armed Forces (Forces Armées Rwandaises, FAR), and militia forces took control of the refugee population in Zaire. Hutu refugees who wished to return to Rwanda were intimidated or eliminated by armed elements in the camps (UNHCR 1997a, 20). Armed elements among the Rwandan refugees also threatened local Zairian Tutsi communities and increased cross-border attacks against Rwanda.

During this period, tension and violence were rising in eastern Zaire. In the North Kivu province, a three-way war was being waged between Hutu, Tutsi, and local peoples such as the Hunde, which resulted in the killing and mass expulsion of many Tutsis. The Banyamulenge, an ethnic Tutsi group with roots in the province of South Kivu, were also harassed and displaced by local Zairians, who were backed by the Kinshasa government.

In October 1996, some of the rebel groups existing in Zaire and the neighboring countries that supported them joined forces with the Alliance of Democratic Forces for the Liberation of Congo-Zaire (Alliance des Forces Démocratiques pour la Libération du Congo, AFDL), under the leadership of Laurent-Désiré Kabila. Most of the rebels were Banyamulenge. The decision in April 1996 by then President Mobutu Sese Seko to deprive the Banyamulenge—who opposed the president—of their nationality and to expel them from the country triggered the fighting in Zaire.

The AFDL, with important backing from Rwanda, Uganda, Burundi, Angola, and other neighboring countries, fought against a coalition of President Mobutu's Zairian Armed Forces (Forces Armées Zairoise, FAZ), ex-FAR members, Rwandan Interhamwe militias, and mercenaries. Hence, the internal conflict within Zaire involved armed elements among the Rwandan refugees and from neighboring countries, making the conflict extremely complex. In addition to the overthrow of President Mobutu, the Rwandan Patriotic Army (RPA) and the AFDL sought to disperse the refugee camps in eastern Zaire, and to bring home hundreds of thousands of civilian refugees as well as members of the ex-FAR and Rwandan Interhamwe.

The Tutsi-dominated uprising that began in eastern Zaire resulted in the ousting of President Mobutu in March 1997. Kabila and his AFDL took power and the Democratic Republic of the Congo was established in May of that year. The Tutsi-dominated authorities in Rwanda, with the active assistance of the authorities in Angola and Uganda, supported and even instigated the rebellion. Therefore, the removal of President Mobutu from power was a regional undertaking, masterminded by the Rwandan government and supported by the governments of Angola, Uganda, Zambia, and Zimbabwe (Centre for Documentation and Research/UNHCR 1998, 6).

In August 1998, a new armed movement, this time against President Kabila, was organized by the Congolese Rally for Democracy (Rassemblement Congolais pour la Démocratie, RCD), based in eastern Congo. The new conflict was the result of the particular situation in that area, the Kivu region—the ethnic composition of the population, the presence of several rebel forces grouped along ethnic lines, and the implications for the internal security of neighboring countries. In November 1998, a second rebel movement, the Movement for the Liberation of Congo (Mouvement pour la Libération du Congo, MLC) emerged in Equateur province. While these two armed groups had once joined forces with Kabila's AFDL in order to overthrow the Mobutu regime, the rebel forces (comprising Congolese soldiers and Congolese Banyamulenge), along with the governments of Rwanda, Uganda, and Burundi, accused President Kabila of having become a dictator and of increasing regional instability through his support for guerrilla groups that opposed the governments of his former allies. The ensuing civil war that erupted in Congo, which pitted the RCD rebels, assisted by Rwandan and Ugandan forces, against President Kabila's AFDL, supported by Zimbabwe, Namibia, Angola, Chad, and Sudan, has been categorized by one UN official as an internal conflict with the participation of foreign armed forces (United Nations [UN] 1999b).

In July 1999, a cease-fire agreement was signed in Lusaka, Zambia, by Angola, Congo, Namibia, Rwanda, Uganda, and Zimbabwe. The MLC and RCD also signed the agreement in August 1999. The conflict, however, rages on across Congo. Following the signing of the cease-fire by all parties, the United Nations Security Council passed a resolution in August 1999 to send up to 90 military observers, who began deploying in mid-September 1999 to the countries involved in the conflict (UN 1999d). The Security Council's resolution in February 2000 further approved the secretary-general's recommendation to increase the size of the UN Organization Mission in the Democratic Republic of the Congo (MONUC) to 500 military observers, supported by some 5,000 UN troops, with the provision that the forces not be deployed before all parties to the conflict had provided guarantees on cooperation (UN 2000a). This resolution authorized MONUC to take necessary action, acting under Chapter VII of the Charter of the United Nations.[4] Although there was initially some delay, as of March 2002, a total of 3,63 uniformed personnel, including 446 military observers, 3,173 troops, and 14 civilian police had been deployed to carry out the MONUC mandate, which includes monitoring the implementation of the cease-fire agreement, maintaining continuous liaison with the headquarters of all the military forces involved, and facilitating humanitarian assistance and human rights monitoring (UN 2002).

Militarization of Refugee Camps

The crucial issue of forced displacement, from the viewpoint of conflict prevention, is that the very existence of refugees has the potential to threaten and destabilize the security of the asylum country. The situation in Zaire was no exception. The volatile security situation in the North and South Kivu provinces, a region with ethnic complexities, seriously threatened the stability of Zaire.

The violence that gripped Rwanda was transported to the refugee camps in eastern Zaire by forced human displacement. Many of the Rwandan refugees themselves were deeply involved in the acts of genocide committed in Rwanda.[5] They were also continuing to participate in the internal war in Rwanda by engaging in cross-border attacks. The lives of refugees and humanitarian staff were endangered, and the delivery of relief and essential services was disrupted by these individuals. Their aim appeared to be to control the refugee population, block their voluntary return to Rwanda, and build resistance against the government in Kigali.

The United Nations High Commissioner for Refugees (UNHCR) conveyed its serious concerns on the security situation of the refugees to the Zairian authorities and to the United Nations secretary-general, and strongly urged the immediate removal of all armed elements from the camps (UNHCR 1994b). The secretary-general's special representative for Rwanda, Shaharyar Khan, similarly stressed that the separation of the ex-FAR, military elements, and militia was the only means to provide security for the refugees and to allow them to choose freely to return to Rwanda (UN 1994a, para. 21). Based on that recommendation, the secretary-general proposed to the Security Council that a United Nations peacekeeping force be deployed to the refugee camps in Zaire, conditional upon gaining the consent of the government of Zaire (UN 1994c, para. 18). The task of such a force would be to provide security for international relief workers, protection for the storage and delivery of humanitarian assistance, and safe passage to the Rwandan border for those refugees who wished to return. The secretary-general further warned that the situation was potentially destabilizing for the host country and for the sub-region as a whole (UN 1995a, para. 2).

The Security Council responded by requesting that the secretary-general consult with potential troop contributors to assess their willingness to participate in a possible peacekeeping operation that would create secure areas within large camp sites and provide safe conditions for the refugees in those areas (UN 1994d). However, only one of the 60 potential troop-contributing countries consulted formally offered a unit. The option of deploying a peacekeeping force to tackle the security issues in the refugee camps in Zaire therefore turned out to be impracticable. Given this situation, UNHCR concluded an agreement with the government of Zaire on January 27,

1995, regarding the deployment of 1,500 Zairian security personnel to work in close liaison with a technical and monitoring team of 50 international security advisors of UNHCR (UNHCR 1995b).

UNHCR warned in October 1994 that the lack of progress in repatriating Rwandan refugees would exacerbate tensions in eastern Zaire, and this indeed became a reality. Extremist elements among the Rwandans in Zaire, many of whom had been defeated in the internal war in their country, committed armed incursions into Rwanda. This resulted in Rwandan support for rebel groups in Zaire, which led to massacres in the North Kivu province in 1994 and in October 1996. Cross-border raids and shelling, and the alleged infiltration of armed groups from Rwanda regionalized the internal conflict in eastern Zaire, straining interstate relations. Armed elements moved much deeper into Zaire and some even reached the Angolan border. From the end of August 1996, fighting also erupted between the Zairian Army and the armed Banyamulenge in South Kivu province. This eventually led to the establishment of a new country, Congo. This case, therefore, clearly shows that the very existence of refugees worsened the security situation of the asylum country, which then led to a prolonged internal war.

It is the primary responsibility of the asylum country to ensure the personal security of refugees and maintain the exclusively civilian and humanitarian character of refugee camps and settlements. While these principles are generally accepted, the political will and, more importantly, the capacity to implement them are often lacking. The international community must therefore urgently examine how it can assist the asylum country in taking the necessary, concrete actions to improve security in refugee camps as a means of preventing further conflicts.

This case also shows a clear linkage between a humanitarian issue and the issue of peace and security. The lack of progress in repatriating Rwandan refugees intensified tensions in eastern Zaire. The presence of former Rwandan government leaders, military personnel, and militia who had committed acts of genocide and were defeated in the internal war in Rwanda, and the fact that these individuals were able to halt the voluntary repatriation of Rwandan refugees, made the refugee camps more political than humanitarian in nature. While UNHCR tried to secure the refugee camps by establishing security forces for them, it is a humanitarian agency by nature and is not capable of assuming full responsibility for this type of effort. This highlights the need to find ways to back up humanitarian agencies in their efforts to provide security management in refugee camps.

Comprehensive Regional Approach to Conflict Prevention

Although the potential for internal conflict clearly existed within Zaire, it was the very presence of refugees that worsened and prolonged the war. The threatening of local Zairian Tutsi communities by military elements among the Rwandan Hutu refugees triggered the internal conflict in Zaire. Cross-border attacks against Rwanda by these same elements also induced the alleged military intervention by neighboring countries, which regionalized and prolonged the internal conflict within Zaire, straining interstate relations. Both the Kabila government and the rebel groups were supported by countries such as Zimbabwe, Namibia, Angola, Rwanda, and Uganda.

Given the scope and complexity of this conflict, clearly it can only be resolved in a regionally oriented and comprehensive manner, rather than through a country-centered approach. In this case, "regionally oriented" and "comprehensive" means that it requires the full commitment of Congo and its neighboring countries, but also of the international community, to address all aspects of the conflict. The essential contribution of the international community should include political backing for initiatives of national reconciliation and assistance to the asylum country, including security management of refugee camps.

In this connection, it should be reiterated that the recommendation of the secretary-general that a UN peacekeeping force be deployed to provide security was not carried out because of insufficient support from the international community. If the international community had intervened substantively and in a timely manner in the conflict in Congo, the fighting would not have been prolonged to the extent that it has been. It is precisely on this point that the situation in the African Great Lakes region differs decisively from the Kosovo case, where there was overwhelming intervention on the part of the international community. It may be argued that the international community was reluctant to intervene in the situation in the African Great Lakes region because major countries (and particularly the United States) did not perceive any national interests in this region, and that the impact of the Somalia debacle and the crisis in Rwanda had a restrictive effect on U.S. policy toward UN operations. However, the degree of human tragedy produced by these conflicts cannot be differentiated. One would hope, therefore, that support from the international community would be more balanced and would not be meted out with double standards.

In terms of a comprehensive approach to conflict prevention in the African Great Lakes region, there are a number of problems that must be considered. For example, the uncontrolled flow of small arms in this region has exacerbated the conflicts. The relative ease with which small arms are trafficked between countries means that the combatants are continuously supplied. This problem must be addressed in order to avoid further conflicts. A second critical issue is that people are indiscriminately struggling for natural resources without considering the consequences. In the African Great Lakes region, controlling natural resources such as oil, diamonds, and wood appears to be an even more pressing concern for governments and rebel groups than taking political power. Ways to prevent illegal trafficking in these natural resources, which contributes financially to those involved in conflicts, should be a serious consideration in the effort to prevent lasting conflicts. While these are just two examples of what a comprehensive approach might entail, sincere steps by the international community to address these problems would certainly pave the way for the prevention of further conflicts.

THE CASE OF THE KOSOVO CRISIS

Background

The Kosovo crisis covers the period from the wake of the North Atlantic Treaty Organization (NATO) airstrikes against the Federal Republic of Yugoslavia (FRY, also referred to as Serbia and Montenegro) on March 24, 1999, to the establishment of a framework for peace in mid-June 1999. The long-simmering conflict in Kosovo represents in many ways a classic secessionist struggle. The text of the 1974 Constitution of the Socialist Federal Republic of Yugoslavia defined the constituent parts of the Yugoslav Federation as comprising not only the six republics (Slovenia, Croatia, Bosnia and Herzegovina, Macedonia, Serbia, and Montenegro), but also Kosovo, which was one of two autonomous provinces (the other being Vojvodina) within the republic of Serbia. As an autonomous province, Kosovo enjoyed virtually the same rights as federal republics and could, to a large extent, make decisions independently on local affairs. In 1989, however, the 1974 Constitution was revised. Kosovo no longer enjoyed that autonomous status and came under the direct control of the central government of Yugoslavia. The majority of the population of Kosovo, which is predominantly ethnic Albanian, were progressively denied the right to govern their own affairs, to earn a living for themselves, to have access to the legal and judicial system, or to be able to educate their children in their own language and culture.

For over a century, Kosovo's ethnic Albanians have sought to form a separate political entity on the basis of the current territory of Kosovo in the form of either autonomy, independence, or union with Albania. In September 1991, the ethnic Albanian population organized an unofficial referendum. The turnout among voters was 85 percent, of whom 99.8 percent voted in favor of a sovereign and independent state of Kosovo (Centre for Documentation and Research/ UNHCR 1996, 4). When Kosovo's status was excluded from the agenda of the 1995 Dayton Peace Accords for the former Yugoslavia, the ethnic Albanians' struggle turned violent. They took up arms and organized themselves into the Kosovo Liberation Army (KLA). But the emergence of the KLA was used by the Yugoslav authorities to justify more violence.

In the years after Kosovo lost its status as an autonomous province, the Serbian authorities committed serious human rights violations against the ethnic Albanian population there, including arbitrary arrests and detention for political activity, violent treatment while in detention by the Serbian police force, restrictions on freedom of association and on freedom of speech and expression, employment discrimination, and discrimination in education and in the medical profession (Centre for Documentation and Research/UNHCR

1996, 5). This deteriorating situation in Kosovo increasingly alarmed the international community, which was concerned about both the human rights situation and the potential spread of instability to neighboring countries in the region. Following the Yugoslav government's indiscriminate military operations against the KLA during the summer of 1998, NATO moved down a path toward military confrontation with Belgrade.

On February 23, 1999, the so-called Contact Group (the United States, United Kingdom, France, Germany, Italy, and Russia) announced a political framework for settlement of the Kosovo crisis, known as the Rambouillet peace plan. The plan defined the terms of an agreement on substantial autonomy for Kosovo, while respecting the national sovereignty and territorial integrity of the FRY, and it provided for a cease-fire, a peace settlement, and the deployment of an international peacekeeping force within Kosovo to uphold that settlement. While the Kosovo Albanians signed the accord, the FRY did not.

NATO began its airstrikes on March 24, 1999, in order to end Serb violence in Kosovo and to make the Yugoslav authorities accept the terms of the Rambouillet plan. Although it was expected that these objectives would be achieved quickly, the NATO strikes were accompanied by escalating violence on the ground and a large refugee outflow that included organized expulsions. Within nine weeks of the beginning of the airstrikes, nearly 860,000 ethnic Albanians fled or were expelled from Kosovo, ending up in Albania (444,600), Macedonia (344,500), and Montenegro (69,900) (Evaluation and Policy Analysis Unit/UNHCR 2000, 6).

In June 1999, the FRY accepted the principles of a political solution to the Kosovo crisis, including an immediate end to the violence and a rapid withdrawal of its military, police, and paramilitary forces. The Security Council of the United Nations therefore adopted a resolution on June 10, 1999, and decided to deploy an international civil and security presence in Kosovo under UN auspices.

Almost immediately after the deployment of this security presence (in the form of a NATO-led international force known as KFOR), refugees began flooding back to Kosovo spontaneously. As of June 2000, more than 850,000 Kosovo Albanians had returned to Kosovo.

It is estimated that some 14,000 refugees from Kosovo, including Albanians, Serbs, and Roma, remain in neighboring countries, while around 220,000 primarily Serbs, Roma, and other minorities from Kosovo are internally displaced in Serbia and Montenegro (UNHCR 2000g).

Humanitarian Intervention and the Mass Exodus of Refugees

In the case of the Kosovo crisis, it is crucial to understand that it was NATO's airstrikes that triggered the humanitarian disaster and thus the mass exodus of refugees.[6] NATO asserted that the airstrikes were intended to end Serb violence perpetrated against the Kosovo Albanians, in other words that it was a humanitarian intervention.[7] It was widely believed that the airstrikes "would be a solution rather than a problem." They were "publicly premised on the notion that the Yugoslav authorities would quickly back down (as they had done in Bosnia and Herzegovina after NATO air power was used)" (Evaluation and Policy Analysis Unit/UNHCR 2000, 18). In fact, however, NATO's airstrikes triggered more intensive Serb military activities and exacerbated the human disaster. While it has been suggested that the Serb offensive against the civilians was planned and that the exodus was therefore a fully organized expulsion, it is clear that, whether directly or indirectly, the airstrikes triggered more intensive Serb military activities on the ground and heightened the violence.

No aid agency anticipated the speed and magnitude of the refugee movement; more than 800,000 people fled Kosovo within an 11-week period, of whom half a million left in the first couple of weeks (Evaluation and Policy Analysis Unit/UNHCR 2000, 17). There seem to have been good reasons for the failure to predict such an exodus: the Yugoslav border was heavily mined, and the army had established a "security zone" along Kosovo's borders with Macedonia and Albania to prevent KLA infiltration. It was expected that the borders would be closed if the conflict worsened. Therefore, an escalation of conflict was expected to entail more massacres and internally displaced persons bottled up in the hills and on the mountainsides. It was also understood that, for the ethnic Albanians in Kosovo who claim self-determination and independence, the evacuation from their homeland would mean a defeat in the secessional war and would assist the Serb policy of ethnic cleansing.[8]

Despite these formidable obstacles, the airstrikes and the resulting intensification of the Serb military activities convinced massive numbers of people to leave. NATO's airstrikes thus proved to be counterproductive, offering a striking example of the fact that, irregardless of humanitarian goals, the use of force—which is by nature not humanitarian—rarely promotes a humanitarian solution.

Burden Sharing by the International Community

It is self-evident that mass inflows of refugees entail significant costs and risks for the first asylum country, as was demonstrated in Macedonia. There was, in this case, a legitimate fear that the small, newly established and ethnically fragile state might disintegrate in the conflict. Macedonia received around 330,000 refugees, of whom about 100,000 came by car and train in a massive wave during the first week of the crisis alone.[9] When well over a hundred thousand Kosovo Albanians had appeared by early April, the Macedonian government began to panic. Widespread local protests against the NATO airstrikes aggravated the situation.

The government initially insisted that it would accept refugees into Macedonia only on a transit basis, and that their status and eventual physical location would have to be clarified prior to entrance. In the meantime, they were trapped at the Blace field on the Macedonian side of the border, receiving minimal assistance. Several thousand were then allowed into camps that were literally built overnight by NATO forces. Another several thousand were evacuated by the government, with U.S. assistance, in a controversial relocation operation to Turkey, Greece, and Albania.

For the Macedonian government, the presence of refugees raised fundamental issues of national security. The sudden refugee inflow, which equaled over 10 percent of the total population of Macedonia, had a serious effect on the delicate ethnic balance between the majority Slav population and the ethnic Albanian minority (Evaluation and Policy Analysis Unit/UNHCR 2000, 10).[10] Macedonia had only gained its independence in 1991, and the refugee inflow occurred only a few months after a new coalition government had been formed in Skopje, which included the most nationalist elements of both the ethnic Slav and the ethnic Albanian populations. As a result, it increased the possibility that Macedonia would be destabilized and pulled into the conflict.[11] Moreover, it could not be assured that the refugees would be in the country on a temporary basis because the duration of asylum is often unpredictable once refugees have been admitted. For these reasons, the Macedonian government was reluctant to accept a major refugee inflow.

As noted above, there was a near disaster at the outset of the crisis, when thousands of refugees were stuck at the Blace crossing point on the border between Kosovo and Macedonia without shelter and with only minimal assistance. Except for a few medical evacuations, tens of thousands of refugees remained trapped in the muddy field. The immediate cause of the crisis was the refusal of Macedonia to admit this massive refugee flow, asserting that the international community had some responsibility for creating the refugee problem and thus a commensurate obligation to solve it. This resulted in a "burden-sharing program," in which the onward passage of refugees to third countries was offered as an incentive for Macedonia to admit refugees, based on the underlying premise that protection is a common responsibility of states. A number of governments took the initiative in these programs—particularly the United States, which was moved by strategic-political interests as well as humanitarian concerns.[12] UNHCR worked with these states to develop and coordinate the plans.

The burden-sharing program developed in this case had two elements, a humanitarian evacuation program (HEP) and a humanitarian transfers program (HTP). HEP evacuated refugees from Macedonia to countries outside the Balkans in an operation of unprecedented speed and scale. By alleviating the burden on the vulnerable asylum country, the operation enabled other refugees to enter Macedonia, thereby enhancing overall protection. HTP, on the other hand, transferred refugees from Macedonia to neighboring Albania. This program was made feasible by Albania's acceptance of refugees, UNHCR's leadership, and the encouragement of key donors.

Blace was unblocked with the help of a package that combined

NATO-built camps with the burden-sharing program and promises of economic assistance. The first buses brought refugees from the "holding area" at Blace to two newly established transit camps on April 4, 1999. Initially, a total of 5,000 refugees were transferred (Evaluation and Policy Analysis Unit/UNHCR 2000, 37). By the end of the emergency in mid-June, when the framework for peace was established, almost 92,000 refugees had been evacuated by HEP to 29 host countries. The scale and speed of such an evacuation were unprecedented. Overall, HEP contributed positively to the protection of the refugees by alleviating the burden on a reluctant Macedonia, which faced the risk of destabilization (Evaluation and Policy Analysis Unit/UNHCR 2000, 95). The case of Kosovo, therefore, might be considered a success in terms of the prevention of further conflict induced by the existence of refugees.

On the other hand, this case raises the issue of the compatibility of the extraordinary burden-sharing program with conventional refugee law. Effective protection of refugees depends, in the first instance, on the assumption by the asylum country of its international responsibilities. Macedonia's unwillingness to grant unconditional asylum raised basic issues of first asylum in relation to the obligations and rights of states. The potential tragedy at the Blace border crossing dramatically juxtaposed the rights of refugees against the interests of states.

At first, UNHCR vigorously defended the position that unconditional first asylum remains the core of international protection, as indeed it might be expected to under the norms enunciated by its Executive Committee (EXCOM). However, it later changed its policy and accepted the need to transfer refugees from Macedonia to third countries. This shift was a reaction to pressure from the United States and the United Kingdom, which were more attuned to the destabilization concerns of Macedonia and worried that the refugee presence would lead the government to withdraw its support for NATO's military campaign, and from Canada and the Nordic countries, which were pushing for evacuation on general humanitarian grounds (Evaluation and Policy Analysis Unit/UNHCR 2000, x). In fact, UNHCR was faced with the unusual situation of having donors competing to take in refugees, and was criticized for not adjusting quickly enough to their demands. The change in UNHCR's policy was formalized in a policy statement by the high commissioner on April 4, which presented "burden sharing" as a possible solution to the first asylum problem in Macedonia.[13]

In this connection, the following 1981 stipulation of EXCOM's Conclusion 22, on the protection of asylum seekers in situations of large-scale influx, should be borne in mind:

> A mass influx may place unduly heavy burdens on certain countries; a satisfactory solution of a problem, international in scope and nature, cannot be achieved without international co-operation. States shall, within the framework of international solidarity and burden-sharing, take all necessary measures to assist, at their request, States which have admitted asylum seekers in large-scale influx situations. (Evaluation and Policy Analysis Unit/UNHCR 2000, 91)

The Kosovo case suggests that burden sharing is essential for small and vulnerable asylum countries that face mass inflows of refugees. Although unconditional first asylum remains an international responsibility, the use of burden-sharing programs as a means of eliminating potential threats to destabilize asylum countries should be reexamined in the context of preventing further conflicts.

The Role of Military Force in Humanitarian Assistance

One of the issues highlighted during the Kosovo crisis in relation to conflict prevention was the role of military force (in this case, the role of NATO), particularly in humanitarian operations.[14] In the operational field, joint air control by NATO and the United Nations was not controversial. In 1992, the United Nations had established a ban on military flights in the airspace over Bosnia and Herzegovina. This ban was not applied to the UN Protection Force (UNPROFOR) flights or to other flights in support of UN operations, and thus humanitarian flights were coordinated with military use of airspace. However, military activities directly related to humanitarian operations, such as transport, logistics, and infrastructure, raised a question.[15] The distinction between military activities and humanitarian assistance was blurred in the case of dual-use facilities (i.e., the use of military planes or airports for the transport of basic materials such as foods and blankets). It was finally erased when NATO forces built refugee camps and provided security and other camp services in Macedonia and Albania.[16]

The relationship between UNHCR and NATO in the Kosovo crisis was different from that in Croatia or in Bosnia and Herzegovina since the NATO forces with which UNHCR worked in the latter cases were deployed in a UN "peace enforcement" capacity. In Kosovo, however, NATO was a direct party to the military conflict and its airstrikes were conducted without a UN Security Council resolution explicitly authorizing the use of force. UNHCR's decision to work with NATO during the airstrikes, therefore, represented a deviation from the traditional norm that humanitarian agencies be impartial and neutral.

There was also a risk that NATO involvement in camp services might expose the camps as targets in the military conflict and facilitate their use by guerrillas for recruitment. Moreover, there was concern on the part of UNHCR that close relations with NATO could jeopardize its relations with Belgrade and undermine its operations in Yugoslavia, including its ability to work in Kosovo. Generally, a close association with military forces could weaken UNHCR's claim to impartiality and hence access to those in need of assistance in future refugee situations (Evaluation and Policy Analysis Unit/UNHCR 2000, 109).

It was therefore difficult for UNHCR as a humanitarian agency to decide to enter into a close operational relationship with NATO during the crisis. As a subsidiary organ of the UN General Assembly, UNHCR was affected by the discrepancy between NATO's actions and the strict rules in the UN Charter governing the use of force. However, the practical challenge of coping with a mass influx of refugees for which UNHCR was unprepared led the high commissioner to accept NATO's support. In the Kosovo case, it seemed to be the only option and was widely accepted by the international community as being necessary in order to save lives (Evaluation and Policy Analysis Unit/UNHCR 2000, 13).

Thus, the Kosovo case set a precedent, validating operational cooperation between UNHCR and a military force that is a belligerent party—not only in the case that the military force is engaged in a UN enforcement action under the Charter and authorized by the United Nations, but also in the case that there is no alternative available for avoiding substantial suffering and loss of life.

Conclusion: Lessons Learned

Stabilization of the Asylum Country

The cases examined in this chapter clearly demonstrate the potential for mass influxes of refugees, and/or the very presence of refugees, to threaten and destabilize the security of an asylum country, which in turn increases the probability of igniting further conflicts. It is therefore critically important to protect and stabilize asylum countries.

The security of the asylum countries we have examined was threatened in two ways. First, in the case of Congo, there were those who took advantage of their refugee status to engage in cross-border attacks against their country of origin or to participate in the internal war within the asylum country. Second, in the Kosovo case, the existence of refugees itself destabilized the volatile ethnic balance in the asylum country of Macedonia.

The former case demonstrates that the separation of armed elements from other refugees is crucial in order to maintain the civilian character of refugee camps. This is the responsibility first and foremost of the asylum country, and not of humanitarian organizations such as UNHCR. If, however, the asylum country cannot take on this responsibility due to its own vulnerable social situation, then the international community must share the burden by providing the necessary assistance to prevent further conflicts. One of the reasons for the failure to prevent the successive prolonged internal conflicts in Zaire and Congo was that the international community failed to respond correctly to the situation. As noted previously, when the UN secretary-general proposed to the Security Council that a UN peacekeeping force be deployed to the refugee camps in Zaire, only one state responded positively to the proposal. The failure on the part of the international community to react to a volatile situation hinders the effective prevention of further violence and conflict and can often make the situation worse. Unless timely and effective assistance is provided to an asylum country, the threat in one country can easily become a threat to the region, as the African Great Lakes case clearly shows, and it can potentially become a threat to international peace and security.

On the other hand, Macedonia's fears of destabilization due to the impact of the refugee population on the ethnic balance, which were shared by many in the international community, generated a burden-sharing program through which a significant number of refugees were transferred to third countries. This case points to the need for further examination of the principle of first asylum in situations of mass influx. The issue of whether first asylum should be considered as an absolute and unconditional legal obligation, consistent with the Convention Relating to the Status of Refugees, should be examined within the context of conflict prevention. Needless to say, however, this does not imply preventing people from seeking safety or protection outside of their country of origin.

In relation to the stabilization of the asylum country, it should also be kept in mind that the causes of internal conflict are not necessarily internal in nature. As the Congo case shows, the internal war was exacerbated by the involvement of neighboring countries. Under such circumstances, conflict is not effectively prevented by a country-oriented approach; rather, a regionally oriented mechanism, utilizing regional or subregional organizations where available, is needed for the prevention and permanent solution of such conflicts.

Moreover, it must be remembered that there is rarely a single reason for a conflict; most conflicts have multiple causes and complex origins. Effective prevention, therefore, requires a comprehensive approach—"comprehensive" in the sense that it covers the whole life of a conflict, from prevention to post-conflict rehabilitation, that it encompasses human rights and long-term development issues as well as security issues, and that it reflects the obligation and responsibility of the international community as a whole, as well as of the subject country or region.

The Refugee Problem as a Political Issue

The fact that the presence of refugees in an asylum country can cause further conflicts means that the refugee problem is not only a humanitarian issue but a political issue as well. Refugees have formerly been considered a byproduct of conflicts. Increasingly, however, they are also viewed as potential participants in, or instigators of, conflict. Armed elements among refugee populations have taken advantage of their refugee status—through which their basic needs for accommodation and food are provided by the government of the asylum country or humanitarian organizations, and their legal status and rights are internationally protected—to participate in fighting or to recruit guerrillas from among those in refugee camps. This kind of politicization of the refugee problem should not be overlooked.

Certainly, the root causes of refugee-producing situations are political. Moreover, while the availability of protection abroad is affected by the possibility of solutions, those solutions cannot be sustained if the conflict that provoked the refugee influx continues and if the security of the returnees is not assured. Therefore, decisive measures by the political organs of the United Nations and the political will of member-states are crucial for the prevention of refugee-induced eruptions of further conflicts.

In this connection, the established principle of unconditional first asylum has to be reexamined. From the standpoint of international refugee law, unconditional first asylum remains the core of international protection. However, as the Kosovo case shows, the unpredictable scale and speed of mass refugee influx can threaten the security of the asylum country and place an excessive burden on it. If refugee management fails, an internal conflict can erupt and devastate the asylum country, as it did in Congo, resulting in violations by parties to the conflict (especially the government) of the human rights and fundamental freedoms of not only the refugee population but also the local people. Therefore, from the perspective of conflict prevention, a new methodology for both stabilization of the asylum country and protection of refugees, such as the transfer program in Macedonia, should be seriously considered on the underlying premise that protection is a common responsibility of states.

Institutional Reform within the UN System

We must also raise here the delicate issue of the balance between the humanitarian and the political—that is, how humanitarian organizations like UNHCR can maintain their impartiality, neutrality, and independence. In the second paragraph of the Statute of the UN High Commissioner for Refugees, it is stipulated that "The work of the High Commissioner shall be of an entirely non-political character; it shall be humanitarian . . . " (UN 1950). This is the formal legal basis of UNHCR's activities, and it is therefore generally understood that UNHCR should refrain from any political consideration of refugee issues.

However, it is very difficult to distinguish a particular type of work as being strictly humanitarian or strictly political.[17] Moreover, cooperation with the political arms of the United Nations is essential for UNHCR in order to resolve or prevent refugee crises. The security conditions on the ground leave UNHCR with little choice (UNHCR 1992). In fact, in the Kosovo case, the imperative of saving lives required UNHCR's close cooperation with NATO, which was simultaneously a party to the war, thereby blurring the distinction between humanitarian and political, as previously noted. Institutional cooperation of this kind can compromise the UNHCR's status as a nonpolitical humanitarian organization, undermine its acceptability as a partner and coordinator to other humanitarian actors, and circumscribe its access to refugees in certain emergency situations.

It is important, however, to note that humanitarian principles such as "neutrality," "impartiality," and "independence" cannot be the founding principles of UNHCR since it is a subsidiary organ, and therefore an integral part, of the United Nations, which is fundamentally a political organization. UNHCR cannot be "neutral" when it is authorized by the United Nations to conduct a particular operation. This is more evident when the United Nations is conducting enforcement actions under Article 42 of the Charter, where the United Nations is a direct party to military operations conducted as a sanction against the violator of the provisions of the Charter. High Commissioner Ogata Sadako also clearly mentioned in 1995 that, once the use of force against one or the other party in a conflict is authorized, humanitarian action associated with such military force is no longer viewed as neutral, and UNHCR therefore opens itself up to retaliation by one or more parties, as occurred in Somalia and in Bosnia (UNHCR 1995c).[18]

It might therefore be suggested that the United Nations should not get directly involved in "humanitarian" relief efforts in conflict situations and should confine its role to "political" functions associated with the resolution of disputes, the prevention of conflicts, and coercive intervention to end them.[19] One could also argue that, if humanitarian assistance must always be neutral and impartial, then UNHCR should be separated from the inherently political United Nations. It is this author's opinion, however, that such a conclusion is fundamentally unrealistic and unwarranted. Turning again to the provision of the Statute of UNHCR, it should be remembered that the wording reads, "*The work* of the High Commissioner shall be of an entirely non-political character . . ." (emphasis added). This means that UNHCR's operational activities—i.e., the provision of legal protection and material assistance for refugees—should be non-political, neutral, and impartial, but it does not mean that UNHCR, as an integral part of the United Nations, must always be neutral, nor that UNHCR should refrain from considering political aspects of refugee-producing situations.

Needless to say, it is not the primary responsibility of UNHCR, being a humanitarian organization, to disarm the armed elements in a refugee camp or to defuse refugee-producing situations. These tasks must be carried out by the political organs of the United Nations. If refugee-induced conflicts are to be effectively prevented, the political organs of the United Nations, such as the Security Council, must seriously tackle the political elements of refugee problems, including the root causes of conflicts, security issues in the vulnerable regions, and national reconciliation in post-conflict situations.

In order both to maintain the humanitarian nature of UNHCR and to tackle the political elements of refugee problems, it is urgently required that the gap between the humanitarian work of UNHCR and the political consideration of refugee issues by the Security Council be more effectively bridged. The high commissioner regularly attends the Security Council meetings and reports on current refugee situations around the world. It is not enough, however, just to report on the situations and to leave the deliberations to the Security Council.

It is widely acknowledged that complex humanitarian emergencies or large-scale humanitarian crises occur usually in complicated political and military environments. Therefore, the United Nations has been trying to establish an effective mechanism of coordination and cooperation within the UN system and to strengthen its capacity for launching coherent and coordinated humanitarian action. Secretary-General Annan's reform process, for example, has included such initiatives as the establishment of the Office of the Emergency Relief Coordinator (ERC) and the Inter-Agency Standing Committee, as well as the introduction of the Consolidated Appeal Process and the Central Emergency Revolving Fund.

This institutional reform process, however, refers only to operational organs of the UN system and not to political organs. This places critical constraints on the functions of these new initiatives. The ERC, for example, should be responsible for seeking durable solutions and appealing for rehabilitation and reconstruction, but its core function is described simply as the "advocacy of humanitarian issues with political organs, notably the Security Council" (UN 1997, para. 186). Humanitarian actions require a wide range of efforts not only to provide emergency relief assistance but also to seek long-term solutions, and thus closer consultation and coordination between the political, military, and humanitarian components are essential at every phase and level of the operation in complex humanitarian emergencies.

For these reasons, a formal institutional framework among UNHCR, the Security Council, and the member-states should be established in order to consider refugee problems from the perspective of conflict prevention and to raise the political will of member-states. The strong political will and commitment of the member-states regarding their common responsibility for refugee protection and conflict prevention is crucial. Otherwise, the impact of the underlying causes of refugee flows in one country will spread throughout the region, with the potential to pose a serious threat to international peace and security.

The African Great Lakes region and Kosovo cases indicate that the capacity of asylum countries is not limitless. It is not enough just to provide humanitarian assistance for refugees. Without the appropriate assistance and a definite political commitment from the international community, further conflicts caused by overwhelming refugee burdens cannot be effectively prevented.

NOTES

1. There is no concrete or formal definition of "forced displacement." It generally means that people are obliged to flee from their own country or community as a result of persecution, armed conflict, or violence (United Nations High Commissioner for Refugees [UNHCR] 1997a, 1). It includes refugees, asylum seekers, returnees, internally displaced persons, and others. These are usually called "persons of concern to the United Nations High Commissioner for Refugees (UNHCR)," who fall under the mandate of the UNHCR. As of January 1, 2000, there were 11.7 million refugees, 2.5 million returnees, 1.2 million asylum seekers, and 6.9 million internally displaced persons and others—a total of 22.3 million individuals who have been forcibly displaced worldwide (UNHCR 2000h).

2. According to Article 1 of the Convention Relating to the Status of Refugees (and of the Protocol Relating to the Status of Refugees), a "refugee" is defined as any person who, "owing to well-founded fear of being persecuted for reasons of race, religion, nationality, membership of a particular social group or political opinion, is outside the country of his nationality and is unable, or owing to such fear, is unwilling to avail himself of the protection of that country."

3. In this connection, it should be clearly kept in mind that any effort in terms of preventive action is not aimed at preventing refugee outflows, or in other words, preventing people from seeking safety or protection abroad. International human rights and refugee protection principles—most notably the right to freedom of movement within the border of each state, the right to leave and return to one's own country, and the right to seek and enjoy asylum in another country—must always be observed (Crisp 1998, 2).

4. Chapter VII of the Charter of the United Nations refers to "action with respect to threats to the peace, breaches of the peace, and acts of aggression." In this context, since the Iraq-Kuwait conflict of 1990, necessary action is taken to include the use of force.

5. According to a 1994 UN report, the population of the camps in Zaire fell into the following categories: (a) political leaders, estimated at approximately 50 heads of family; (b) uniformed military elements of the former Rwandan Armed Forces (ex-FAR), estimated at 16,000 and accompanied by their families, bringing the total to approximately 80,000; (c) militia, whose number is unknown since they have mingled with the refugees; and (d) ordinary refugees, estimated at about 1 million persons (UN 1994a, para. 19).

6. In 1998, UNHCR estimated that there were over 200,000 victims of forced displacement, most of whom were internally displaced persons remaining in Kosovo (UNHCR 1998b). After NATO's airstrikes, however, more than 800,000 people fled to neighboring countries as refugees.

7. It should be noted that the NATO member-states, which are also members of the United Nations, used force for humanitarian intervention in

Kosovo without a solid legal basis under the Charter of the United Nations. First, the use of force is generally prohibited under Article 2, paragraph 4. Second, although the use of force for the purpose of self-defense is permitted under Article 51, no armed attack had occurred against a NATO member, thus precluding that justification for NATO actions. Third, although the use of force in the application of enforcement measures under Chapter VII of the Charter is permitted, the United Nations was not taking such enforcement measures, nor had the Security Council authorized the member-states to use military force by its resolution.

In certain kinds of humanitarian situations, the participation of military personnel in the exercise of international humanitarian intervention would be required and is thus justifiable. It is, however, strongly recommended that objective criteria and procedures be established, based on which a judgement can be made as to whether or not humanitarian intervention in a specific case would be permitted.

8. In this connection, the concept of "the right to remain"—underlining the need to protect the basic right of the individual not to be forced into exile—must be seriously considered as one of the fundamental human rights and freedoms. It is inherent in Article 9 of the Universal Declaration of Human Rights that no one shall be subjected to arbitrary exile (UNHCR 1993).

9. UNHCR estimated an inflow of 20,000 refugees only (Evaluation and Policy Analysis Unit/UNHCR 2000, 25).

10. As of 1994, the ethnic breakdown of the population in Macedonia was as follows: Macedonians 66 percent, Albanians 23 percent, Turks 4 percent, Serbs 2 percent, and other 5 percent ("Ethnic Makeup" 2002).

11. NATO had given de facto security guarantees to Skopje when launching the airstrikes against FRY. Even so, the Macedonian government occasionally threatened publicly to demand the withdrawal of NATO troops from its territory. The threat was a critical factor in negotiations over refugee admissions (Evaluation and Policy Analysis Unit/UNHCR 2000, 10).

12. U.S. prominence on the asylum issue reflected its important political role in the region and in the Kosovo conflict. U.S. acceptance of the government's premise that the refugees represented a national security threat was largely to secure Macedonian cooperation during the NATO military campaign.

13. The statement came the day after the Macedonian government had agreed to unblock Blace (Evaluation and Policy analysis Unit/UNHCR 2000, 39).

14. The quickest way of constructing refugee camps was to use the NATO forces already deployed in Macedonia. On April 1, the government of Macedonia formally agreed to request that NATO build the camps. The Macedonian decision was relayed to UNHCR, but the high commissioner initially objected to the proposal. While she preferred that civilians construct the camps, there was no civilian alternative to NATO forces that could have established camps

overnight, as the situation required (Evaluation and Policy Analysis Unit/ UNHCR 2000, 113). In the end, the imperative of saving lives convinced UNHCR to accept NATO's assistance.

15. In Kosovo, NATO member troops managed the airports, unloaded humanitarian supplies, transported them to refugee camps or distribution centers in Albania and Macedonia, and expanded the airport and improved roads in Albania that had dual military and humanitarian use.

16. For example, a special NATO force to Albania (AFOR) has a strictly humanitarian mission.

17. Moreover, UNHCR's involvement in certain situations has been vested with the purely "political" organ of the United Nations, the Security Council. For example, the Security Council urged and supported the secretary-general's decisions to send UNHCR to places like the African Great Lakes region in order to defuse those situations (UN 1996; 1995b).

18. UNHCR's humanitarian activities in Bosnia and Herzegovina during 1992–1995 were closely linked to the military mandates of the United Nations Protection Force (UNPROFOR), which included the protection of humanitarian activities. Since UNPROFOR was authorized to use air power in and around the safe areas—in which Muslim civilians were under siege from the Bosnian Serb forces—to protect them, the risk of retaliation toward civilian humanitarian staff increased, and 12 UNHCR and other humanitarian staff were killed. In Somalia, similarly, the United Nations Force (the United Nations Operation in Somalia, or UNOSOM II) was authorized to and did in fact use force for humanitarian purposes. The UN force thus became a party to the conflict in Somalia and was attacked by a Somali group, the United Somali Congress/Somali National Alliance, resulting in nearly 100 UNOSOM II personnel killed or wounded in 1993 (UNHCR 1994c).

19. See James Ingram's 1993 *National Interest* article, "The Politics of Human Suffering," as referred to in Sugino (1998, 46).

BIBLIOGRAPHY

Annan, Kofi A. 1999. *The Question of Intervention*. New York: United Nations Department of Public Information (DPI/2080).

Centre for Documentation and Research/UNHCR. 1996. "Background Paper on Refugees and Asylum Seekers from Kosovo." Geneva: UNHCR.

———. 1998. "Background Paper on Refugees and Asylum Seekers from the Democratic Republic of the Congo." Geneva: UNHCR.

———. 2000. "Background Paper on Refugees and Asylum Seekers from the Democratic Republic of the Congo." Geneva: UNHCR.

Copson, Raymond W. 2000. "Congo (formerly Zaire)." Washington, D.C.: Congressional Research Service.

Crisp, Jeff. 1998. "UNHCR's Role in the Prevention of Refugee-Producing Situations." UNHCR internal document.

Cutts, Mark. 1999. "The Humanitarian Operation in Bosnia, 1992–95: Dilemmas of Negotiating Humanitarian Access." UNHCR Working Paper No. 8. Geneva: UNHCR.

Embassy of the Federal Republic of Yugoslavia in Tokyo. 1999. "Basic Facts on Kosovo and Metohija Province." <http://www.twics.com/~embtokyo/homepage/k31.htm.> (8 February 2001).

"The Ethnic Makeup of the Republic of Macedonia." 2002. <http://faq.macedonic.org/information/ethnic.makeup.html> (13 March).

Evaluation and Policy Analysis Unit/UNHCR. 2000. *The Kosovo Refugee Crisis: An Independent Evaluation of UNHCR's Emergency Preparedness and Response.* <http://www.unhcr.ch/evaluate/kosovo/toc.htm> (14 July).

Gilbert, Geoff. 1998. "Rights, Legitimate Expectations, Needs and Responsibilities: UNHCR and the New World Order." *International Journal of Refugee Law* 10(3): 349–388.

Honma Hiroshi. 1990. *Nanmin mondai towa nanika* (What is a refugee problem?). Tokyo: Iwanami Shoten.

Hoshino Toshiya. 2000. "Beikoku no Kosobo funsō kainyū: sono dōgisei, gōhōsei, seitōsei" (U.S. intervention in the Kosovo conflict: Its morality, legality, legitimacy). *Kokusai Mondai,* no. 479: 17–29.

Independent Commission on International Humanitarian Issues. 1990. *Nanmin-ka no rikigaku.* Trans. by Ogata Sadako. (Originally published as *Refugees: The Dynamics of Displacement: A Report for the Independent Commission on International Humanitarian Issues.*) Tokyo: Daisan Bunmei-sha.

Jentleson, Bruce W., ed. 2000. *Opportunities Missed, Opportunities Seized: Preventive Diplomacy in the Post–Cold War World.* Lanham, Md.: Rowman & Littlefield Publishers.

Kikkawa Gen, ed. 2000. *Yobō gaikō (Preventive diplomacy).* Tokyo: Sanrei Shobo.

Kourula, Pirrko. 1999. "Governance and Co-ordination in Conflict and Post-Conflict Situation: Challenge or Maze?" In Guy S. Goodwin-Gilland and Stefan Talmon, eds. *The Reality of International Law: Essays in Honour of Ian Brownlie.* Oxford, U.K.: Oxford University Press.

Koizumi Kōichi. 1994. "Nanmin to kaihatsu: Rinen no suii to ryōsha no tsunagari" (Refugees and development). *Kokusai Kaihatsu Kenkyū,* no. 3: 155–161.

———. 1998. *"Nanmin" towa nanika* (Who are refugees?). Tokyo: San'ichi Shobo.

Lund, Michael S. 1996. *Preventing Violent Conflicts: A Strategy for Preventive Diplomacy.* Washington, D.C.: United States Institute of Peace.

———. 2000. "Preventive Diplomacy for Macedonia, 1992–1999: From Containment to Nation Building." In Bruce W. Jentleson, ed. *Opportunities Missed, Opportunities Seized.* New York: Rowman & Littlefield Publishers.

Makonnen, Yilma. 2000. "Natural-Resource-Based Violent Intra-State Conflict: Towards the Development of Social Responsibility Guidelines for Non-state

Actors in Conflict Prevention and Peace-building." New York: United Nations.

Minear, Larry. 1999. "Partnerships in the Protection of Refugees and Other People at Risk: Emerging Issues and Work in Progress." UNHCR Working Paper No. 13. Geneva: United Nations High Commisioner for Refugees.

Ninomiya Masato. 1995. "Nanmin mondai kaiketsu e no kokuren no apurochi ni kansuru ichi kōsatsu" (A study on the United Nations' approach to finding a permanent solution to the problem of refugees). *Gaikō Jihō*, no. 2: 26–41.

———. 1997. "Nanmin mondai no kōkyūteki kaiketsu to jihatsuteki kikan" (A durable solution to the situation of refugees through voluntary repatriation). *Kitakyūshū Daigaku Kaigaku 50 Shūnen Kinen Ronbunshū* (March): 47–68.

North Atlantic Treaty Organization. 1999. "NATO's Humanitarian Mission to Albania." <http://www.afsouth.nato.int/operations/harbour> (9 February 2001).

Ogata Sadako. 1995. "Jindō bunya ni okeru kokuren katsudō" (Humanitarian action by the United Nations). *Kokusai Mondai*, no. 428: 50–62.

Roberts, Adam. 1998. "More Refugees, Less Asylum: A Regime in Transformation." *Journal of Refugee Studies* 11(4): 375–395.

Rutinwa, Bonaventure. 1999. "The End of Asylum? The Changing Nature of Refugee Policies in Africa." UNHCR Working Paper No. 5. Geneva: UNHCR.

Stremlau, John. 1998. *People in Peril: Human Rights, Humanitarian Action, and Preventing Deadly Conflict*. Washington, D.C.: Carnegie Commission on Preventing Deadly Conflict.

Sugino Kyoichi. 1998. "The 'Non-Political and Humanitarian' Clause in UNHCR's Statute." *Refugee Survey Quarterly* 17(1): 33–59.

Suhrke, Astri. 1998. "Burden-sharing during Refugee Emergencies: The Logic of Collective Versus National Action." *Journal of Refugee Studies* 11(4): 396–415.

United Nations. 1950. "Statute of the Office of the United Nations High Commissioner for Refugees." Document A/RES/428(V) ANNEX (14 December).

———. 1994a. "Progress Report of the Secretary-General on the United Nations Assistance Mission for Rwanda." Document S/1994/1133 (6 October).

———. 1994b. "Statement by the President of the Security Council." Document S/PRST/1994/59 (14 October).

———. 1994c. "Report of the Secretary-General on Security in the Rwandan Refugee Camps." Document S/1994/1308 (18 November).

———. 1994d. "Statement by the President of the Security Council." Document S/PRST/1994/75 (30 November).

———. 1995a. "Second Report of the Secretary-General on Security in the Rwandan Refugee Camps." Document S/1995/65 (25 January).

———. 1995b. "Statement by the President of the Security Council." Document S/PRST/1995/41 (23 August).

———. 1996. "Statement by the President of the Security Council." Document S/PRST/1996/1 (1 January).

———. 1997. "Secretary-General's Report, Renewing the United Nations: A Programme for Reform." Document A/51/950 (14 July).

———. 1999a. "Assistance to Refugees, Returnees and Displaced Persons in Africa." Document A/RES/53/126 (12 February).

———. 1999b. "Report on the Situation of Human Rights in the Democratic Republic of the Congo submitted by the Special Rapporteur, Mr. Roberto Garreton." Document E/CN.4/1999/31 (8 February).

———. 1999c. "Security Council Resolution 1234 (1999) on the Situation Concerning the Democratic Republic of Congo." Document S/RES/1234(1999). (9 April).

———. 1999d. "Security Council Resolution 1258 (1999) on the Situation in the Democratic Republic of Congo." Document S/RES/1258(1999). (6 August).

———. 1999e. "Security Council Resolution 1265 (1999) on the Protection of Civilians in Armed Conflict." Document S/RES/1265(1999). (17 September).

———. 1999f. "Security Council Resolution 1273 (1999) on the Situation Concerning the Democratic Republic of Congo." Document S/RES/1273(1999). (5 November)

———. 1999g. "Security Council Resolution 1279 (1999) on the Situation Concerning the Democratic Republic of Congo." Document S/RES/1279(1999). (30 November).

———. 2000a. "Security Council Resolution 1291 (2000) on the Situation Concerning the Democratic Republic of Congo." document S/RES/1291(2000). (24 February).

———. 2000b. "Security Council Resolution 1296 (2000) on the Protection of Civilians in Armed Conflict." Document S/RES/1296(2000). (19 April).

———. 2000c. "Security Council Resolution 1304 (2000) on the Situation Concerning the Democratic Republic of Congo." Document S/RES/1304(2000). (16 June).

———. 2002. "Democratic Republic of the Congo: MONUC Facts and Figures." <http://www.un.org/depts/dpko/monc/moncF.htm> (19 April 2002).

United Nations High Commissioner for Refugees. 1992. "Refugees: Challenge of the 1990s—Statement by Mrs. Sadako Ogata, United Nations High Commissioner for Refugees, at the New School for Social Research." New York, 11 November 1992. <http://www.unhcr.ch/cgi-bin/texis/vtx/print?tbl=ADMIN&id=3ae68fae18> (13 March 2002).

———. 1993. "Statement by Mrs. Sadako Ogata, United Nations High Commissioner for Refugees to the Forty-ninth Session of the Commission on Human Rights." Geneva, 3 March 1993. <http://www.unhcr.ch/cgi-bin/texis/vtx/print?tbl=ADMIN&id=3ae68fad1c> (13 March 2002).

———. 1994a. *Sekai nanmin hakusho: nanmin hogo e no charenji* (The state of the world refugees: the challenge of protection). Translated by the UNHCR office, Japan. Tokyo: Yomiuri shimbunsha.

——. 1994b. "Statement by Mrs. Sadako Ogata, United Nations High Commissioner for Refugees to the 45th Session of the Executive Committee of the High Commissioner's Programme." Geneva, 3 October. <http://www.unhcr.ch/cgi-bin/texis/vtx/print?tbl=ADMIN&id=3ae68fc818> (13 March 2002).

——. 1994c. "Humanitarianism in the Midst of Armed Conflict." Presentation by Mrs. Sadako Ogata, United Nations High Commissioner for Refugees, at Brookings Institution, Washington D.C., 12 May. < http://www.unhcr.ch/cgi-bin/texis/vtx/print?tbl=ADMIN&id=3ae68faa10> (14 March 2002).

——. 1995a. "Statement by Mrs. Sadako Ogata, United Nations High Commissioner for Refugees to the Informal Meeting of the Executive Committee." Geneva, 17 January. <http://www.unhcr.ch/cgi-bin/texis/vtx/print?tbl=ADMIN&id=3ae68fa94> (13 March 2002).

——. 1995b. "Statement by Mrs. Sadako Ogata, United Nations High Commissioner for Refugees to the Regional Conference on Assistance to Refugees, Returnees and Displaced Persons in the Great Lakes Region." Burundi, 15 February. <http://www.unhcr.ch/cgi-bin/texis/vtx/print?tbl=ADMIN&id=3ae68faa20> (13 March 2002).

——. 1995c. "International Security and Refugee Problems after the Cold War: 'Assuring the Security of People: the Humanitarian Challenge of the 21st Century' Old Palme Memorial Lecture by Mrs. Sadako Ogata, United Nations High Commissioner for Refugees at the Stockholm International Peace Research Institute." Stockholm, 14 June. <http://www.unhcr.ch/refworld/unhcr/hcspeech/14ju1995.htm> (19 July 2000).

——. 1996a. Sekai nanmin hakusho: kaiketsu o motomete. Trans. by UNHCR office in Japan. Tokyo: Yomiuri shimbunsha. Originally published as The State of the World Refugees 1995: In Search of Solutions (Oxford: Oxford University Press Inc, 1995).

——. 1996b. "Remarks by Mrs. Sadako Ogata, United Nations High Commissioner for Refugees to the UN Security Council." New York, 28 June. <http://www.unhcr.ch/cgi-bin/texis/vtx/print?tbl=ADMIN&id=3ae68fae10> (13 March 2002).

——. 1996c. "Remarks by Mrs. Sadako Ogata, United Nations High Commissioner for Refugees to the UN Security Council." New York, 25 October. <http://www.unhcr.ch/refworld/unhcr/hcspeech/25oc1996.htm> (27 July 2000).

——. 1997a. Sekai Nanmin Hakusho: Jindō kōdō no kadai (The state of the world's refugees: A humanitarian agenda). Translated by the UNHCR Office, Japan. Tokyo: Yomiuri shimbunsha.

——. 1997b. "Crisis in the Great Lakes." Refugees, no. 110 (winter).

——. 1997c. "Remarks by Mrs. Sadako Ogata, United Nations High Commissioner for Refugees to Conference of the Carnegie Commission on the prevention of Deadly Conflict and UNHCR, on a Humanitarian Response and the Prevention of Deadly Conflict." Geneva, 17 February. <http://www.unhcr.ch/refworld/unhcr/hcspeech/17fe1997.html> (11 July 2000).

———. 1997d. "Remarks by Mrs. Sadako Ogata, United Nations High Commissioner for Refugees to the UN Security Council." New York, 28 April. <http://www.unhcr.ch/cgi-bin/texis/vtx/print?tbl=ADMIN&id=3ae68fbb1c> (13 March 2002).

———. 1998a. "Statement by Sadako Ogata, United Nations High Commissioner for Refugees and Salim Ahmed Salim, Secretary-General, Organization for African Unity." Kampala, 9 May. <http://www.unhcr.ch/cgi-bin/texis/vtx/print?tbl=ADMIN&id=3ae68fcc30> (13 March 2002).

———. 1998b. "Opening Statement by United Nations High Commissioner for Refugees at the Forty-ninth Session of the Executive Committee of the High Commissioner's Programme." Geneva, 5 October. <http://www.unhcr.ch/refworld/unhcr/hcspeech/05oc1998.htm> (10 August 2000).

———. 1998c. "Statement by Mrs. Sadako Ogata, United Nations High Commissioner for Refugees, to the Euro-Atlantic Partnership Council." Brussels, 18 November. <http://www.unhcr.ch/refworld/unhcr/hcspeech/981118.htm> (7 August 2000).

———. 1999a. "Kosovo—One Last Chance." *Refugees,* no. 116.

———. 1999b. "The Democratic Republic of Congo." <http://www.unhcr.ch/world/afri/zaire.htm> (14 July 2000).

———. 2000a. *1999 Global Report: Achievements and Impact.* <http://www.unhcr.chfdrs/gr99/toc.htm> (14 July)

———. 2000b. *2000 Global Appeal—Strategies and Programmes.* <http://www.unhcr.ch/fdrs/ga2000/toc.htm> (14 July)

———. 2000c. "Briefing by Mrs. Sadako Ogata, United Nations High Commissioner for Refugees, to the Security Council of the United Nations on the Situation of Refugees in Africa" New York, 13 January. <http://www.unhcr.ch/refworld/unhcr/hcspeech/000113.html> (2 February 2000).

———. 2000d. "Statement by the United Nations High Commissioner for Refugees, Mrs. Sadako Ogata, on the Occasion of Africa Refugee Day." Adjumani, Uganda, 20 June. <http://www.unhcr.ch/refworld/unhcr/hcspeech/000620.html> (14 July).

———. 2000e. "Keynote Speech by Mrs. Sadako Ogata, United Nations High Commissioner for Refugees, at the International Symposium on Human Security (Bridging the G8 Kyushu-Okinawa Summit and the UN Millennium Summit)—Enabling People to Live in Security." Tokyo, 28 July. <http://www.unhcr.ch/cgi-bin/texis/vtx/home/opendoc.htm?tbl=ADMIN&id=3ae68fcac> (13 March 2002).

———. 2000f. "Country Update: Africa Fact Sheet, May 2000." <http:www.unhcr.ch/news/cupdates/0005afri.htm> (14 July).

———. 2000g. "Southeast Europe Update: 15 June 2000." <http:www.unhcr.ch/world/seo/ud000615.htm> (14 July).

——. 2000h. "Refugees by Numbers 2000." <http:www.unhcr.ch/un&ref/numbers/numb2000.pdf> (5 February 2001).

——. 2001. *The State of the World's Refugees 2000: Fifty Years of Humanitarian Action.* London: Oxford University Press.

Working Group on International Refugee Policy. 1998. "Report of the International Conference on the Protection Mandate of UNHCR." *Journal of Refugee Studies* 12(2): 203–220.

CHAPTER FIVE

Preventive Diplomacy and the Reform of the United Nations

Shōji Mariko

FOLLOWING the cold war, new types of conflicts have increased in the world, requiring us to redefine the boundaries between internal and external conflicts (Rupesinghe 1992, 1). The most common kinds of conflict today are internal, or intrastate, conflicts. An "internal" conflict, however, does not always remain within a single state; many have in fact spread to surrounding states, thus making the intrastate conflict an international concern. The conflicts in Kosovo, Somalia, and Rwanda exemplify this problem. To date, however, the United Nations (UN) has been reactive rather than proactive on the matter of intrastate conflicts, and more attention must be focused on how to address this new challenge to international security.

As the frequency of intrastate conflicts has increased, the types of nonstate actors involved have also increased. Conflicting parties in almost all intrastate conflicts tend to include nonstate actors such as ethnic groups, religious groups, and other kinds of communal groups. Nongovernmental organizations (NGOs) have also begun to play a more significant role as preventers of conflicts.[1] Despite these new developments, however, the framework of the United Nations remains fundamentally based on state sovereignty, thus hampering its ability to interact with this wide range of actors.

There is in fact a structural obstacle to the United Nations per-forming peacekeeping activities in intrastate conflicts. Article 2, clause 7 of the UN Charter, the principle of domestic jurisdiction, dictates that the United Nations cannot readily intervene in states' internal affairs. The United Nations is swayed by the interests of member-states. As James Sutterlin explains, "If conflicts continue to be pre-dominantly internal in nature, the United Nations cannot meet its mandate to preserve peace without dealing with them—without seek-ing in every appropriate way to prevent or mitigate social tensions that derive from such factors as ethnic or religious division or human rights violations, before they escalate into armed violence" (1995, 12). Given that most conflicts today involve nonstate actors, the United Nations must find a way to involve nonstate actors in the process of its preventive diplomacy.

For the purposes of this chapter, we will begin by considering the meaning of various technical terms related to preventive diplomacy. The meanings of these terms seem to differ slightly depending on the place and organization. It is important for these terms to have com-mon meanings and definitions, however, in order to avoid confusion and to allow the United Nations to apply measures on preventive diplomacy effectively. We will then examine the current mechanisms within the United Nations for conducting preventive diplomacy and the current and potential role of regional organizations in this effort. In doing so, we will seek to present effective ways in which to involve nonstate actors—both NGOs and nonstate conflicting parties—in the United Nations' efforts toward preventive diplomacy as a means to overcome the obstacles posed by article 2, clause 7 of the UN Charter.[2]

CONCEPT AND FRAMEWORK OF PREVENTIVE DIPLOMACY

The Definition of Preventive Diplomacy

There are many definitions of preventive diplomacy. Michael Lund has defined preventive diplomacy as "action taken in vulnerable places and times to avoid the threat or use of armed force and related forms of coercion by states or groups to settle the political disputes that can arise from the destabilizing effects of economic, social, political, and international change" (1997, 37). A 1995 report of the Joint Inspection Unit of the United Nations (JIU Report) stressed, "The notion of preventive (pre-conflict) peace-building/'preventive development' must be clearly and fully integrated/incorporated into the substantive as well as operational programmes of the United Nations system as a complement to preventive diplomacy" (Hernandez and Kuyama 1995).

While there is a need for preventive diplomacy in the context of these broader meanings of the term (as I will return to later), if the definition is too broad, it can hamper the efforts of the United Nations to take concrete measures. Secretary-General Kofi Annan responded to the JIU Report as follows: "Their emphasis on 'preventive development' may have caused them to give undue prominence to only one of the various types of preventive action which the United Nations system can undertake and to move the security and political dimensions of conflict prevention into the background" (United Nations General Assembly 1997, par. 55). Before we examine concrete measures of preventive diplomacy, however, let us first consider the various explanations of preventive diplomacy offered by some of the UN secretary-generals over the years.

Historically speaking, preventive diplomacy was originally proposed by Dag Hammarskjöld, the second secretary-general, who viewed preventive diplomacy as a means to fill the power vacuum between the cold war powers of the Western and Soviet blocs. Hammarskjöld stated, "Experience indicates that the preventive diplomacy, to which the efforts of the United Nations must thus to a large extent be directed, is of special significance in cases where the original conflict may be said either to be the result of, or to imply risks for, the creation of a power vacuum between the main blocs. Preventive action in such cases must in the first place aim at filling the vacuum so that it will not provoke action from any of the major parties, the initiative for which might be taken for preventive purposes but might in turn lead to counter-action from the other side" (1960, 1–8). In this sense, he also imagined that the notion of preventive diplomacy could be used to explain the activities of the UN Peacekeeping Operations (PKOs).

Javier Pérez de Cuéllar, the fifth secretary-general, also stressed the preventative role of the United Nations. According to Pérez de Cuéllar,

"The prevention of armed conflicts is a mandate envisaged in the provisions of the Charter relating both to the Security Council and to the responsibilities of the Secretary-General. Article 34 speaks of any situation which might lead to international friction or give rise to a dispute and Article 99 of any matter which in the Secretary-General's opinion may threaten the maintenance of international peace and security" (1991, 228). During his tenure, he strengthened the early-warning capacity of the United Nations—one of the many methods of preventive diplomacy—by setting up the Office for Research and the Collection of Information (ORCI) in the UN Secretariat to engage in fact-finding and the investigation of disputes.

Boutros Boutros-Ghali, the sixth secretary-general, defined preventive diplomacy in his report, *An Agenda for Peace,* as follows: "Preventive diplomacy is action to prevent disputes from arising between parties, to prevent existing disputes from escalating into conflicts and to limit the spread of the latter when they occur" (1992, 11). In comparison to his predecessors, Boutros-Ghali thought of preventive diplomacy as a very broad concept, including peaceful means and the good offices of the secretary-general, as defined in the UN Charter, as well as certain kinds of peacekeeping operations. He believed that preventive diplomacy should incorporate confidence-building measures, fact-finding, early warning, preventive deployment and, in some situations, the establishment of demilitarized zones.

Annan, the current secretary-general, accepted this broad meaning of preventive diplomacy as given by Boutros-Ghali. Annan, however, renamed these activities "preventive action." Annan explained, "Although diplomacy is a well-tried means of preventing conflict, the United Nations experience in recent years has shown that there are several other forms of action that can have a useful preventive effect: preventive deployment; preventive disarmament; preventive humanitarian action; and preventive peace-building, which can involve, with the consent of the Government or Governments concerned, a wide range of actions in the fields of good governance, human rights and economic and social development. For this reason, the secretary-general has decided to rename the activity called 'preventive diplomacy' as 'preventive action'" (UN Department of Political Affairs 1999). Subsequently, Annan redefined preventive diplomacy as one element of preventive action.[3]

Some differentiate between two aspects of preventive diplomacy: early prevention and late prevention. As Gareth Evans explains, "The difference is not between tardiness and timeliness, but rather between different time perspectives and different goals" (1993, 65). Early prevention falls within the range of peaceful dispute resolution methods mentioned in Article 33 of the UN Charter. The term "peacemaking," it should be noted, is used to represent these same methods when used after a dispute has become an armed conflict (Peck 1996, 132). Under a late-prevention approach, the United Nations would monitor situations around the globe, doing little or nothing even when it is fairly certain that a particular dispute was about to cross the threshold into armed conflict. This is synonymous with early warning. Evans points out that late-prevention action relies heavily on adequate intelligence information (1998, 64). According to these studies, "early warning" and "early action" are the main measures of preventive diplomacy.

In his 1999 annual report, Annan referred not only to preventing war, but also to preventing humanitarian and natural disasters (1999). The aim of this chapter, however, is to focus on finding effective means for preventing war or conflict. The notion of preventive diplomacy in this chapter will be actions that are, in Annan's words, "non-coercive, low-key and confidential" (1999, 11). We will therefore not include preventive deployment or preventive disarmament in our concept of "preventive diplomacy."[4] We will instead focus primarily on the narrow sense of preventive diplomacy—mainly on early warning and peaceful settlement activities (e.g., negotiation, enquiry, mediation, conciliation, and good offices)—and in the broader context, will also examine confidence-building measures and peacebuilding. The meanings of these four preventive diplomacy measures will be examined in greater detail below.

Confidence-Building Measures (CBMs)

Confidence-building measures (CBMs) are said to be useful instruments for preventing wars, bringing about arms control and disarmament agreements, and facilitating conflict resolution.[5] The term CBMs has two aspects, one broader and one more limited. Both should be pursued in the process of preventive diplomacy. Marie-France

Desjardins defines CBMs as actions falling into one or more of the following categories (1996, 5):
- · exchanging information and/or increasing communication between parties;
- · exchanging observers and/or conducting inspections;
- · establishing "rules of the road" for certain military operations;
- · applying restraints on the operation and readiness of military forces.

Igor Shcherbak offers the following definition of CBMs (1991, 8):

Confidence-building measures in the military sphere are unilateral, bilateral or multilateral actions carried out by states through the adoption of special political or military measures to ensure the predictability of the political intentions of States and their military activities with the help of adequate information and verification, so as to rule out the risk of misinterpretation of the military activity of States, and to prevent a surprise attack as well as an armed conflict or an incident occurring as a result of accidents or unauthorized actions. Steps to strengthen international security, stabilize the strategic and regional situation and create a favourable political climate for the conclusion and effective implementation of agreements on arms limitation and reduction are also covered by such measures.

Arun Elhance and Moonis Ahmar also prefer a broader definition: "Although the establishment of military CBMs may help prevent an inadvertent war between India and Pakistan in the short run, substantial progress also needs to be made in establishing nonmilitary CBMs in the environmental, economic, technical, cultural, and social arenas to moderate and perhaps eliminate the possibility of an undesired and unintended war in the long run" (1996, 132).

In contrast, Tsubouchi Jun asserts that the meaning of CBMs should be limited to the narrower sense, to be applied to the restricted area of repressing hostility. CBMs were not originally measures for friendship (1999, 78). He states that CBMs are measures "to contribute to the prevention of emerging armed conflict by notifying that there is no aggressive intention, in the short term, and in the long term, by reducing mutual distrust on military security" (1999, 93).

The term CBM in this chapter is mainly used in the limited sense, referring to the field of military security. These measures are basically related to the exchange of information on, notification of, and observation of major military activities, with the ultimate goal of reducing the risk of a surprise attack. On the other hand, CBMs in the broader sense should also be put into perspective. The philosophy of CBMs can be applied to any other arena, such as conflict prevention, or economic, social, and cultural relations. CBMs are useful for areas where deep-rooted suspicions and mistrust continue to frustrate the quest for peaceful coexistence among nations (Elhance and Ahmar 1996, 131). The aim of CBMs is stability, transparency, and predictability in various regions. The essential purpose is to "build confidence," as the name implies, and thus they seek to promote change in the psychological dimensions of security relationships between states (UN Office for Disarmament Affairs 1993, 4). However, when referring to CBMs, it is important to differentiate between these two aspects of the term.

Early Warning

The most important measure of preventive diplomacy is early warning.[6] For preventive diplomacy to succeed, it is critical to collect information in a timely manner and to analyze the information perceptively. As noted above, the UN ORCI was established in 1987 to engage in fact-finding, inquiries, and investigations of disputes, thus establishing an early-warning capacity in the UN Secretariat. But the United Nations does face some difficulties in performing this early-warning function.

Sutterlin points out two problems—the inadequacy of the early-warning system and the nonavailability of crucial information. Adding to the problem is the fact that the United Nations members do not relish being spied on by their own organization (1995, 13). Rupesinghe, however, denies these two elements of the problem, asserting that an early-warning system is different from a secret intelligence system. Early warning is an activity related to protecting the socially weak. Early-warning mechanisms concentrate on the following three functions: (1) collecting information, (2) analyzing and understanding the collected information, and (3) judging appropriate measures (1998, 91–92).

In 1992, the General Assembly of the United Nations confirmed the importance of early warning in a resolution that stated, "Recognizing the need to strengthen the capacity of the United Nations for early-warning, collection of information and analysis, [the General Assembly] invites the Secretary-General to strengthen the capacity of the Secretariat for the collection of information and analysis to serve better the early-warning needs of the Organization and, to that end, encourages the Secretary-General to ensure that staff members receive proper training in all aspects of preventive diplomacy, including the collection and analysis of information" (UN General Assembly 1992).

In this chapter, I will use the following definition of early warning: For the purpose of conflict prevention, early warning in the United Nations is intended to collect information on the symptoms of dispute as early as possible, to analyze that information accurately, and to choose appropriate measures for preventive diplomacy, before any dispute or conflict occurs.

Peaceful Settlement for Preventive Diplomacy

Originally, peaceful settlement of disputes was stipulated in Articles 33, 34, and 99 of the UN Charter. In those articles, concrete measures for peaceful settlement were enumerated, including negotiation, enquiry, fact-finding, investigation, mediation, good offices, conciliation, arbitration, judicial settlement, resort to regional agencies or arrangements, or other peaceful means.[7] Boutros-Ghali mentioned peacemaking in his report, *An Agenda for Peace.* He stated that we must look primarily to peacemaking "if we hope to enhance the capacity of the Organization for achieving peaceful settlement" (1992, 20–21). He considered peacemaking and peaceful settlement to be synonymous terms. At his instruction, the Office of Legal Affairs, Codification Division in the UN Secretariat, published in 1992 a *Handbook on the Peaceful Settlement of Disputes between States.* In this book, the United Nations presented a precise and professional analysis of peaceful settlement.

However, I believe that the above-mentioned concept of peaceful settlement described in the UN Charter, or the concept of peacemaking, is fundamentally different from peaceful settlement for preventive diplomacy. While the methods are the same, the traditional concept of peaceful settlement implies measures to be taken after the outbreak of a conflict, whereas peaceful settlement for preventive diplomacy should be applied before a conflict erupts, while a problem is still in the stage of a petty dispute or a potential conflict. Peck points out that the difference between early prevention and traditional approaches to peaceful settlement is the early use of such procedures as described in the UN Charter (1996, 44). Moreover, the *Handbook on the Peaceful Settlement of Disputes between States* applies the method of peaceful settlement only to disputes between states, and shows little intention of applying it to deal with disputes involving nonstate parties.

The traditional procedures described in the Charter were carried out principally by the Security Council. In contrast, peaceful settlement for preventive diplomacy can utilize many actors, including primarily the secretary-general, the staff of the UN Secretariat, or others in the United Nations. Evans points out that placing priority on early prevention (i.e., peaceful settlement for preventive diplomacy) has a number of significant advantages, including motivation, effectiveness, completeness, and cost (1993, 70).[8]

Peacebuilding

Boutros-Ghali describes post-conflict peacebuilding in his report, *An Agenda for Peace*, as "action to identify and support structures which will tend to strengthen and solidify peace in order to avoid relapse into conflict" (1992, 11). He enumerated preventive diplomacy, peacemaking, peacekeeping, and post-conflict peacebuilding alternatively. But not everyone agrees that peacebuilding is an alternative measure to preventive diplomacy. A. B. Fetherston points out that "as a means of preventing the recurrence of hostilities, reconstructing economic and social interactions and facilitating resolution, peacebuilding is crucial" (1994, 131). Sutterlin states that peacebuilding can be seen as the macro approach to the prevention of war (1995, 71). In the broader sense, then, peacebuilding should be included as a measure of preventive diplomacy.

Evans gives a more precise explanation for peacebuilding: "'Peace building' is used here to describe a set of strategies which aim to ensure that disputes, armed conflicts and other major crises do not arise in the first place—or if they do arise that they do not subsequently recur" (1993, 9). He describes two categories of these strategies: international regimes and "in-country peacebuilding." International regimes consist of international law, norms, agreements, and such arrangements as arms control and disarmament treaties, international dispute resolution mechanisms (e.g., the International Court of Justice), and multilateral dialogue and cooperation forums (e.g., the ASEAN Post-Ministerial Conference). In-country peacebuilding refers to national and international efforts aimed at economic development, institution building, and, more generally, to the creation or restoration within countries of the conditions necessary to make them stable and viable states (1993, 9). Certainly, the United Nations should get involved in conflict prevention not only in the post-conflict stage but also in the pre-conflict stage.[9]

Peacebuilding encompasses all efforts to prevent conflict and to strengthen international security such as economic and social development, democratization, observance of fundamental human rights, the elimination of all forms of discrimination, and so on. Originally, the United Nations was set up to achieve international cooperation in solving international problems of an economic, social, cultural, or humanitarian character, and in promoting and encouraging respect for human rights and for fundamental freedoms for all without distinction as to race, sex, language, or religion—all for the purpose of international peace and security (UN Charter art. 1, cl. 3). Many scholars consider peacebuilding in the broader dimension. Evans pays particular attention to democratic institutions and economic reconstruction. Sutterlin explains that the reason why peacebuilding is considered in the broader dimension is that "now, with the increased interdependence of peoples as well as of states, and the transparency that brings instantaneous global awareness of all serious threats to human well-being, the common understanding of international security has changed and continues to evolve" (1995, 73). He also mentions economic and social development, and democracy. Alger argues for "governance for the global commons" as the new tool for peacebuilding. He also refers to the fact that many historical tools for peacebuilding and all the approaches exploited in the United Nations contribute to peacebuilding comprehensively (1996, 340–345).

Peacebuilding in this chapter consists of activities performed not only in the post-conflict stage but also in the pre-conflict stage. Peacebuilding includes almost all activities conducted by the United Nations, including good governance, development, democratization, and the protection of human rights. The meaning of peacebuilding is very broad and ambiguous. The measures for peacebuilding are flexible enough to leave room for the root causes approach,[10] the approach for good governance,[11] carrot and stick (incentive) approach for conflict prevention,[12] long-term strategy,[13] and so on.[14]

Concluding Observations

As stated above, the main purpose of this chapter is to seek ways to involve nonstate actors in the system of UN preventive diplomacy. We have already discussed concrete measures of preventive diplomacy. Based on the above-mentioned definitions, we will mainly analyze early warning and peaceful settlement for preventive diplomacy. In the broader sense, CBMs and peacebuilding are also included among the measures of preventive diplomacy. CBMs in the narrower sense are sometimes categorized as "late prevention." But while the philosophical sense of CBMs and peacebuilding are too broad and too ambiguous, we cannot eliminate these ambiguities. Although these measures will be considered as a secondary issue in this chapter rather than the main issue, there are two reasons for leaving these ambiguous measures in the scope of this chapter. First, many scholars recognize CBMs in the broad sense and peacebuilding as an important method for preventive diplomacy. Second, there is a need to widen the viewpoint of research in the broad and comprehensive context, so that we can consider the involvement of nonstate actors. The narrower focus on early warning and peaceful settlement leaves fewer openings for the involvement of nonstate actors than do CBMs and peacebuilding measures.

The need for a comprehensive approach in the reform process of the United Nations has been repeatedly emphasized (Shōji 1993, 10–20). One JIU report suggested a "comprehensive conflict prevention strategy" that would comprise the following major elements: "(a) preventive diplomacy as a specific and well defined sub programme and (b) pre-conflict peace-building or activities addressing root causes of conflicts in a pre-conflict situation" (Hernandez and Kuyama 1995, para. 105). Similarly, Annan stated in his 1997 report on the reform of the United Nations, "It is now widely accepted that present day conflicts have many dimensions that must be addressed comprehensively and require more integrated and coordinated action" (1997, para.117). After much debate, the Department of Political Affairs (DPA) in the United Nations initiated reforms on an experimental basis in early March 1998. The plan identified a number of steps to be taken with a view to creating a comprehensive strategy for conflict prevention (Boothby and D'Angelo 2000, 5).

Accordingly, it is important that we analyze the issues from the viewpoint of a comprehensive approach for preventive diplomacy. What is a comprehensive approach? Is there any difference between a comprehensive approach and a "jack-of-all-trades" approach? Evans criticizes "comprehensive security" because it is so all-embracing as to lose much of its descriptive force (1993, 15). In this author's view, a comprehensive approach is neither a jack-of-all-trades approach nor comprehensive security. The comprehensive approach that we will examine in this chapter pays attention to the following four points:

(1) *Actors*: Many actors can get involved in the process of preventive diplomacy—the UN families, specialized agencies, regional organizations, NGOs, civil societies, and conflicting parties. Evans call such an approach "cooperative security" (1993, 16).[15]

(2) *Time and space*: A comprehensive approach implies the need to cover a broader range of time and space. The United Nations should engage in conflict prevention based on a more constant watch rather than on an ad hoc basis, and it should also engage in a global watch.

(3) *Multidimensional or interdisciplinary approach*: A multidimensional or interdisciplinary approach should be utilized. Not only peace and security, but also economic, social, and cultural dimensions should be considered by related organs independently or functionally.

(4) *Coordination*: Coordination is the most important factor for this comprehensive approach. Multidimensional functional

actors should not be unified under a single authority of the United Nations. Many actors should be coordinated under the auspices of the United Nations as an accountable organ for coordination.

The comprehensive approach described in this chapter is a practical tool for analyzing the United Nations' mechanism for preventive diplomacy. It is an approach that is needed for the United Nations as a worldwide system.

PREVENTIVE DIPLOMACY BY THE UNITED NATIONS

In this section, we will review the preventive diplomacy activities of the United Nations. There are many divisions within the United Nations that handle preventive diplomacy, such as DPA, the Department of Disarmament Affairs (DDA), and the Department of Peacekeeping Operations (DPKO), the secretary-general, the Security Council, the Department of Economic and Social Affairs, and the UN Development Programme (UNDP). In examining these various UN organs, we will consider the types of activities that are currently used, and the extent to which the comprehensive approach is applicable from the viewpoint of early warning, peaceful settlement, CBMs, and peacebuilding.

DPA in the UN Secretariat

The work of the DPA in the UN Secretariat in the area of conflict prevention is very important, as it has the primary responsibility for early warning regarding potential conflicts. For preventive diplomacy, it is important to deal with symptoms of disputes as early as possible.

Historically speaking, the DPA took over the work of ORCI, which had been established in accordance with an announcement of Secretary-General Pérez de Cuéllar on March 1, 1987, and was then dissolved into DPA in 1992. ORCI was "responsible among other things, for gathering information, conducting research, assessing global trends, and bringing potential trouble spots and critical security situations to the attention of the Secretary-General" (Ramcharan 1991, 44). In 1997, Annan assigned the responsibility for early warning to the DPA. The DPA also considers appropriate follow-on actions for preventive measures and endeavors to take a comprehensive approach.

Before the Security Council can take up a dispute òn its agenda, there are a number of administrative procedures that must be carried out. First, the regional divisions in the DPA conduct a global watch for early warning. There are four regional divisions, two for Africa, one for Asia, and one for the Americas and Europe. The desk officer of each division identifies potential crisis areas and monitors the potential conflict or dispute. The desk officer requires an official report from member-states. After that, the desk officer prepares analytical briefs and/or in-depth studies, focused on emerging trends bearing on peace and security. Despite recent improvements in communications technology, information collection is not sufficient for the desk officer to provide a firm basis for early warning.

There is a need for a comprehensive approach for early warning and fact-finding. For that purpose, a DPA Prevention Team was created in March 1998 by Sir Kiera Prendergast, under-secretary-general for political affairs. It is an intradepartmental forum for peer review and cross-fertilization of experience in order to develop various possible preventive actions in DPA (Kanninen 1999, 1-6; Boothby and D'Angelo 2000, 8-9).

In order to enhance the effectiveness of the comprehensive approach, the General Assembly resolved to create a new mechanism, the Interdepartmental Framework for Coordination (UN General Assembly 1997). The objective was to ensure that the pertinent departments of the Secretariat would coordinate their respective activities in the planning and implementing of such operations through the sharing of information, consultations, and joint action. An important element of the Framework for Coordination is the provision for staff-level consultations among the relevant departments and other parts of the organization to undertake joint analyses and to formulate joint recommendations.

A Framework Team for Peace and Security was then organized to facilitate preventive diplomacy. Members of the team are drawn from the DPA, DPKO, the Office for Humanitarian Affairs (OCHA), the UNDP, the UN High Commissioner for Refugees (UNHCR), the UN

Children's Fund (UNICEF), the Food and Agricultural Organization (FAO), the World Food Programme (WFP), and the World Health Organization (WHO). More recently, the World Bank was also invited to join. On behalf of the Framework Team, the UNDP is in charge of obtaining appropriate input from the UN resident coordinators in the specific countries of concern (Boothby and D'Angelo 2000, 7–8).

If some preventive effort is found to be necessary, the Framework Team presents recommendations to the high-level Executive Committee on Peace and Security. Again, to ensure a comprehensive approach, the Executive Committee is composed of representatives from all of the above-mentioned UN departments and agencies, including the Center for Human Rights. The Executive Committee convenes once a month and is chaired by the under-secretary-general for political affairs in DPA.[16] After discussion in the committee, the desk officer in charge of the area concerned provides an early warning to the secretary-general on the developments and situations affecting international peace and security. In accordance with this early warning, the secretary-general decides on an appropriate course to be taken for preventive diplomacy. All of these procedures are part of the early-warning system, which was designed to detect symptoms of a dispute as early as possible.

Based on this examination, we can see that the main activity of DPA is early warning, and DPA also considers appropriate follow-up actions for preventive measures. DPA makes full use of the comprehensive approach. Three stages of comprehensive mechanisms are devised: the Prevention Team, which is an intradepartmental mechanism, the Framework for Coordination, which is an interdepartmental mechanism, and the Executive Committee, which ensures a high-level discussion within the UN family.

Despite this extensive and comprehensive set of mechanisms, however, the DPA still faces a number of major challenges in the area of preventive diplomacy. First, the relationship between state sovereignty and fact-finding by the United Nations should be reconsidered. It is very difficult for the United Nations to collect information relating to disputes because of obstacles of state sovereignty. One recent example of this was the rejection in April 2002 by the government of Israel of a UN fact-finding team that was to be sent to investigate the situation in Jenin and other areas in which civilians were said to have been killed by the Israeli military ("Awaiting Formal Reply" 2002). It is important to seek ways to perform fact-finding, inquiry, and investigation in a manner acceptable to sovereign states, while recognizing the reality that official reports from member-states do not always represent impartial information.

Second, under the current system, it takes too long to issue an early warning. As noted above, the DPA carefully examines symptoms of dispute through a four-layered process, going first through a desk officer, then the Prevention Team, then the Framework for Coordination, and finally, through the Executive Committee. As a result, it is impossible for the DPA to give warnings expeditiously.

Third, most of the department's energy is consumed not by preventive diplomacy but by coordination. By constructing so many coordination mechanisms for the sake of a comprehensive approach, the DPA has included too many participants, making communication difficult. A comprehensive approach is needed, but we must also recognize that the coordination of so many actors is a problem.

Fourth, while the DPA has constructed an excellent early-warning system, how the DPA can carry out early preventive action is a question. There is a need to improve the department's ability to produce coherent and compelling arguments for taking preventive action. In addition, the DPA does not have sufficient authority at present to decide and carry out early action.

Fifth, at present, the DPA does not have a mechanism to involve NGO staff in its coordination and comprehensive approach. Only a few staff from the UN specialized agencies can commit to this process, and they have no representatives from active NGOs in the field. If it is to undertake a truly comprehensive approach, the DPA needs to develop the capacity to coordinate among the many actors involved.

Finally, without consent from member-states, the DPA cannot develop appropriate mechanisms for carrying out preventive diplomacy, which will deprive the DPA of undertaking conflict prevention at an early stage. The five obstacles mentioned here will need to be addressed if the DPA is going to conduct preventive diplomacy with a comprehensive approach.

DDA in the UN Secretariat

The DDA mainly carries out confidence-building measures. As noted above, crisis management and preventive diplomacy are related to CBMs. Measures of openness and transparency can provide useful early-warning indicators in the process of preventive diplomacy (UN Office for Disarmament Affairs 1993, 4).

One of the DDA's tasks is to pay attention to "micro-disarmament." It attaches primary importance to curtailing illicit trade in small arms, light weapons, and ammunition. After the cold war, small arms, light weapons, and ammunition have become more easily available to groups and individuals. Intrastate conflicts do not need high-technology weapons. Disarmament of small arms and light weapons will lead to a reduction in intrastate conflicts. DDA cooperates with regional organizations, allowing those organizations to incorporate in their early-warning mechanisms information on disarmament, such as information on the flow of illicit arms into conflict areas, the number of armed groups operating in an area, countries or organizations providing military assistance to such groups, as well as any other information that might assist in determining the level of militarization of a particular conflict situation (United Nations 1999, 25).

DDA contributes to preventive diplomacy by CBMs and disarmament of small arms, light weapons, and ammunitions. And DDA cooperates with regional organizations for a comprehensive approach. The problem of trade in small arms, light weapons, and ammunition is closely related to intrastate conflicts involving nonstate conflicting parties. While it is very difficult for the United Nations to intervene in intrastate micro-disarmament, there is some possibility of involving nonstate actors in the process of UN preventive diplomacy in this area. NGOs can monitor small arms trade in the field without violating the principle of state autonomy.

DPKO in the UN Secretariat

The DPKO is not a main actor for preventive diplomacy. Originally, peacekeeping was a consequence of the failure of preventive diplomacy and peacemaking (Zacarias 1996, 192). But PKOs and preventive diplomacy are closely related for several reasons. First, PKOs save lives by preventing violence. Second, because the range of peacekeeping activities has been widened, PKOs include many activities which can be called preventive diplomacy and peacebuilding.

Basically, a PKO cannot intervene in a conflict without the consent of conflicting parties. As we have noted, however, the majority of conflicts since the cold war have been intrastate rather than interstate, and thus the disputes involve nonstate actors. PKOs have increasingly been forced to intervene in these intrastate conflicts and have been compelled to get the consent of nonstate conflicting parties. The intervention is consensual and its functions can extend to consensual disarmament, election supervision, and human rights monitoring (White 1997).

One case in point was Cambodia, where there were four conflicting parties: Hun Sen (the People's Republic of Kampuchea; Phnom Penh government), Prince Norodom Sihanouk (the United National Front for an Independent, Neutral, Peaceful and Cooperative Cambodia; FUNCINPEC), Son Sann (Khmer People's National Liberation Front; KPNLF), and Pol Pot (the Party of Democratic Kampuchea; Khmer Rouge). In 1990, the Phnom Penh government occupied a seat in the United Nations, and the other three opposing parties, who were nonstate conflicting parties, contested the legitimacy of the government. In October 1991, the Agreement on a Comprehensive Political Settlement of the Cambodia Conflict (the so-called Paris Agreement) was concluded among three of the conflicting parties, with the exception of the Khmer Rouge. The agreement, signed by the nonstate parties, provided that not only peacekeeping but also post-conflict peacebuilding were to be carried out by the United Nations Transitional Authority in Cambodia (UNTAC).

Here, a number of points can be presented about the activities of PKOs and the DPKO. First, by nature, PKOs are essentially a post-conflict activity and not a pre-conflict activity. PKOs undertake their activities after a cease-fire agreement is concluded and PKOs cannot intervene in conflicts without the consent of conflicting parties in principle. Second, because of the extension of the role of PKOs after the cold war, PKOs now contribute to post-conflict peacebuilding in addition to their peacekeeping activities.[17] Third, PKOs sometimes undertake early warning to prevent the recurrence of a dispute or a potential conflict. Once a PKO has been dispatched to an area of conflict, the PKO observes a cease-fire and warns of any symptoms of a recurrence of the dispute. Fourth, nowadays PKOs are compelled to intervene in intrastate conflicts. And in such conflicts, PKOs must deal with nonstate conflicting parties. Fifth, at the UN Secretariat level, there are problems related to the relationship between the DPA and the DPKO. Once the matter of conflict falls within the jurisdiction of the DPKO through the decision of the Security Council, the DPA may no longer have a hand in the matter. Long-term commitment is important, however, in dealing with a conflict. There should be a mechanism that allows the DPA a channel for a continuing commitment to the settlement of a conflict.

The Secretary-General

Article 99 of the UN Charter prescribes, "The Secretary-General may bring to the attention of the Security Council any matter which in his opinion may threaten the maintenance of international peace and security." According to this article, the secretary-general has four powers to prevent a conflict. First, he has the right to investigate a symptom of dispute or potential conflict for the purpose of early warning and to bring the matter to the attention of the Security Council. Second, the secretary-general plays the role of good offices for conflicting parties at any time, in the pre-conflict stage or ongoing conflict stage. Third, the secretary-general has the right to choose any appropriate measures for preventive diplomacy, peacekeeping, or peacebuilding, and to recommend those measures to the Security Council. Fourth, the secretary-general encourages efforts undertaken at the regional level to prevent disputes or conflicts.

In accordance with any early warning given by the DPA, the secretary-general considers the following three alternative processes. Based on Article 99, the first possible measure is to dispatch a personal representative or personal envoy to areas of actual or potential conflict for the purpose of fact-finding, peacemaking, or other kinds of preventive efforts. The secretary-general does not have to wait for the decision of the Security Council. He can dispatch a mission on his own authority. The size of these missions is very small. Ordinarily, only one person is dispatched to the field on behalf of the secretary-general. A personal envoy engages in shuttle diplomacy, going back and forth between the UN Secretariat and the site of trouble. A personal representative has the prerogative of the secretary-general to negotiate, mediate, play good offices, and make arrangements on behalf of the secretary-general. As Thomas Frank (1991, 92) pointed out, the stationing of personal representatives of the secretary-general in 20 to 30 key countries, with regional responsibilities, would add immeasurably to the sensitivity that is conducive to the successful discharge of the good offices function.

The second course that the secretary-general can take is to bring a matter to the attention of the Security Council, and to request the dispatch of a special representative or a special envoy for preventive diplomacy. A special representative or a special envoy must be authorized by a decision or resolution of the Security Council, whereas a personal representative or personal envoy can be dispatched at the discretion of the secretary-general. Sutterlin points out that there are "limitations on the capacity of the Secretary-General, acting independently, to prevent conflict. He has only the power of persuasion. He can recommend but he cannot initiate measures for conflict deterrence" (1995, 17). And Ismat Kittani stresses that "the independence of the Secretary-General is more constrained now than in the Cold War years, because the deliberative organs (i.e., the Security Council) are more capable of acting" (1998, 102).

The third possibility for the secretary-general is to cooperate with a group of states that might offer to assist the efforts of the secretary-general to perform good offices and other methods of preventive diplomacy. There is no necessity to get authorization from the Security Council if a voluntary ad hoc group, usually referred to as the "Friends of the Secretary-General" can support the task of the secretary-general. For example, in the case of El Salvador, a "four plus one" group, consisting of Colombia, Mexico, Spain, and Venezuela, supported the good offices effort by the secretary-general. In the case of Haiti, the "Friends of Haiti" (Argentina, Canada, France, the United States, and Venezuela), in the case of Angola, the "troika" (Portugal, Russia, and the United States), and in the case of the former Yugoslavia, "the Contact Group for the former Yugoslavia" (France, Germany, Russia, United Kingdom, the United States, and sometimes Italy) played the important role of "Friends of the Secretary-General."

There are various merits and demerits of the role of the secretary-general for preventive diplomacy. On the positive side, it is very important for early action and preventive diplomacy to be able to dispatch investigative and/or good offices missions readily to areas of dispute. To this end, a personal envoy or a personal representative who is appointed by the secretary-general solely on his own authority plays an important role for preventive diplomacy. Similarly, because of their flexibility, the "Friends of the Secretary-General" groups are very useful for preventive diplomacy. The secretary-general also is at an advantage in that he can intervene in an intrastate conflict. For example, in the case of El Salvador, the secretary-general met with both sides of the conflicting parties—the government of El Salvador and the Frente Farabundo Martí para la Liberacíon Nacional (FMLN) —first separately and then jointly (Ramcharan 1991, 24). Through the good offices of the secretary-general, a series of peace agreements were concluded between the two sides from April 1991 to January 1992. Moreover, conflicting parties sometimes favor the low-key involvement of the secretary-general as an alternative to the high-profile Security Council consideration of the matter (Kittani 1998, 101).

And last, the secretary-general plays an important role in terms of establishing a comprehensive approach. As Article 98 of the UN Charter prescribes, the secretary-general has the ability to get involved in almost all fields of UN activities (although he has no authority to control the main organs of the UN without the Secretariat). For the purpose of coordinating among other organizations and actors, he has endeavored to make three coordinative entities more effective. Within the main bodies of the United Nations, including all the subsidiary organs of the United Nations, the secretary-general established the Executive Committee structure to act as a decision-making mechanism to cover the five main areas of UN concern—peace and security, economic and social affairs, development cooperation, humanitarian affairs, and human rights. In the broader UN System, including all the specialized agencies and the World Trade Organization, the secretary-general established the Administrative Coordination Committee under the auspices of the Economic and Social Council (ECOSOC). Acting under instructions from ECOSOC, the secretary-general can serve as its agent in exercising a degree of supervision over the specialized agencies. The secretary-general also convenes biennially a high-level meeting with regional organizations. (We will return to the issue of coordination and cooperation between the United Nations and regional organizations in further detail below.) Although he has no power to control or dictate to these coordinative entities, he serves as permanent chairman, thus assuring him the status of *primus inter pares* and giving him the possibility to pursue a comprehensive approach that will involve many actors.

Despite these advantages, some scholars point out that the secretary-general should have much more authority or ability independent from the deliberative organs (i.e., the Security Council and General Assembly) and member-states. As Sutterlin (1995, 129) proposed, it would be of high humanitarian and moral value if the secretary-general had the authority and the capacity to quickly send a UN guard contingent adequately trained and armed to afford protection to UN and other international humanitarian personnel present in the area. This perspective was also reflected in the 2000 "Brahimi Report" of the Panel on United Nations Peace Operations (United Nations 2000). The secretary-general does have the ability to appoint and dispatch a small-sized mission of fewer than 100 personnel. But there still remains the problem of the secretary-general's good offices. As Kittani describes, "A risk of the Secretary-General is that his good offices can create the illusion of action, providing a convenient smokescreen for intransigent parties and an excuse for inaction by the Security Council and General Assembly" (1998, 102).

Finally, the secretary-general needs substantially more resources and staff members. Within the limited availability of resources and staff members, the secretary-general should perform his duty, not only in the area of preventive diplomacy but also other tasks that cover all activities of the United Nations.

The Security Council

In the United Nations, the Security Council has the primary responsibility for preventive diplomacy as well as for the maintenance of peace and security in general (Article 24 of the UN Charter). And it is only the Security Council that has the authority to establish and dispatch missions for preventive diplomacy to trouble spots (Article 29). Without authoritative support from the Security Council, preventive diplomacy efforts become uncertain. The decisions of the Security Council are legally binding on all member-states of the United Nations (Article 25). Of course, the Security Council is a deliberative organ by nature, and does not typically conduct preventive diplomacy itself. Rather, the Security Council reinforces the efforts of missions or individuals for preventive diplomacy by signaling its concern about a particular dispute and its willingness to intervene if necessary.

There are three types of missions that the Security Council can authorize. First, as discussed above, the Security Council can authorize a special representative or a special envoy of the secretary-general. Second, through a decision or resolution by the Security Council or General Assembly, a DPA-led mission for preventive diplomacy can be established. The mandate of the DPA-led mission is restricted to the performance of preventive diplomacy, such as investigation, fact-finding, early warning, good offices, and other similar activities. DPA-led missions cannot perform peacekeeping activities. The size of these missions are comparatively small; ordinarily, the personnel involved are less than 30 in number. A DPA-led mission is easier for conflicting parties to accept than a PKO. For example, on June 11, 1999, the Security Council established the United Nations Mission in East Timor (UNAMET), which was a DPA-led mission. UNAMET oversaw the transition period pending the implementation of the decision of the East Timorese people regarding independence. Indonesia agreed to the dispatch of a DPA-led mission, but did not agree to the setting up of a PKO at that time. It is possible that the government of Indonesia was cautious about the nature of a PKO, suspecting that its mandate might be extended to include military action. Similarly, in the case of Afghanistan, the Taliban, one of the major parties to the conflict, agreed to accept a DPA-led mission in the occupied area in 1998.

Third, the Security Council can decide to organize and dispatch a PKO to an area that may threaten international peace and security. In the case of peacekeeping operations, the DPA will not be in charge of the matter; the DPKO will take over the work of political guidance and support for the secretary-general. As noted previously, the DPKO does not conduct preventive diplomacy in the strict sense, but carries out peacekeeping operations and nowadays often carries out peacebuilding.

It should be emphasized that the Security Council has the power to make member-states obey if it decides to send these three types of missions. But there are a number of problems with preventive diplomacy as conducted by the Security Council. First, it takes an excessive amount of time for the Security Council to negotiate and reach a decision. In terms of preventive diplomacy, there is the important question of how to deal with symptoms of disputes as early as possible, before the Security Council takes up the matter. If the DPA or some organ could start dealing with symptoms of disputes earlier, it would be better than just waiting idly for a decision or recommendation to be agreed upon by the Security Council.

Second, sometimes a UN peace verification mission can be more useful and effective than an early-warning system. The above-mentioned case of Afghanistan illustrates the problem of early warning. Early-warning systems consist of a series of work by the DPA, the secretary-general, and the Security Council. If the United Nations steps in too early to warn disputing parties, those disputing parties may harden their attitudes. On the other hand, if the United Nations sends a peace verification mission, it may be more easily accepted by the disputing parties. In the process of negotiation, the representative of the United Nations explained that the nature of the UN mission would be neither peacekeeping activity to watch for any breach of peace, nor investigative activity for early warning about potential conflict. The nature of the mission was to verify that the Taliban would not infringe on human rights. This was a "peace verification mission" by the United Nations (Kawabata 1999, 176).[18]

Third, the meaning of the term "preventive action" is very ambiguous, encompassing preventive diplomacy as well as preventive deployment, preventive peacebuilding, and other actions that can have a useful, preventive effect. Originally, however, the term "preventive action" implied "provisional measures" in Article 40 of the UN Charter. The word "action" is used in Chapter VII of the UN Charter, which provides for coercive action by the United Nations. Article 40 states, "In order to prevent an aggravation of the situation, the Security Council may . . . call upon the parties concerned to comply with such provisional measures. . . ." "Provisional measures" are those used to prevent the aggravation of a situation.[19] There is another question about the relationship between the phrases "a threat to the peace"

(Article 39 of Chapter VII) and "endanger the maintenance of international peace and security" (Article 33 of Chapter VI). In case of the former—but not the latter—the United Nations has the possibility to intervene in intrastate conflict coercively (Article 2, Clause 7). We can interpret the phrase to mean that the United Nations has a mandate to intervene in an intrastate conflict coercively for the purpose of preventive action, including preventive diplomacy. But this interpretation is unrealistic. In practice, the United Nations does not exercise coercive power in the area of preventive diplomacy.[20]

Fourth, the system for involving NGOs in the UN secretary-general's decision-making process should be considered. Under the contemporary system, as Yoshida Yasuhiko states, "No official status has been accorded under the Charter to those NGOs working in the fields of peace, security, and disarmament. The Charter does not provide NGOs with any means of consultation with the Security Council" (1997, 161). But Article 33 of the UN Charter recognizes nonstate conflicting parties: "If it is a party to a dispute under consideration by the Security Council, it shall be invited to participate, without vote." The Khmer Rouge in Cambodia or the Macedonian rebels, for example, can participate in Security Council discussions. However, nonstate actors and NGOs working in the fields of peace, security, and disarmament do not have any official status to participate in either the General Assembly or the Security Council and thus cannot join in this process as third parties to a dispute under consideration. Peter Willetts states, "If NGOs were accepted in the assembly's discussions on questions concerning conflicts, peacekeeping, and arms control, then it would be illogical to exclude NGOs from the Security Council" (2000, 199).[21]

The ECOSOC and the UNDP

The ECOSOC does not have primary responsibility for dealing with preventive diplomacy, and its role in that process is thus limited. However, there is the possibility for ECOSOC to contribute to preventive diplomacy through its close relationship with the UNDP. The UNDP is in a position to contact and coordinate with nonstate actors through its resident coordinators.

Unlike other organs under the UN Charter, the ECOSOC has a

mandate to involve NGOs in the decision-making process. As described in Article 71 of the UN Charter—"The Economic and Social Council may make suitable arrangements for consultation with non-governmental organizations which are concerned with matters within its competence"—ECOSOC can enter into arrangements with NGOs. Once an NGO has gained consultative status, its representatives are admitted to all meetings of ECOSOC and its official subsidiary bodies. The role that an NGO can play varies with the organization itself and the forum within ECOSOC. As Willetts states, "The smaller the decisionmaking body, the lower its public profile, the more technical the subject matter, and the more experienced the NGO representatives, the more likely it becomes that the NGOs can take a full part in the discussions and exercise significant influence" (2000, 193). But NGOs have only consultative status within ECOSOC. It should be noted, however, that NGOs have the right to participate in and the right to speak in the ECOSOC, but they do not have the right to vote.

In a recent report by the UNDP, that organization discusses its efforts in the area of "Capacity Building in Conflict Resolution" (United Nations Development Programme 2000). The object of this project is to develop diagnostic, analytical, planning, and training instruments that will help African governments and their civil society partners to formulate proactive policies and strategies for managing disputes and diversity in their societies in preemptive, constructive, nonviolent ways. To this end, the report closely examines the following four thematic areas: (1) developing capacity for conflict analysis and early response; (2) national capacity building in conflict management; (3) dispute resolution skills development; and (4) integrating conflict management tools into development work.

On the positive side, the approach outlined in this report is truly comprehensive, encompassing every actor and method of preventive diplomacy. If implemented, nonstate actors would be able to participate in preventive diplomacy by the United Nations. As a result, it would be possible to catch subtle symptoms of conflict at an early stage and to judge whether early action is required. Of course, this would depend both on the UNDP's internal capabilities and its ability to interact effectively and in a timely way with the other UN agencies and departments. However, this approach would also allow the United Nations to provide assistance to nonstate and other actors.

Nonetheless, this proposed approach has many problems as well. There should be a way to receive input from nonstate actors, but the question is which organ of the United Nations can authoritatively receive and deal with this kind of information or petition. The Security Council has primary responsibility in the field of peace and security, but the UNDP does not have a very strong connection with the Security Council. It is an autonomous subsidiary organ under the General Assembly. And it is strongly linked with ECOSOC and related divisions dealing with economic and social development in the UN families. Finally, the UNDP approach is too broad, as it attempts to deal with economic and social development as well as peace and security concerns. All of the problems and all of the actors are given equal status. The United Nations should create different mechanisms to deal with nonstate conflicting parties, NGOs, or regional organizations respectively in one accountable organ.

Concluding Observations

We have examined preventive diplomacy efforts by the United Nations, and have seen that in the UN Secretariat, the DPA is the principal organ in charge of preventive diplomacy. But there remain some problems for a comprehensive approach. From this study, we may conclude that there is a possibility to involve nonstate actors in the process of preventive diplomacy by the secretary-general and/or UNDP. These two organs are flexible and already open to nonstate actors. But there are some limitations to these organs and the other organs of the United Nations, such as the DDA, the DPKO, the Security Council, and ECOSOC, have even greater limitations.

COORDINATION AND COOPERATION BETWEEN THE UN AND REGIONAL ORGANIZATIONS

Since 1994, the secretary-general has been convening biennial meetings with the heads of regional organizations. In particular, the secretary-general has endeavored to promote "cooperation for conflict prevention" between and among the United Nations and regional organizations. The main purpose of this section is to study the ways in which these organizations can coordinate and cooperate with the United Nations and other regional organizations, and how the United Nations can utilize them for the purpose of a comprehensive approach to preventive diplomacy.

In the following sections, we will examine regional organizations for preventive diplomacy in four regions: the ASEAN Regional Forum (ARF), the Organization of American States (OAS), the Organization of African Unity (OAU), and the Organization for Security and Cooperation in Europe (OSCE).

ARF

In 1994, the first meeting of ARF was held in Bangkok. From the start, ARF was not expected to play an important role in the fields of disarmament, peacekeeping operations, or peacebuilding. ARF does not have the experience needed to seriously engage in arms control or to develop formal dispute settlement mechanisms. Nonetheless, ARF is a very valuable forum in the sense that it can get member-states to sit down at the same table.

ARF has adopted a gradual, evolutionary approach for sustaining and enhancing peace and security. As described in "Concept and Principles of Preventive Diplomacy" (ASEAN Regional Forum [ARF] 2002), the members have agreed to progress in three stages: Stage I is the promotion of confidence-building measures; Stage II is the development of preventive diplomacy mechanisms; and Stage III is the development of conflict resolution mechanisms. In Stage III, ARF might conceivably set up peacekeeping operations or dispatch peacekeeping missions. For now, however, ARF is still seeking a way to meet its Stage I objectives. The CBMs projected for Stage I are basically the convening of meetings or seminars with member-states to talk and learn about CBMs (ARF 2002).[22] In Stage II, the "preventive diplomacy" measures being considered for ARF involve the issue of overlap between CBMs and preventive diplomacy, and the ministers at the sixth ARF in 1999 instructed the Meeting of the ARF Inter-sessional Support Group on CBMs to further explore this question.

Preventive diplomacy measures of ARF could include the following:

a) Confidence-building efforts—Continuous efforts to build mutual trust and confidence between states, which are essential for the successful application of preventive diplomacy.

b) Norms building—The nurturing of accepted codes or norms of behavior guiding the relationships among states in the Asia-Pacific region. To the extent that these norms enhance predictability and strengthen cooperative behavior in ensuring regional peace, they can enhance trust between and among states in the region.

c) Enhancing channels of communication—The promotion of open, easy, and direct communications or channels among ARF participants, which can serve to enhance transparency with a view to avoiding misperceptions or misunderstanding.

d) Creating a role for the ARF Chair—The setting of some role for the ARF Chair, as determined by the ARF members.

Although ARF has held many seminars, meetings, and training programs related to CBMs and preventive diplomacy since its inception, it does not have any organized mechanism for implementing concrete measures for preventive diplomacy or peacekeeping. There are many reasons for this, mostly relating to what is widely known as the "Asian way" of addressing Asian problems. One reason is that there is little imminent conflict for ARF to settle, except for tensions in the Korean peninsula. A second reason is the diversity of ARF member-states with respect to history, culture, ethnicity, and political, social, and economic backgrounds (Tsubouchi 2000, 265–269). Third, member-states share a common feeling of domestic insecurity, referred to as the problem of "internal collective security."[23] Most member-states have residual, unresolved territorial or other disputes. Fourth, most member-states are still in the process of achieving independence and thus adhere to the concept of state sovereignty. They give exceedingly high priority to state sovereignty over individual human rights. The political democracy of these states is still far from being mature. For these reasons, ARF still has a long way to go before contributing to peacebuilding.

To date, ARF has not participated in the above-mentioned biennial meetings convened by the secretary-general, and there are in fact a number of obstacles for ARF cooperation with the United Nations. ARF is as yet too immature and the United Nations already has many mechanisms in the field of peace and security, as seen in the cases of Cambodia and Myanmar, thus leaving little room for ARF's involvement in the process of conflict prevention. Moreover, ARF is not likely to push hard for closer interinstitutional cooperation with the present United Nations, because it may fear the loss of national and regional autonomy (Peou 1998, 450). Yet, while it may develop in ways quite different from the historical UN development in this area, we might eventually see a new path emerge toward peace and security. We should wait and see whether this "Asian way" evolves from ARF.

OAS

The OAS creates harmonious, loose ties among its member-states. Since its creation as the Pan-American Union in 1989, the OAS has experienced a long history as a regional organization. At the same time, there has been a long history of strong attitudes among its members in support of the principle of nonintervention. The principle has two motivations. One is to avoid intervention in the domestic jurisdiction of member-states. The other is the fear of a U.S. invasion of Latin American countries. In the wake of the cold war, however, the OAS has changed its style. Since there is no threat of communism, the OAS is now intended to work only by consensus, without taking any enforcement action.

Given this background, preventive diplomacy by the OAS does not fall within the narrow sense of early warning and peaceful settlement, but rather in the broad sense of CBMs and post- conflict peacebuilding. Discussion of confidence- and security-building measures (CSBMs) became part of the agenda of the OAS in 1991. The OAS also contributes to conflict prevention through numerous agreements on disarmament and arms reduction, such as the 1995 Declaration of Santiago and 1998 Declaration of San Salvador on Confidence- and Security-Building Measures, and the 1999 Inter-American Convention on Transparency in Conventional Weapons Acquisitions.

In the field of post-conflict peacebuilding, it contributes to the

defense and promotion of democratic institutions and their stability, and to the debate over the new paradigms and concepts that
should shape the hemispheric security agenda (Granada 1999, 46).
The most important objective for preventive diplomacy by the OAS
is to promote democratic institutions within member-states. In this
regard, the OAS works toward the development and use of conflict
resolution methods and the design of long-term conflict prevention
mechanisms within a member-state, and supports national and local
efforts to foster dialogue, build consensus, and develop joint solutions to important social and political problems (Soto 1999, 4).

Traditionally speaking, member-states of the OAS have strongly
adhered to the principle of nonintervention, but the OAS can play
an important role in intrastate matters of promoting democratic institutions for preventive diplomacy. This is because, as was proposed
in the Declaration of Managua (1993) through the notion of "effective and ethical governance," promoting and strengthening democracy has become a common agenda for member-states.[24] And as the
inter-American system of human rights protection is gradually becoming "depoliticized," making it more responsive to peoples' needs
as opposed to government agendas, the OAS is expected to become
more directly involved in this area as well (Thérien, Fortmann, and
Gosselin 1996, 220).

Cooperation and coordination between the United Nations and
the OAS on conflict prevention is just beginning. The third meeting
between the United Nations and regional organizations was held in
July 1998. Unlike other regional organizations, the OAS focused not
on concrete measures of early warning or peaceful settlement, but
on CBMs and post-conflict peacebuilding. The OAS pointed to its
use of "pacific means" to help produce a stable environment within
its region and noted its efforts to promote long-term solutions (UN
1998b, 7). Following that meeting, a tripartite meeting among the
OAS, CARICOM (the Caribbean Community), and the United Nations was held in December 1998. At that meeting, they agreed to appoint a special representative of the secretary-general to deal with
early warning and conflict prevention. Which organization will act
as the lead player will be determined on an ad hoc basis, with consideration to the ability of each organization or actor to deal with a
specific matter (UN/CARICOM/OAS 1998). "Previously, for example,

the OAS and the UN had jointly created missions to Nicaragua and Haiti."²⁵ The mandates of these missions differ on a case-by-case basis, and the division of labor also depends on the case. Given its lack of concrete measures for early warning or peaceful settlement, the OAS is inherently less prepared than the United Nations to deal with conflict, but it may be useful in cases of conflict as a supplement to the United Nations through its declarations regarding CBMs and its concrete mechanisms for promoting democratic institutions. On the political level, however, certain OAS members fear that delegating power to the United Nations might result in the subordination of the OAS to the global body (Thérien, Fortmann, and Gosselin 1996, 229). It should be noted that from the standpoint of the OAS, the United Nations plays an important role in deterring a U.S. invasion of member countries.

OAU

The OAU was established in 1963, and as of 2000, it had become the largest regional organization in the world in terms of membership, with a total of 53 member countries. The OAU's charter prescribes the principle of nonintervention in the domestic jurisdiction of member-states (Art. 3, cls. 2–3). That principle is a significant obstacle in terms of the OAU's ability to manage conflict prevention smoothly. It also places limitations on the extent to which an individual country's internal matters can be probed in hidden conflict situations (Attah-Poku 1998, 128).

In 1993, the OAU created a Mechanism on Conflict Prevention, Management and Resolution (MCPMR). Since the establishment of this main organ, the OAU has dealt with many cases of conflict prevention, including the facilitation of the Arusha Peace Treaty between Burundi and Rwanda in 1993. And in the field of peacebuilding, the OAU was able to observe nearly 40 elections or referendums in 25 member-states in the period from 1993 to 2000, which accelerated the democratization of domestic political institutions in many member-states of the OAU.

The creation of the MCPMR has enabled the OAU to promote peaceful settlements through preventive diplomacy, such as the good offices of the OAU secretary-general, direct negotiations with conflicting parties and the governments of the countries concerned, and the sending of missions to conflict areas. The MCPMR also contributed to the OAU endeavor to set up a regional early-warning system. Furthermore, the OAU promotes confidence-building measures in the context of the philosophical sense of CBMs, devoting itself to fostering conversation and mutual understanding among the various actors—member-states, conflicting parties, and others. As Salim Ahmed Salim states, thanks to the MCPMR, "the OAU was able to inspire the confidence of the negotiators enough to spell out the most minute details of the peace agreement" (1998, 249).

Another contribution by the OAU is the establishment of organs and operations in the areas of preventive diplomacy and preventive deployment. In the cases of Congo and Gabon in 1997, the OAU attempted preemptive involvement of the organization in lingering conflicts with the intention of offering the protagonists an opportunity for dialogue and accommodation. And in the case of Burundi in 1993, the OAU sent an observer mission composed of military and civilian components. Ali Mazrui proposes the establishment of a pan-African emergency force under an African security council, complete with permanent members, in the style of the UN Security Council (1998, 242–243). A report by the Stockholm International Peace Research Institute also points out the need for a permanent decision-making body (Stockholm International Peace Research Institute 1998, 52). In spite of these recommendations, the OAU's lack of financial resources makes it difficult to establish an OAU peacekeeping operation or deployment mission for the present (Aoki 2000a, 120–121).

It may be realistic for the OAU to support the efforts of subregional organizations, such as the Economic Community of West African Countries (ECOWAS) and the Southern African Development Community (SADC). And for the purpose of cooperation and coordination, the OAU should serve as a center for conflict prevention, which can approach many actors—not only subregional organizations, but also NGOs in this region.

The Department of Political Affairs of the United Nations attaches great importance to conflict prevention in Africa.[26] As noted above, that department has set up four regional divisions, and two of them are in charge of conflict prevention in Africa. In 1998, the secretary-general of the United Nations offered a report on "The causes of conflict and the promotion of durable peace and sustainable development in Africa," in which the United Nations encourages that conflict prevention in Africa be conducted by Africa for Africa (Shōji 2000, 39–41).

Attah-Poku has pointed out that "the OAU comes nowhere near [the United Nations] in terms of political and economic resources and power. It should therefore not surprise one if the OAU handed over [peacekeeping operations] to [the United Nations]" (1998, 92). On the other hand, the United Nations cannot react to the symptoms of conflict speedily because of the impediments of its tedious legal political procedures and its physical distance from the African region. It is important for preventive diplomacy to firmly grasp the cultural, geographical, and historical conditions of conflicting parties. The OAU has taken a position neither too far nor too near to conflicting parties in comparison with the United Nations and other subregional organizations. The primary responsibility for preventive diplomacy in Africa should rest with the OAU, and the United Nations should play an assistant and subordinate role to that organization.

OSCE

The machinery of the OSCE for preventive diplomacy is more advanced than those of other international regional organizations, comprising a number of organs for preventive diplomacy. The Office for Democratic Institutions and Human Rights (ODIHR), for example, contributes to early warning and peacebuilding by monitoring the implementation of OSCE commitments in the fields of human rights and democracy (the "human dimension"), promoting democratic elections, and if necessary, observing national elections. The function of the High Commissioner on National Minorities (HCNM) is to identify and seek early resolution of ethnic tensions by promoting dialogue, confidence-building, and cooperation between concerned parties. These methods include early warning, peaceful settlement for preventive diplomacy, and confidence-building in the philosophical sense of the term. The Representative on Freedom of the Media

(FOM) addresses serious problems caused by the obstruction of media activities and unfavorable working conditions for journalists. The mission of the FOM depends on its activities in early warning. The Forum for Security Cooperation (FSC) is responsible for negotiations and consultations among participating states on military security and stability for the purpose of CBMs. And the Conflict Prevention Centre (CPC), which is within the OSCE Secretariat, supports OSCE peace missions and CBMs.

The OSCE has dispatched many kinds of missions for preventive diplomacy to such locations as Kosovo, Sanjak, Vojvodina, Belarus, Croatia, and Slovenia. The Secretariat maintains contacts with international and nongovernmental organizations, providing conference and language services, as well as administrative, financial, and personnel services. OSCE involves nonstate actors in the process of preventive diplomacy.

OSCE's preventive diplomacy is characterized by the following four aspects. First, OSCE utilizes diverse measures for preventive diplomacy—early-warning systems, peaceful settlement for preventive diplomacy, confidence-building measures, peacebuilding measures, and so on. Second, OSCE takes a comprehensive approach to preventive diplomacy, employing many kinds of organs (including those described above), and tackling problems in many fields, such as human rights, democracy, minority issues, security, military, media, and so forth. Many actors are involved in this process of preventive diplomacy—not only sovereign states, but also nonstate actors. Third, OSCE has overcome the principle of nonintervention in domestic jurisdiction by focusing on specific issues, such as human rights, democracy, minority issues, and the media (Kikkawa 1999, 39). Fourth, OSCE uses soft power and soft measures (Kikkawa 1999, 46; Nowak 1999, 140). OSCE has an attractive power to draw concerned actors toward common values and norms such as democratization, respect for human rights, the rule of law, and so on. And measures of preventive diplomacy such as early warning, fact-finding, rapporteur, good offices, and monitoring missions make flexible and effective use of soft measures, while hard measures are undertaken for peacekeeping operations or military operations. Finally, OSCE cooperates with, and has established links to, many external actors such as the North Atlantic Treaty Organization (NATO), the West European Union

(WEU), the European Union (EU), and the United Nations. Through cooperation with these organizations, OSCE compensates for its own deficiencies. For example, OSCE does not have the capacity to undertake enforcement action, which the WEU, NATO, and the United Nations all have. The EU also has the economic power to carry out economic assistance and economic sanctions, which OSCE does not. By contrast, OSCE can deal with the problems of new states that were formerly part of the Soviet Union, where NATO, the EU, and the WEU have no legal jurisdiction.

Concluding Observations

On the one hand, preventive diplomacy by regional organizations has many merits. In the field of preventive diplomacy, the efforts of regional organizations command priority over those of the United Nations. Article 52, clause 2 of the UN Charter provides for the "priority of the use of regional arrangements for peaceful settlement." In other words, the Security Council should first encourage the development of peaceful settlement and preventive diplomacy of local disputes through regional organizations, which are better situated to address domestic problems in their member-states than is the United Nations. As discussed above, for example, OSCE in particular has overcome the principle of nonintervention in domestic jurisdiction on specific issues. On account of a slow "depoliticization," the OAS will be able to get directly involved in the area of human rights protection. In the case of ARF, member-states share a common feeling of domestic security, which is called "internal collective security."

Regional organizations are more favorably situated geographically than the United Nations for the purpose of early warning. It is important for those conducting preventive diplomacy to have a firm grasp of the cultural, geographical, and historical conditions of conflicting parties. Geographical proximity also gives member-states of regional organizations a chance to foster a sense of belonging to a "security community" (Satō 2000, 5). The presence of a security community contributes to the development of CBMs and allows neighboring states to employ peer pressure on conflicting parties.

Finally, it should be noted that many regional organizations have not yet rigidly institutionalized the mechanisms of preventive diplomacy and have kept loose ties among member-states. The flexibility of regional organizations makes the soft characteristics of measures taken under preventive diplomacy smooth and effective, while the hard measures of peacekeeping or military action do not require such flexibility.

In addition to these positive aspects, however, there are also certain demerits of preventive diplomacy exercised by regional organizations. First, a number of the regional organizations (although not all) have no concrete mechanisms to enforce their measures toward conflicting parties. Sometimes, regional organizations are too loose and too weak. ARF, for example, represents only a loose tie among member-states, with the only obligation being to come to the same table for meetings. OAS prefers not to use concrete measures like early warning. And OSCE does not have the ability to take any enforcement action. Second, preventive diplomacy by regional organizations sometimes falls into an impartiality crisis. Regional organizations sometimes end up playing the role of helping a hegemonic power in the region. And in other cases, member-states of the regional organization compete for their respective interests in a conflicting area. Third, most regional organizations do not have sufficient financial, logistical, or human resources to carry out preventive diplomacy.

Given these various demerits of the regional organizations, there is a need for cooperation and coordination by the United Nations. As noted above, in July 1998, the secretary-general convened the Third High-Level Meeting between the Secretary-General and Heads of Regional Organizations.[27] Participants at that meeting endorsed the "Suggested Practical Modalities for Cooperation between the UN and Regional Organizations" (United Nations 1998b). This document mentions 13 modalities for cooperation for conflict prevention, including joint training and meetings for early warning and conflict prevention, the development of an early-warning capacity, and the promotion of more effective mobilization of resources through cooperation between the United Nations and regional organizations.[28]

In this author's estimation, these last two points in particular stand out. Although a central role for the United Nations is vital for preventive diplomacy, the body is already overburdened in this field.

The best coordination and cooperation is driven by necessity, and in this case, such coordination is useful both to the United Nations and to the regional organizations.

There are four potential benefits to this approach. First, financial, logistical, and personnel resources can be more effectively shared. For example, the United Nations, the OAU, and the ECOWAS do not normally share their resources in these areas, but in 1993–1997 they cooperated to pool their resources and send a joint PKO mission to Liberia.

Second, this approach can help address the problem of division of labor and task sharing. Through coordination and cooperation, organizations can avoid overlapping activities, as occurred in the Dominican Crisis in 1965, when the OAS and the United Nations competed for jurisdiction over a single dispute. It can also alleviate the problem of gaps in activities, as was seen in the case of Somalia in 1995. The United Nations Operation in Somalia II (UNOSOM II) withdrew from Somalia and no other international organization could access that country because it was too dangerous. And it can ensure that organizations avoid the type of dropped hand-offs of activities that occurred with the Grenada Invasion in 1983. The United Nations, OAS, CARICOM, and OECS were involved in the dispute, but after the dispute ended, none of them remained eager to engage in peacebuilding.

Third, the United Nations is able to use coercive measures, particularly economic sanctions, which can improve the effectiveness of preventive diplomacy. Unlike when a world body such as the United Nations enforces sanctions, when a regional organization like the EU enforces economic sanctions alone, they are ineffective because they can be enforced only through the regional organization's member-states.

Fourth, according to Article 53, clause 1 of the UN Charter, the United Nations can authorize enforcement actions by regional organizations. The United Nations thus has the ability to give legitimacy and authority to the activities of regional organizations. Not only legal legitimacy but also political legitimacy is crucial for the activities of regional organizations, and the political legitimacy provided by the United Nations can make it easier and smoother for regional organizations to conduct preventive diplomacy. Furthermore, the involvement of the United Nations guarantees impartiality and thus offers conflicting parties a sense of protection against the possible manipulation of the regional organization by a regional hegemonic power.

CONCLUSION

In this chapter, we have sought ways in which the United Nations can deal with the proliferation of intrastate conflicts. As the frequency of intrastate conflicts has increased, the types of nonstate actors involved have also expanded. Another aim of this chapter has thus been to seek an effective way to involve nonstate actors in the preventive diplomacy efforts of the United Nations.

We examined each of the relevant organs of the United Nations related to preventive diplomacy—the DPA, the DDA, the DPKO in the UN Secretariat, the secretary-general, the Security Council, ECOSOC, and UNDP. Under the present system, there is little possibility of involving nonstate actors. Against this reality, Willetts proposes that the Security Council should be reformed as a hybrid organization that admits NGOs on an equal status with states, in the same fashion as the tripartite system of the International Labor Organization (2000).[29] In the distant future, this proposal may be realized. Certainly, there are many kinds of actors in the world, such as international organizations, sovereign states, nonstate actors, and so on. But sovereign states are still the most important actors for sustaining peace and stability, and member-states are unlikely to yield their sovereignty to make room for NGOs in the Security Council. Thus, the proposal to reform the Security Council as a hybrid organ is unrealistic in the immediate future.

Among the existing organs, the secretary-general and/or UNDP have the possibility of involving nonstate actors in the process of preventive diplomacy. But there remain some problems. It would be better for preventive diplomacy if the office of the secretary-general were independent of member-states, and if it were expanded in terms of its personnel and financial resources. But if such a proposal were realized, the decisive and impartial ability of the secretary-general would be needed. Unless such discretion and impartiality were guaranteed, there would be a danger of the secretary-general to becoming a dictator in world affairs. As argued in this chapter, UNDP is the preferable organ to involve nonstate actors.[30] But UNDP, as it is, is not the proper organ to deal with international peace and security.

As has been discussed, regional organizations can address intrastate conflicts more easily than the United Nations. We examined the conditions relating to coordination and cooperation between the United Nations and regional organizations. It is realistic and possible, for the present, to develop a more effective worldwide network for an early-warning system through cooperation between the United Nations and regional organizations. Coordination and cooperation for peaceful settlement, CBMs, and peacebuilding will have to be considered gradually, in keeping with the gradual development of the measures themselves. For the purpose of cooperation and coordination between the United Nations and regional organizations, Peck suggests the creation of "UN Regional Centres for Sustainable Peace," saying that the proposed centers "could also liaise closely with appropriate NGOs. . . ." In her vision, the centers could be established under the auspices of the DPA (1999, 435). For effective diplomacy, such a center is needed.

Many scholars argue for including NGOs in the process of UN preventive diplomacy.[31] Because NGOs have their own bases for activities in the field, they can provide live information on potential conflicts to the United Nations, thereby enhancing the organization's capacity for early warning. And they also have the ability to appeal or petition on behalf of conflicting parties lacking the capability to articulate their position internationally. Their nongovernmental character is another advantage for NGOs regarding preventive diplomacy. Not having to contend with the principle of noninterference in domestic affairs, NGOs can play the role of good offices and help conflicting parties to use confidence-building measures on behalf of the United Nations. Certainly it would be better if NGOs could easily join in the process of UN preventive diplomacy.

We should also consider another kind of nonstate actor—the conflicting parties themselves. Most potential conflicting parties cannot easily approach the United Nations because they do not have access to the appropriate networks. Sometimes there is no international entity appropriate to accept their petition or appeal. Some type of international body is needed to improve the ability to accept petitions or appeals from conflicting parties. Resident representatives and resident coordinators in UNDP have the ability to receive requests from groups of inhabitants who need some kind of development assistance. It would be helpful if a similar system were established to allow resident staff of the United Nations to receive petitions or appeals from conflicting parties.

It is the opinion of this author that a new mechanism for preventive diplomacy is needed as an autonomous subsidiary organ under the UN Security Council. On the one hand, preventive diplomacy for intrastate conflicts is a matter for which the Security Council has primary responsibility. On the other hand, the issue of nonstate conflicting parties is a matter of collective human rights. Like the High Commissioner on National Minorities of OSCE, which handles minority human rights, the United Nations should take up this problem as a collective human rights issue. So that the new mechanism can have the authority to accept the petitions of nonstate conflicting parties and undertake preventive diplomacy, the new mechanism should be established as an autonomous subsidiary organ of the United Nations, similar to UNDP and United Nations University. Autonomous subsidiary organs of the United Nations enjoy autonomy within the UN system, and this autonomy should enable the organ to dispatch its own missions readily to deal with potential conflicts or disputes in the field.[32]

For the purpose of a comprehensive approach, it is also very important to engage many actors in conflict prevention, such as the United Nations, specialized agencies, regional organizations, NGOs, and civil society. The United Nations, by setting up this new mechanism, should be the focus of coordination and cooperation for conflict prevention among these actors. Another important point is to respect the independence of these actors from one another. Coordination and cooperation can be best achieved when the various actors are treated as equals, rather than creating hierarchical relationships.

The most important purpose of the United Nations, as stated in the UN Charter, is "to maintain international peace and security, and to that end, to take effective collective measures for prevention and removal of threats to the peace" (Article 1, Clause 1). But it is not a world government in a centralized society. There is a broad range of actors involved in international peace and security today, and each actor has decentralized power. A decentralized society, however, is different from a disordered society. A disordered society is an anarchical society, while a decentralized society needs a kind of focal entity. If the United Nations can serve as the focus of coordination and cooperation for many actors in the world for the purpose of conflict prevention, it can contribute to ensuring that the world in the coming 21st century will not become a disordered society. And if the United Nations can involve nonstate actors in its system for conflict prevention, it will be able to perform a more effective role in the world.

NOTES

1. See, for example, Miall, Ramsbotham, and Woodhouse on "preventers of non-interstate conflict," and the critical role of indigenous peacemakers and peacebuilders within the potential conflict area (1999, 107–109).

2. Makinda suggests a reinterpretation of state sovereignty and security, stating, "The fact that most conflicts now take place within rather than between states means that the UN can only postpone, but not completely avoid, considering a reinterpretation of state sovereignty. This interpretation would be easier if the definition of security that stresses social, political, economic, and cultural aspects was widely accepted. Such a broad concept of security would incorporate institution building, demands for self-determination, and the effect of poverty and economic stagnation on regional and international stability" (1996, 165). Doyle, Johnstone, and Orr propose multidimensional peace operations. They suggest "a subtle and dynamic redefinition of the evolving notion of sovereignty, by which the parties agreed to UN involvement in areas long thought to be the exclusive domain of domestic jurisdiction . . ." (1997, 19).

3. It should also be noted that Annan has stressed the cost-effectiveness of preventive diplomacy, stating, "Preventive diplomacy is particularly favoured by Member States as a means of preventing human suffering and as an alternative to costly politico-military operations to resolve conflicts after they have broken out." These cost-effective aspects of preventive diplomacy are verified in Brown and Rosecrance (1999).

4. This demarcation is explained, for example, by Connie Peck, who states, "It should also be noted that preventive deployment, although a type of preventive action is not preventive diplomacy" (1996, 228).

5. Krepon refers not only to CBMs but also to Conflict Avoidance Measures (CAMs). CAMs are best characterized by initial steps to avoid unwanted wars and unintended escalation. They can be used even when states have not established diplomatic relations. One reason to implement CAMs is to provide a cooling-off period after wars or periods of high tension. "Buying time" is a neutral profession. By contrast, CBMs are not value neutral; they will always be shaped by the motivation of national leaders over preferred end-states (1999, 6).

6. For analyses of "early warning," see Ramcharan (1991) and Shōji (1997, 66–71).

7. From the study of peaceful settlement by the United Nations, five points are counted as the merits of having the United Nations conduct peaceful settlement activities as opposed to nation-states or other organizations: 1) the United Nations can carry out its task permanently and independently; 2) peaceful settlement by the United Nations is more systemic than that in general international law; 3) the United Nations can use coercive measures along with peaceful measures; 4) peaceful settlement by the United Nations is more effective than that of general international law; and 5) peaceful measures by the United Nations have politically authoritative effect. These merits are applicable to the peaceful settlement for preventive diplomacy (Shōji 1996).

8. Evans explains each advantage as follows: "motivation: parties are more likely to accept assistance while issues are still specific, and before grievances accumulate and the desire for retribution becomes paramount; effectiveness: prevention is more likely to be effective before issues have generalised, issues and parties have multiplied, positions have hardened and actions have turned into ever-more hostile reverberating echoes of threat and counter-threat; completeness: since the goal of early prevention is resolution rather than containment, it is more likely that the dispute will be resolved and will not recur; and cost: early prevention is likely to be more cost-effective in both financial and human terms" (1993, 70).

9. For a different opinion on this issue, see for example de Soto, who asserts that peacebuilding should be performed only in the post-conflict stage. "Governance is, after all, typically a matter that falls within the domestic jurisdiction of states. The reluctance of member-states to accord such a general mandate to the Secretary-General is particularly strong as regards the 'pre-conflict' stage, though somewhat less so, assuming a case-by-case treatment, after a conflict" (1997, 140).

10. Holl introduces a root causes approach. She thinks resolving root causes includes strategies to build intercommunal confidence and overcome deeply held distrust and enmity. Her approach, however, may well be classified with CBMs in the broad sense (1997, 119). Attali categorizes different types of economically driven conflicts. He thinks that, while there are conflicts with no economic causes and no economic solutions, there are often economically driven conflicts in the world. Economically driven conflicts can be prevented only if

massive financial assistance is given (1997, 127–130). Peck also discerns the root causes of conflict: when the physical safety or cultural identity of an identity group is threatened, they may mobilize to express their collective concern and seek redress (1999, 430).

11. Joyner studies the relationship between the United Nations and democracy (1999, 333–357). Unwin and Biagiotti analyze good governance from the viewpoint of political conditionality on human rights, democracy, governance, and military spending (1996, 377–400). Peck thinks that one goal of prevention should be to provide assistance in building human security through the development of an international architecture made up of the building blocks of good governance structures (1999, 431). Rupesinghe also considers good governance for conflict prevention of intrastate conflict. He proposes conflict transformation (1992, 1–26).

12. Cortright and Lopez study a carrot and stick approach and they assert that sanction and incentives are needed for conflict prevention (1998, 113–134). See also the edited volume of Cortright on the carrot and stick approach (1997).

13. Alger points out the need for long-term strategies for violence prevention (1996, 351–356). Otunnu believes that conflict can be prevented if we are prepared to act in a way that is serious and systematic, deploying long-term strategies (1997, 75).

14. Soros proposes the concept of an "open society." The concept actually provides a different view of the world and serves as a common value that could then help create a world order in which there could be a reasonable degree of stability (1997, 80–81). The *International Journal of Psychology* recently published a special issue on "Diplomacy and Psychology," in which it is pointed out that war is increasingly societal and involves nonstate actors. With regard to diplomacy employed for conflict prevention and management, this raises profound psychological issues of how to handle nongovernmental actors, who gets to go to the negotiating table, and the perceived legitimacy of the representatives of the other side (Gärling et al. 2000, 81–86).

15. Evans explains that cooperative security "assumes that states are the principal actors in the security system, but accepts that nonstate actors may have an important role to play" (1993, 16). The concept of cooperative security is also studied by Yamamoto (1995a and 1995b).

16. Interview with Den Hitoki, senior political affairs officer, assistant to the under-secretary-general for political affairs in DPA, on March 1, 2000.

17. See White's analysis of this new type of PKO, which is endowed with many types of activities such as observation and fact finding, supervision, disarmament/demobilization, human rights monitoring, referendum/election monitoring, and humanitarian assistance (1997, 248–284).

18. Based on interview with Kawabata Kiyotaka, Political Affairs Officer, DPA, on March 2, 2000.

19. Goodrich, Hambro, and Simons offer the following explanation: "The

primary intent of Article 40 was to empower the Council to take measures to prevent a threat to the peace from developing into actual breach." They refer to "preventive action" as follows: "There would appear to have been an assumption, however, at least by the Secretary-General, that the measures were to be considered as 'preventive action' requiring the support of all members." And they go on to say, "It is not clear whether they come within the scope of 'preventive' action, thus providing grounds for suspension in the event of noncompliance and requiring members to refrain from giving assistance to states that refuse to carry out the Council's resolutions" (1969, 303–307).

20. Goodrich, Hambro, and Simons explain Article 2, Clause 7 of the UN Charter as follows: "Thus, the Council's actions under Article 41 and 42 are exempt from the 'domestic jurisdiction' clause, but this exception does not extend to all actions by the Council under Chapter VII" (1969, 292).

21. Willetts goes on to say, "Ironically, the Provisional rules of procedure of the Security Council already provide for the possibility of NGO participation: Rule 39" (2000, 199).

22. The meetings and seminars include the ARF Meetings of Heads of Defense Colleges and Institutions, the ARF Foreign Affairs and Defense Officials Professional Development Program, the Seminar on the Law of Armed Conflict, the Seminar on the Production of Defense Policy Documents, and the Symposium on Tropical Hygiene and Prevention and Treatment of Tropical Infectious Diseases. For further discussion of the need for more CBMs in the ARF context, see Haas (1997, 345).

23. It was the national regimes in power, which shared the same interest in self-preservation and the same perception of common internal enemies, that motivated the formation of ASEAN (Peou 1998, 447).

24. The Declaration of Managua defined "effective and ethical governance" as the right of people to demand that the government improve legal and administrative structures so as to prevent the obstruction of governance (preamble and art. 7).

25. The International Verification and Support Commission (CIAV) was established in 1989 for Nicaragua to implement a work plan designed to demobilize, repatriate, and voluntarily relocate members of the irregular forces (the Contras) and their families. And the International Civilian Mission in Haiti (MICIVIH) was set up in 1993 to defend and promote human rights, support the consolidation of democracy, and make an effort to strengthen institutions.

26. Aoki points out that the United Nations shows a lack of effort in the report of the UN secretary-general, "The causes of conflict and the promotion of durable peace and sustainable development in Africa" (Aoki 2000b, 37).

27. I am indebted to Dr. Jehangir A. Khan, of the DPA of the UN Secretariat, with whose permission many unpublished documents about this meeting were made available (interview, March 3, 2000).

28. The other modalities include better coordination and consultation between regional organizations and the United Nations, both at the headquarters level and in the field; better flows of information through systemic mechanisms between regional organizations and the United Nations; exchanges of staff between the United Nations and regional organizations; and follow-up meetings.

29. Willetts states, "Hybrid organizations can take two forms: the bicameral form, where NGOs and governments must vote separately and each produce majority approval for a decision; and the unicameral form, where they vote together" (2000, 204).

30. See Sollis on the role of UNDP in involving NGOs (1996, 200–203).

31. Alger explains the opinions of a number of scholars on involving NGOs in the process of UN preventive diplomacy (1996, 354–357). Childers and Urquhart (1994, 112–118) and Natsios (1996, 67–81) insist that, especially in the field of humanitarian emergencies, there is a necessity to set up some kind of coordinating or operational body. Yoshida (1996) also is in favor of involving NGOs, and lists up a range of merits for the inclusion of NGOs in preventive diplomacy.

32. The new mechanism for preventive diplomacy could be set up by the name of, for example, High Commissioner for Conflict Prevention as an autonomous subsidiary organ of the UN Security Council. The proposed new organ should:

- have the ability to undertake preventive diplomacy at its discretion;
- create an early-warning network among the UN families, specialized agencies, regional organizations, sovereign states, NGOs, civil societies, and conflicting parties;
- analyze the information collected;
- constantly observe root causes of conflicts, symptoms of disputes, and on-going conflicts;
- undertake post-conflict peacebuilding;
- collect all necessary information for conflict prevention on an on-going basis;
- be able to respond and provide good offices readily in the face of disputes on its own authority; and
- be able to dispatch missions to conflicting areas readily and speedily.

BIBLIOGRAPHY

Alger, Chadwick F. 1996. "Thinking About the Future of the UN System." *Global Governance* 2(3): 335–361.

Annan, Kofi A. 1997. *Report of the Secretary-General.* United Nations Official Record of General Assembly (A/51/950). 14 July. <http:www.un.org/reform/track2> (16 July).

———. 1999. *Preventing War and Disaster: A Growing Global Challenge.* (1999 Annual Report on the Work of the Organization.) New York: United Nations.

Aoki Kazuyoshi. 2000a. "Reisen-go Afurika ni okeru funsō taiō mekanizumu" (Mechanisms for countering conflict in post-cold war Africa). *Kokusai Seiji,* no. 123: 110–126.

———. 2000b. "Afurika ni okeru funsō mondai no akutā no hensen to OAU" (The transition of actors in the conflicts in Africa and the OAU). *NIRA Seisaku Kenkyū* 13(6): 32–37.

ASEAN Regional Forum. 1998 "The ASEAN Regional Forum: A Concept Paper." <http://www.asean.or.id/politics/arf_ch2c.htm> (12 August).

———. 2002. "ASEAN Regional Forum. "Concept and Principles of Preventive Diplomacy." <www.aseansec.org/view.asp> (10 June).

Attah-Poku, Agyemang. 1998. *African Ethnicity: History, Conflict Management, Resolution and Prevention.* Lanham, Md.: University Press of America.

Attali, Jacques. 1997. "Economic and Social Dimensions of Preventing Conflict." In Aspen Institute, ed. *Conflict Prevention: Strategies to Sustain Peace in the Post–Cold War World.* Aspen, Colo.: Aspen Institute.

"Awaiting Formal Reply on Jenin, Annan Says UN Did all to Meet Israeli Concerns." 2002. *UN News* (30 April). <http://wwwO.un.org/apps/news/story .asp>.

Boothby, Derek, and George D'Angelo. 2000. "Building Capacity within the United Nations: Cooperation on the Prevention of Violent Conflicts." An unpublished report (ppu/UNU/#12, 23 February).

Boutros-Ghali, Boutros. 1992. *An Agenda for Peace, Preventive Diplomacy, Peacemaking and Peace-Keeping.* New York: United Nations Department of Public Information.

Brown, Michael E., and Richard N. Rosecrance, eds. 1999. *The Cost of Conflict: Prevention and Cure in the Global Arena.* Lanham, Md.: Rowman & Littlefield.

Childers, Erskine, and Brian Urquhart. 1994. *Renewing the United Nations System* (Development Dialogue 1994: 1). Uppsala, Sweden: Dag Hammarskjöld Foundation.

Cortright, David, ed. 1997. *The Price of Peace: Incentives and International Conflict Prevention.* New York: Rowman & Littlefield.

Cortright, David, and George A. Lopez. 1998. "Carrots, Sticks, and Cooperation: Economic Tools of Statecraft." In Barnett R. Rubin, ed. *Cases and Strategies for Preventive Action.* New York: Century Foundation Press.

Desjardins, Marie-France. 1996. *Rethinking Confidence-Building Measures: Obstacles to Agreement and the Risks of Overselling the Process.* Oxford, U.K.: Oxford University Press.

de Soto, Alvaro. 1997. "Political Dimensions of Conflict Prevention: Post-Conflict Peacebuilding." In Aspen Institute, ed. *Conflict Prevention: Strategies to Sustain Peace in the Post-Cold War World.* Aspen, Colo.: Aspen Institute.

Doyle, Michael W., Ian Johnstone, and Robert C. Orr. 1997. *Keeping the Peace:*

Multidimensional UN Operations in Cambodia and El Salvador. Cambridge, U.K.: Cambridge University Press.

Elhance, Arun P., and Moonis Ahmar. 1996. "Nonmilitary CBMs." In Michel Krepon and Amit Sevak, eds. *Crisis Prevention, Confidence Building, and Reconciliation in South Asia.* New Delhi: Manohar.

Evans, Gareth. 1993. *Cooperating for Peace: The Global Agenda for the 1990s and Beyond.* St. Leonard's, NSW, Australia: Allen & Unwin.

———. 1998. "Preventive Action and Conflict Resolution." In Olara A. Otunnu and Michael W. Doyle, eds. *Peacemaking and Peacekeeping for the New Century.* Lanham, Md.: Rowman & Littlefield.

Fetherston, A. B. 1994. *Towards a Theory of United Nations Peacekeeping.* London: Macmillan.

Frank, Thomas M. 1991. "The Good Offices Function of the UN Secretary-General." In Adam Roberts and Benedict Kingsbury, eds. *United Nations, Divided World: The UN's Roles in International Relations.* Oxford: Clarendon Press.

Gärling, Tommy, et al. 2000. "Diplomacy and Psychology: Psychological Contributions to International Negotiations, Conflict Preventions, and World Peace." *International Journal of Psychology*, no. 35: 81–86.

Goodrich, Leland M., Eduard Hambro, and Anne Patricia Simons. 1969. *Charter of the United Nations: Commentary and Documents.* New York: Columbia University Press.

Granada, Camilo. 1999. "Lessons Learned and Moving Forward—Regional Organizations Report (OAS)." In Winrich Kühne, ed. *The United Nations and Regional Security Arrangements: Towards More Effective Task-sharing and Cooperation.* Ebenhausen: Stiftung Wissenschaft und Politik.

Haas, Michael. 1997. "ASEAN's Pivotal Role in Asian-Pacific Regional Cooperation." *Global Governance* 3(3): 329–348.

Hammarskjöld, Dag. 1960. "Introduction to the Annual Report of the Secretary-General on the Work of the Organization, 16 June 1959–15 June 1960." In *General Assembly, Official Records* (15th Session, Supplement 1A).

Hernandez, Homero L., and Sumihiro Kuyama. 1995. *Strengthening of the United Nations System Capacity for Conflict Prevention.* Joint Inspection Unit of the United Nations (A/50/853 and JIU/REP/95/13), 22 December.

Holl, Jane. 1997. "A Report on Work in Progress: Second Report, Carnegie Commission on Preventing Deadly Conflict." In Aspen Institute, ed. *Conflict Prevention: Strategies to Sustain Peace in the Post–Cold War World.* Colorado: Aspen Institute.

Joyner, Christopher C. 1999. "The United Nations and Democracy." *Global Governance* 5(3): 333–357.

Kanninen, Tapio. 1999. "Recent Initiatives by the Secretary-General and the UN System in Strengthening Conflict Prevention Activities." A paper presented at the Max van der Stoel Symposium, Lund, Sweden. 3–4 December.

Kawabata Kiyotaka. 1999. "Tariban: Nazo no shidōsha Omaru-shi kaikenki."

(Interview with Mohammad Omar, mysterious leader of the Taliban). *Sekai*, no. 659 (March): 172–179.

Kikkawa Gen. 1994. *Yōroppa Anzen Hoshō Kyōryoku Kaigi (CSCE): Jinken no kokusaika kara minshuka shien e no hatten* (The Conference on Security and Co-operation in Europe: From the internationalization of human rights to support for democratization). Tokyo: Sanrei Shobō.

———. 1999. "Ōshū Anzen Hoshō Kyōryoku Kikō (OSCE) no yobō gaikō" (Preventive diplomacy by the Organization for Security and Co-operation in Europe). *Kokusai Mondai*, no. 477: 36–49.

Kittani, Ismat. 1998. "Preventive Diplomacy and Peacemaking: The UN Experience." In Olara A. Otunnu and Michael W. Doyle, eds. *Peacemaking and Peacekeeping for the New Century*. Lanham, Md.: Rowman & Littlefield.

Krepon, Michael. 1999. "Conflict Avoidance, Confidence Building, and Peacemaking." In Michael Krepon, Michael Newbill, Khurshid Khoja, and Jenny S. Drezin, eds. *Global Confidence Building: New Tools for Troubled Regions*. New York: St. Martin's Press.

Kühne, Winrich. 1999. "Executive Summary and Recommendations." In Winrich Kühne, ed. *The United Nations and Regional Security Arrangements: Towards More Effective Task-sharing and Co-operation*. Ebenhausen: Stiftung Wissenschaft und Politik.

Lund, Michael S. 1997. *Preventing Violent Conflicts: A Strategy for Preventive Diplomacy*. Washington, D.C.: United States Institute of Peace.

Makinda, Samuel M. 1996. "Sovereignty and International Security: Challenges for the United Nations." *Global Governance* 2 (2): 149–168.

Mazrui, Ali A. 1998. "The Failed State and Political Collapse in Africa." In Olara A. Otunnu and Michael W. Doyle, eds. *Peacemaking and Peacekeeping for the New Century*. Lanham, Md.: Rowman & Littlefield.

Miall, Hugh, Oliver Ramsbotham, and Tom Woodhouse. 1999. *Contemporary Conflict Resolution: The Prevention, Management and Transformation of Deadly Conflicts*. Malden, Mass.: Polity Press.

Natsios, Andrew S. 1996. "NGOs and the UN System in Complex Humanitarian Emergencies: Conflict or Cooperation?" In Thomas G. Weiss and Leon Gordenker, eds. *NGOs, the UN, and Global Governance*. Boulder, Colo.: Lynne Rienner.

Nowak, Jerzy M. 1999. "The Organization for Security and Co-operation in Europe." In Trevor Findlay, ed. *Challenges for the New Peacekeepers* (SIPRI Research Paper No. 12). Oxford: Oxford University Press.

Otunnu, Olara A. 1997. "Conflict Prevention: Opening Remarks." In Aspen Institute, ed. *Conflict Prevention: Strategies to Sustain Peace in the Post–Cold War World*. Aspen, Colo.: Aspen Institute.

Peck, Connie. 1996. *The United Nations as a Dispute Settlement System: Improving Mechanisms for the Prevention and Resolution of Conflict*. The Hague: Kluwer Law International.

———. 1999. "UN Preventive Action." In Muthiah Alagappa and Takashi Ino-
guchi, eds. *International Security Management and the United Nations*. Tokyo:
United Nations University Press.

Peou, Sorpong. 1998. "The Subsidiary Model of Global Governance in the
UN-ASEAN Context." *Global Governance* 4(4): 439–459.

Pérez de Cuéllar, Javier. 1991. *Anarchy or Order: Report of the Secretary-General on
the Work of the Organization, 1989, Annual Reports 1982–1991*. New York: United
Nations.

Policy Planning Unit, Department of Political Affairs, United Nations Secretariat. 1999. "Current United Nations Conflict Prevention Activities." A
presentation to G-8 development ministers (9 April).

Ramcharan, B. G. 1991. *The International Law and Practice of Early-Warning and Preventive Diplomacy: The Emerging Global Watch*. Dordrecht: Martinus Nijhoff
Publishers.

Rupesinghe, Kumar. 1992. "The Disappearing Boundaries Between Internal
and External Conflicts." In Kumar Rupesinghe, ed. *Internal Conflict and Governance*. London: Macmillan Press Ltd.

———. 1998. *Yobō gaikō* (Preventive diplomacy). Translated by Kayoko Tatsumi.
Tokyo: Diamondo-sha.

Salim, Salim Ahmed. 1998. "The OAU Role in Conflict Management." In Olara
A. Otunnu and Michael W. Doyle, eds. *Peacemaking and Peacekeeping for the
New Century*. Lanham, Md.: Rowman & Littlefield.

Satō Hideo. 2000. "Leadership for a Pacific Security Community: Japan and
Korea." In Kwang Il Baek, ed. *Prospects for Cooperation between Korea and Japan
in the 21st Century*. Seoul: Korean Association of International Studies and
Japanese Association of International Relations.

Shcherbak, Igor N. 1991. *Confidence-building Measures and International Security:
The Political and Military Aspects—a Soviet Approach*. New York: United Nations.

Shōji Mariko. 1993. "Kokuren no kikō kaikaku kōsō: Gari kokuren jimu sōchō
no kikō kaikaku to hachi-jū nendo nakaba ikō no kaikaku kōsō rongi" (A
Comparative Study of the proporsals for the reform of the United Nations—
the reform plans of Secretary-General Boutros-Ghali and other proposals
from 1985-1993). *Kokusai Seiji*, no. 103: 10–27.

———. 1996. "Ippan kokusaihō no funsō no heiwateki kaiketsu ni kansuru kenkyū: Kokuren ni yoru heiwateki kaiketsu to no hikaku kara" (Peaceful settlement of international disputes in general international law—comparison
with the peaceful settlement mechanisms of the United Nations). *Kankyō
Jōhō Kenkyū*, no. 4: 77–95.

———. 1997. "Kokuren ni okeru yobō gaikō no gainen ni kansuru ichi kōsatsu" (A
study on the concept of preventive diplomacy in the United Nations). *Kankyō
Jōhō Kenkyū*, no. 5: 57–80.

———. 2000. "Kokuren no yobō gaikō" (Preventive diplomacy of the United

Nations). In Kikkawa Gen, ed. *Yobō gaikō* (Preventive diplomacy). Tokyo: Sanrei Shobō.

Sollis, Peter. 1996. "Partners in Development: The State, NGOs and the UN in Central America." In Thomas G. Weiss and Leon Gordenker, eds. *NGOs, the UN, and Global Governance*. Boulder, Colo.: Lynne Rienner.

Soros, George. 1997. "Conflict Prevention: Can We Meet the Challenge?" In Aspen Institute, ed. *Conflict Prevention: Strategies to Sustain Peace in the Post–Cold War World*. Aspen, Colo.: Aspen Institute.

Soto, Yadira. 1999. "The Role of the OAS in Conflict Prevention: From Rhetoric to Policy—Towards Workable Conflict Prevention at the Regional and Global Level." Outline of a presentation given at Stanford in Washington seminar on "Preventing Conflict in the 21st Century," May 20.

Stockholm International Peace Research Institute. 1998. *Peace, Security and Conflict Prevention: SIPRI-UNESCO Handbook*. Oxford: Oxford University Press.

Sutterlin, James S. 1995. *The United Nations and the Maintenance of International Security: A Challenge to Be Met*. Westport, Conn.: Praeger.

Thérien, Jean-Philippe, Michel Fortmann, and Guy Gosselin. 1996. "The Organization of American States: Restructuring Inter-American Multilateralism." *Global Governance* 2(2): 215–240.

Tsubouchi Jun. 1999. "Shinrai jōsei gainen no sai-kōchiku ni mukete: reisen-gata teigi kara no dakkyaku to fuhenteki kanōsei" (Toward the re-construction of the concept of confidence-building). In Yamamoto Takehiko, ed. *Kokusai anzenhoshō no shin-tenkai: reisen to sono go* (New development of international security: The cold war and after). Tokyo: Waseda Daigaku Shuppan-bu.

———. 2000. "Ajia Taheiyō no yobō gaikō" (Preventive diplomacy in the Asia Pacific region). In Kikkawa Gen, ed. *Yobō gaikō* (Preventive diplomacy). Tokyo: Sanrei Shobō.

United Nations. 1995. *The United Nations and Cambodia 1991–1995*. Blue Books Series, Vol. II.

———. 1997. "Comments of the Secretary-General and the Administrative Committee on Coordination," A/52/184 (24 June).

———. 1998a. "Draft Discussion Paper: Possible Methods for Implementing Proposed Modalities of Co-operation between the UN and Regional Organizations in the Field of Early Warning and Conflict Prevention" (17 November).

———. 1998b. "Report on Third Meeting between the United Nations and Regional Organizations." Unofficial memo for the information of participants based on the results of meeting held in New York, 28–29 July.

———. 1998c. "The Causes of Conflict and the Promotion of Durable Peace and Sustainable Development in Africa." In *The Report of Secretary-General*, A/52/871-S/1998/318 (13 April).

———. 1999. "Summary of the Result of the Joint Working Groups on the

Modalities of Prevention." Follow-up meeting between the United Nations and regional organizations, "Cooperation for Conflict Prevention," in New York, on December 10–11, 1998. (19 March).

———. 2000. "Report of the Panel on United Nations Peace Operations" (The Brahimi Report). Report submitted to the General Assembly and the Security Council. A/55/305-S/2000/809 (21 August).

United Nations, Department of Political Affairs. 1999. "Preventive Action and Peacemaking." <http://www.un.org/Depts/dpa/docs/peacemak.htm> (4 November).

United Nations, Office of Legal Affairs, Codification Division. 1992. *Handbook on the Peaceful Settlement of Disputes between States.* New York, NY: United Nations.

United Nations Development Programme. 2000. "Capacity Building in Conflict Resolution." UNDP Africa Region. <http://www.un.org/esa/governance/conflictpg.htm> (2 March).

United Nations General Assembly. 1992. 47th Session. UN General Assembly Resolution 120, A/RES/47/120 (New York, 18 December).

———. 1997. 51st Session. UN General Assembly 242, A/RES/51/241 (New York, 26 September).

United Nations, Office for Disarmament Affairs. 1993. *Regional Approaches to Confidence and Security-building Measures, Disarmament.* Topical Papers 17. New York: United Nations.

UN Secretariat. 1998. "Organization of the Department of Political Affairs." *Secretary-General's Bulletin*, ST/SGB/14 (20 August).

UN/CARICOM/OAS. 1998. "UN/CARICOM/OAS Cooperation in the Field of Early Warning and Conflict Prevention." Internal memorandum (December 10).

Unwin, Peter, and Isabelle Biagiotti. 1996. "Global Governance and the 'New' Political Conditionality." *Global Governance* 2(3): 377–400.

White, N. D. 1997. *Keeping the Peace: The United Nations and the Maintenance of International Peace and Security*, 2nd ed. Manchester, U.K.: Manchester University Press.

Willetts, Peter. 2000. "From 'Consultative Arrangements' to 'Partnership': The Changing Status of NGOs in Diplomacy at the UN." *Global Governance* 6(2): 191–212.

Yamamoto Yoshinobu. 1995a. "Kyōchō-teki anzen hoshō no kanōsei: kisoteki na kōsatsu" (A basic study on the feasibility of cooperative security). *Kokusai Mondai,* no. 425(August): 2–20.

———. 1995b. "Reisen-go no kokusai anzen hoshō shisutemu" (International security system in the post–cold war era). In Satō Seizaburō, Imai Ryūkichi, and Yamanouchi Yasuhide, eds. *Kiro ni tatsu Kokuren to Nihon gaikō* (The United Nations at a crossroad and Japanese diplomacy). Tokyo: Mita Shuppankai.

Yoshida Yasuhiko. 1996. "New Role of Non-Governmental Organizations in a Global Civil Society." *Saitama Daigaku Kyōyō Gakubu* 32(2): 163–181.

——. 1997. "The Role of the United Nations Security Council in Conflict Resolution in the New Global System." *Saitama Daigaku Kyōyō Gakubu* 33(1): 111–120.

Zacarias, Agostinho. 1996. *The United Nations and International Peacekeeping.* London: I.B. Tauris.

About the Contributors

SATŌ HIDEO was Senior Adviser to the Rector at the United Nations University (UNU) and a member of the UNU's senior academic staff responsible for the Capacity Building Programme. He earned his M.A. in International Relations and his Ph.D. in Political Science from the University of Chicago. He was on the Foreign Policy Studies research staff at the Brookings Institution from 1972 to 1976 and taught political science at Yale University as Assistant/Associate Professor from 1976 to 1982. After returning to Japan in 1982, he joined the University of Tsukuba as Professor of International Relations, and served as Dean, College of International Relations and as Dean, Graduate School of International Political Economy before joining the UNU in 1998, where he worked until 2001. Dr. Satō was President of the Japan Association of International Relations from 1996 to 1998, Vice-President of the International Studies Association from 1996 to 1997, and a Member of the Science Council of Japan. Dr. Sato authored or edited thirteen books on U.S.-Japan relations, foreign policy and international relations, and published about a hundred book chapters and articles in Japanese and international academic journals, including *International Studies Quarterly*, *International Journal of Public Administration*, *International Spectator*, *Current History*, *Journal of Northeast Asian Studies*, *The Pacific Review*, *The Korean Journal of International Studies*, and *Japan Review of International Affairs*.

AKIZUKI HIROKO is Professor of International Law at Asia University. Dr. Akizuki earned a B.A. in Social Science at International Christian University, and an M.A. in Public Administration and a Ph.D. in International Law from the same university in 1984 and 1997, respectively. Before assuming her current position in 1999, Dr. Akizuki taught as Assistant Professor and Associate Professor at the University of Kitakyūshū from 1993 to 1999; she was a Programme Officer of the United Nations Development Programme in Jakarta from 1987 to 1989. Her publications include *Kokurenhō josetsu* (Introduction to the law of the United Nations, 1999), "Jinken" (Human rights) in *Kokusai kikō ron* (International organizations, 2001 [new edition]), and *Kokusai hō nyūmon* (Introduction to international law, 1999).

HOSHINO TOSHIYA is Associate Professor of International Security Studies at Osaka University. Professor Hoshino was graduated from Sophia University and obtained his M.A. in International Relations in 1986 from the University of Tokyo, where he finished his doctoral course. He was a political analyst at the Japanese Embassy in Washington, D.C., from 1988 to 1991 and a visiting fellow at the Woodrow Wilson School of Princeton University from 1992 to 1993. He had served as a research fellow and later a senior research fellow at the Japan Institute of International Affairs since 1991 until he took up his current position in 1998. Professor Hoshino's recent publications include "Pursuing 'Informal' Human Security: A Track II Status Report" in *Asia's Emerging Security* (2000), "Nichibei dōmei to Ajia no takokukan anzen hoshō: Nippon no shiten kara" (Japan-U.S. alliance and multilateral security in Asia) in *Ajia taiheiyō no chiiki chitsujo to anzen hoshō* (Regional order and security in Asia Pacific, 1999), and "Beikoku no Kosobo funsō kainyū: Sono dōgisei, gōhōsei, seitōsei" (U.S. intervention in the Kosovo conflict: Its morality, legality, and legitimacy) in *Kokusai mondai* (International affairs, 2000).

KIKKAWA GEN is Professor of International Law at Kobe University Graduate School of Law. Graduated from Sophia University, Professor Kikkawa earned an M.A. and Ph.D. in Law from the Graduate School of Hitotsubashi University in 1978 and 1995, respectively. He taught at Hiroshima Shūdō University as Lecturer from 1982, then as Associate Professor from 1983 and Professor from 1992, and served as Professor of International Relations at Kobe University from 1998 until he took his current position in 2000. His recent publications include *Yobō gaikō* (Preventive diplomacy, 2000), *Naze kaku wa nakunaranai no ka: Kaku heiki to kokusai kankei* (Why nuclear power survives: Nuclear weapons and international relations, 2000), *Yōroppa anzen hoshō kaigi OSCE* (Organization for Security and Cooperation in Europe, 1994), and "OSCE no anzen hoshō kyōdōtai sōzō to yobō gaikō" (The OSCE's creation of a cooperative security body and preventive diplomacy) in *Kokusaihō gaikō zasshi* (Journal of international law and diplomacy, 2000).

MIYAWAKI NOBORU is Associate Professor of International Relations at Matsuyama University. Professor Miyawaki earned his B.A. in Political Science from Hōsei University, and his M.A. in Political Science in 1994 at the Graduate School of Political Science at Waseda University, where he also earned a Ph.D. in Political Science in 2001. He served as a Research Fellow of the Japan Society for the Promotion of Studies from 1994 to 1996 and Assistant Professor at Matsuyama University from 1996 to 1999, and has been in his current position since 1999. His publications include "Japan and the CFSP" in *Die Europaeische Sicherheits- und Verteidigungspolitik: Positionen, Perzeptionen, Probleme, Perspektiven* (The European security and defense policy: Positions, perceptions, problems, perspectives, 2002), "Minshuteki heiwa to minshuka shien: Minshu seido, jinken jimusho wo chūshin ni" (Democratic peace and supporting democratization: Focusing on office for democratic institute and human rights), and "Esutonia Ratovia ni okeru yobō gaikō" (Preventive diplomacy in Estonia and Latvia) in *Yobō gaikō* (Preventive diplomacy, 2000).

SHŌJI MARIKO is Professor in the Faculty of International Studies at Keiai University. Professor Shōji earned a B.A. in International Relations from the Department of Liberal Arts at Saitama University and an M.A. in International and Cultural Studies in 1982 at the Graduate School of Tsuda College, where she also completed her doctoral course work in 1985. She was a Lecturer and Associate Professor at Chiba Keiai Junior College, from 1990 to 1993 and from 1993 to 1997, respectively, and Associate Professor at Keiai University from 1996 to 2002. Her publications include "The UN and East Asian Regional Security: A Japanese Perspective" in *UN, PKO and East Asian Security: Currents, Trends and Prospects* (2002), "Kokuren no yobō gaikō" (United Nations' preventive diplomacy) in *Yobō gaikō* (Preventive diplomacy, 2000), and "Kokusai kikō sōgo no kankei" (Relations among international organizations) in *Kokusai kikō ron* (International organizations, 1998).

Index

Japan Center for
International Exchange

Founded in 1970, the Japan Center for International Exchange (JCIE) is an independent, nonprofit, and nonpartisan organization dedicated to strengthening Japan's role in international affairs. JCIE believes that Japan faces a major challenge in augmenting its positive contributions to the international community, in keeping with its position as one of the world's largest industrial democracies. Operating in a country where policymaking has traditionally been dominated by the government bureaucracy, JCIE has played an important role in broadening debate on Japan's international responsibilities by conducting international and cross-sectional programs of exchange, research, and discussion.

JCIE creates opportunities for informed policy discussions; it does not take policy positions. JCIE programs are carried out with the collaboration and cosponsorship of many organizations. The contacts developed through these working relationships are crucial to JCIE's efforts to increase the number of Japanese from the private sector engaged in meaningful policy research and dialogue with overseas counterparts. JCIE receives no government subsidies; rather, funding comes from private foundation grants, corporate contributions, and contracts.